THE 12 LAWS OF
DATING
DYNAMICS

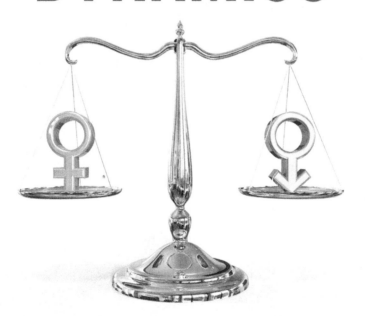

**HOW TO BALANCE THE POWER AND
AVOID** ONE-SIDED RELATIONSHIPS

MANUEL SANTANA

Although the publisher and the author have made every effort to ensure that the information in this book was correct at press time and while this publication is designed to provide accurate and authoritative information regarding the subject matter covered, the publisher and the author assume no responsibility for errors, inaccuracies, omissions, or any other inconsistencies herein and hereby disclaim any liability to any party for any loss, damage, or disruption caused by errors or omissions, whether such errors or omissions result from negligence, accident, or any other cause. This publication is meant as a source of valuable information for the reader, however, it is not meant as a replacement for direct expert assistance. If such level of assistance is required, the services of a competent professional should be sought.

The 12 Laws of Dating Dynamics

Copyright © 2025 by **Manuel Santana**

All rights reserved.

No part of this book may be used or reproduced by any means, graphic, electronic, or mechanical, including photocopying, recording, taping, or by any information storage retrieval system, without the written permission of the author or publisher except in the case of brief quotations embodied in critical articles and reviews.

To request permissions, contact the publisher at contact@penmierpublishing.com

ISBN: 979-8-218-67748-0 (Paperback)

Published By
Penmier Publishing
1325 Avenue of the Americas
New York, NY 10019

www.penmierpublishing.com

Dedication

I would like to dedicate this book to men and women who have been hurt emotionally, mentally, verbally, and physically. Dating & relationships can be very difficult and can take a toll on someone. As a society, we need to speak up and come together and find a way to minimize the pain that a lot of people are currently feeling.

Table of Contents

ACKNOWLEDGEMENTS 1

FOREWORD 3

INTRODUCTION 5

SECTION 1: THE FUNDAMENTALS 9

    CHAPTER 1: THE LAW OF NATURAL PRIORITY 10

    CHAPTER 2: THE LAW OF RELATIONSHIP FORMATS 30

    CHAPTER 3: THE LAW OF DATING SCARCITY 50

    CHAPTER 4: THE LAW OF RELATIONAL MODES 71

SECTION 2: THE PRINCIPLES 93

    CHAPTER 5: THE LAW OF LEADING AND RESULTING ... 94

    CHAPTER 6: THE LAW OF PROGRESSING AND REGRESSING 117

    CHAPTER 7: THE LAW OF RUNNING AND CHASING 139

    CHAPTER 8: THE LAW OF WITHHOLDING AND ACTIVATING 164

SECTION 3: THE ESSENTIALS 189

    CHAPTER 9: THE LAW OF RELATIONAL RESPECT 190

    CHAPTER 10: THE LAW OF DATING CONNECTIONS 216

    CHAPTER 11: THE LAW OF INTENTIONAL INTEREST 243

    CHAPTER 12: THE LAW OF MARKET LEVERAGING 270

CONCLUSION 299

Acknowledgements

I would like to say thanks to everyone who supported me from the very beginning and helped make this book become a reality. First and foremost, I would like to thank my mother and my little sister for always being there for me throughout this journey. Words can't explain what you two mean to me. I love you both to the moon and back. I would like to thank all my "big brothers" and my "big sisters" throughout my teenage years, my 20s and my 30s who gave me advice and always had my back. I would like to say thanks to Greg, Arch, Limage, Etohn, Chris, RC, Ruben, James, Bobby, and O'Neal because I learned so much from you guys. And I would like to say thanks to Kiesha, Monica, Helena, Elicia, Candace, Bridget and Isa for always being there to lend an ear when I needed to vent. You all helped me get through some tough times. I would like to also give a special thanks to my big Brother from another Mother Erik. Words can't explain the gratitude I have for you. You're a key factor in my personal growth and I'm forever grateful. Thanks for trying to help solve the relational situation I had even though it ended in heartbreak. I would also like to give a special thanks to my good friend Sam. Even though we stopped seeing eye to eye, our 10 years of friendship will always be one of my most important friendships of my life. You were always there to lend an ear when I had girl problems and for that I'm forever grateful. We spent years trying to "crack the code" and we figured out a lot of key factors in this book. I would like to give another very special shout out to The Glass Slipper Gentleman's Club in Boston. The two plus years of employment can never be matched. I've built a close bond with so many people, and everyone is like family to me. This book literally would not have been made possible if it wasn't for all the support and feedback you all have given me. Thanks Mike, Billy, and Wally for giving me the opportunity to be your employee. I would also like to give a special shout out to Chloe. You were there for me during some of toughest years. You always supported me and you were always there for me without judgment. Just kindness and understanding. I will forever be grateful. I would also like to give a special shout out to Stephanie. You've been there with me through this journey every step of the way. Always had motivational words when I felt like giving up. And you were always there as my wingwoman and gave me relationship advice from a female point of view. And enough words to say thank you to you. I would like to give another special shout out to Tamara. You have been the best mentor I could have asked for. You've coached me and believed in me since day one. Even when I felt like giving up and suffered from imposture syndrome, you knew I had a special gift and that I was born to do what I'm doing now. I couldn't have done any of this without you. I will forever be grateful. Finally, I would like to say thanks to my twin brother Miguel, my father, and my cousin Ruthy. Even though sometimes we don't see eye to eye, family will always be family, and family will always come first. You all have helped me in ways you may not see and even in ways you may not know. Thanks, from the bottom of my heart.

Foreword

By Tamara Payton Bell

Whether you are new to dating, building confidence, or strengthening a relationship, this book provides essential tools for creating healthy partnerships. Drawing on matchmaking, coaching, and personal experience, the author delivers a practical guide for mastering romantic connections in "The 12 Laws of Dating Dynamics" This guide presents twelve principles to develop balanced relationships by fostering mutual respect, effective communication, recognizing emotional imbalances, and establishing boundaries. It assists readers in identifying red flags, protecting emotional well-being, and constructing partnerships founded on equality and understanding. The book aims to help readers avoid one-sided relationships, reclaim personal autonomy, and comprehend the complexities of modern dating. I had the pleasure of meeting Manuel while he was enhancing his coaching skills and matchmaking abilities. He is dedicated to assisting individuals and solving problems effectively. His insights, teachings, and creations are thoughtful and impactful. Manuel Santana is a relationship coach, author, and podcaster from Boston, MA. He has several forthcoming books on dating, love, and relationships, and is widely recognized as an expert and thought leader in advancing intersexual dynamics in contemporary society. It is both a privilege and an honor to provide this foreword for what is anticipated to be a New York Times Bestseller in 2025. I am a certified sexologist, love coach, master sexpert, and publisher of the blog site, Sexpert.com and Home Party Review magazine. I hold degrees in business management, family studies, and psychology/sociology. I have been cited in numerous books related to business and relationship building and have served on various panels and boards within the adult industry. My passion for business and relationship building led me to Manuel, and I am deeply honored to call him my colleague and friend. I trust you will find the necessary tools to achieve your dating goals and enjoy his books as much as I do.

Tamara Payton Bell

Certified Clinical Sexologist, Loveologist & Love Coach

Ambassador to Students at Loveology University and Administrator for the Sexual

Wellness Professional Alliance (SWPA)

Introduction

What is a law?

A law is a rule or principle that governs behavior, actions, or interactions, designed to create order and fairness. In its broadest sense, a law can be societal, like those created by governments to regulate communities, or natural, like the fundamental principles of physics that govern the universe. In relationships, laws often exist as unspoken agreements—mutual understandings and boundaries that guide how two people treat and respond to each other. These relational "laws" are built on trust, respect, and shared values, and when broken, they can lead to conflict, imbalance, or disconnection.

What is a dynamic?

A dynamic is the energy and movement that flows between two people in a relationship. It's the invisible force that defines how partners interact, connect, and communicate. Dynamics encompass habits, routines, and unspoken agreements, shaping the relationship's tone and rhythm. Healthy dynamics foster growth, understanding, and compassion, while imbalanced ones can breed frustration, resentment, or emotional distance.

What is balance?

Balance is the state of equilibrium where neither partner feels overwhelmed, neglected, or overly responsible for the relationship's well-being. It's about fairness, mutual respect, and reciprocity—qualities that allow each person to feel seen, heard, and valued. A balanced relationship lets each partner give and receive, support and be supported, and navigate life's changes together, harmoniously.

What is power?

Power is the ability to influence, shape, or impact a situation or person. In relationships, power is subtle, fluid, and often invisible, but it underlies every interaction. It's about the roles and boundaries that each partner creates and respects. Power can uplift and empower, or it can limit and undermine—its effects depend on how it is expressed and perceived.

What is a one-sided relationship?

A one-sided relationship is a connection where the effort, energy, and emotional investment are disproportionately placed on one person. In such relationships, one partner may consistently give, compromise, and support, while the other takes without reciprocating in equal measure. This imbalance can manifest emotionally, physically, or practically, leaving the more invested partner feeling unappreciated, unimportant, or drained. A one-sided relationship lacks mutuality—the give-and-take that forms the foundation of healthy, thriving connections. Over time, it can lead to resentment, loneliness, and a sense of invisibility.

The 12 Laws of Dating Dynamics are organized into three sections: The Fundamentals, The Principles, and The Essentials. Each section serves as a building block, guiding you toward understanding and mastering the dynamics of healthy and fulfilling relationships.

The Fundamentals

The Fundamentals are the foundational truths that underlie all successful relationships. These are the basic building blocks of human connection—self-awareness, communication, and emotional intelligence. Without these, any relationship is bound to falter. The Fundamentals teach you to understand your own needs, recognize your patterns, and approach dating with clarity and purpose. They are the "rules of the game" that help you establish a solid groundwork for love and connection.

The Principles

The Principles are the guiding philosophies that shape how you navigate relationships. These go beyond the basics to explore the deeper truths about trust, respect, and power. Principles help you understand the flow of influence and balance within a relationship and teach you how to maintain harmony and mutual appreciation. They are the compass that ensures you stay true to your values and maintain healthy dynamics as relationships evolve.

The Essentials

The Essentials are the actionable steps and strategies that you can apply in real-life dating situations. These are the practical tools and techniques that help you handle challenges, set boundaries, and nurture emotional intimacy. While Fundamentals and Principles focus on understanding, the Essentials focus on doing. They empower you to turn knowledge into action, so you can create and sustain meaningful, balanced relationships.

By mastering these three sections—The Fundamentals, The Principles, and The Essentials—you'll gain the insight and skills needed to navigate dating with confidence, authenticity, and clarity. Together, they form a roadmap to transform how you approach relationships, ensuring that your connections are grounded in balance, mutual respect, and genuine love.

As you turn these pages, you're about to embark on a journey to understand *why*. Why do you feel unappreciated in your relationships? Why does it feel like the emotional effort is often one-sided? Why do you attract people who don't seem to want you as much as you want them? And why are you drawn to people who don't reciprocate fully?

Through this exploration, you'll uncover the patterns, influences, and dynamics at play within your relationships, empowering you to build deeper, more balanced connections. Welcome to *The 12 Laws of Dating Dynamics: How to Balance the Power and Avoid 1-sided Relationships.* Let's dive in.

SECTION 1

THE FUNDAMENTALS

Chapter 1

The Law of Natural Priority

Human relationships have long been studied, dissected, and categorized, but few aspects of interpersonal dynamics are as fundamental—and as contentious—as the balance between sex and romance. While many discussions focus on what individuals should do to create equilibrium between these two powerful forces, it's equally important to explore why people differ in their priorities. The Law of Natural Priority states that individuals tend to prioritize sex over romance, or romance over sex when it comes to their dating and relationship decisions, and such prioritization is largely influenced by and dictated by one's biological and physiological propensity and inclination. But why is it that some people seem driven almost entirely by sexual desire, while others are more invested in emotional intimacy? To understand this, we must delve into the deeper biological and psychological mechanisms at play.

At the heart of this question lie the distinct tendencies among three archetypal groups: Alphas, Betas, and Omegas. These labels, while simplistic, offer a useful framework for exploring why different people prioritize sex or romance to varying degrees. Alphas, often seen as dominant, assertive, and competitive, tend to lean heavily into sexual prioritization. Betas, generally characterized as more cooperative, balanced, and adaptable, have a more fluid approach, capable of shifting between sexual and romantic priorities. Finally, Omegas, typically perceived as introspective, nurturing, and less concerned with social dominance, place a greater emphasis on romance.

These tendencies are not simply personality traits or social roles but are rooted in our biology. Specifically, hormones and neurotransmitters like testosterone and oxytocin play pivotal roles in shaping our desires and emotional drives, explaining why these archetypes differ in their relationship priorities.

Alpha Males and Alpha Females: The Priority of Sex

Alpha males and alpha females are often seen as the embodiment of strength, confidence, and leadership. These individuals are typically driven by a desire to conquer challenges and assert their dominance in social and personal spheres. It's no surprise, then, that they often prioritize sex over romance in relationships. But why is this the case? The answer lies in their biology, particularly in the role of testosterone.

Testosterone, often called the "male hormone" but present in both sexes, is a potent driver of sexual desire. Higher levels of testosterone are linked to increased libido, a heightened focus on physical attraction, and a more urgent need for sexual fulfillment. Alpha individuals, by nature or circumstance, tend to have higher baseline levels of testosterone than their Beta or Omega counterparts. This hormonal profile fuels their sexual prioritization, making physical intimacy a primary goal in relationships.

For Alpha males, sex can be seen as an extension of their dominance. It's an arena where they can assert control, experience pleasure, and reaffirm their masculinity. Their higher testosterone levels drive them toward frequent and sometimes more adventurous sexual encounters. The act of sex itself becomes a form of control, a way to bolster their confidence and reinforce their status, not just with their partners but within their broader social circles.

Alpha females, though often thought of as emotionally driven, also exhibit a tendency to prioritize sex when testosterone is a key factor. These women, while fully capable of forming deep emotional connections, may seek sexual satisfaction to reinforce their independence and power. For Alpha females, sexual encounters can serve as a declaration of agency, emphasizing that they are in control of their desires and their bodies. Just as with their male counterparts, their sexual drive is amplified by elevated testosterone levels, making the pursuit of physical connection a dominant force in their relationships.

While Alphas are certainly capable of forming romantic bonds, these relationships often start with or are sustained by the sexual connection. Romance, for them, is a secondary layer—something that may deepen over time but is rarely the initial priority. Their primary focus remains on the physical and the immediate gratification that comes from sexual intimacy.

Beta Males and Beta Females: The Fluidity of Prioritization

Betas, whether male or female, offer a more adaptable approach to relationships. Neither dominated by the intense sexual drive of Alphas nor the deep emotional longing of Omegas, Betas exist in a middle ground where both sex and romance are important, but neither takes precedence in all situations. The key to understanding Beta priorities lies in their flexibility and responsiveness to their environment.

Betas typically have more balanced levels of testosterone and oxytocin, allowing them to shift between sexual and romantic priorities depending on the circumstances. If they are in a relationship where sexual attraction is high, they may lean into that dynamic, embracing physical intimacy as a central aspect of the connection. However, if they find themselves drawn to someone on a more emotional level, they are equally capable of prioritizing romance, investing time and energy into building emotional bonds, and fostering intimacy.

This fluidity makes Betas highly adaptable in relationships. They can navigate the sexual intensity of an Alpha partner or the emotional depth of an Omega partner with relative ease. Their biological profiles, with moderate levels of both testosterone and oxytocin, enables them to respond to the needs and desires of their partners without becoming overly focused on either sex or romance.

For Beta Males, this adaptability can manifest as a willingness to be led by their partner's priorities. They are often described as more cooperative and less assertive than their Alpha counterparts, but this does not mean they lack sexual drive or emotional depth. Instead, they can balance these forces, making them more attuned to their partner's desires. A Beta Male in a sexually charged relationship may prioritize physical intimacy, while in a more emotionally driven partnership, he may focus on creating a strong emotional connection.

Beta Females exhibit similar adaptability. They can easily oscillate between prioritizing sex or romance based on the dynamics of the relationship and their partner's needs. While they may not have the same raw sexual drive as Alpha Females, they are more than capable of engaging in and enjoying physical intimacy. At the same time, their moderate level of oxytocin makes them attuned to the emotional needs of their partners, allowing them to prioritize romance when the situation calls for it.

Betas are, in many ways, the most balanced of the three archetypes. Their ability to prioritize both sex and romance, depending on the relationship and context, gives them a unique advantage in navigating the complexities of interpersonal dynamics. They are not bound by a single hormonal driver, making them versatile and adaptable partners.

Omega Males and Omega Females: The Priority of Romance

At the opposite end of the spectrum from Alphas, we find Omegas—individuals who tend to prioritize romance over sex. Omegas are often introspective, empathetic, and deeply connected to their emotions. Their relationships are typically defined by emotional intimacy, trust, and long-term bonding rather than physical attraction or sexual fulfillment. This focus on romance is largely influenced by their higher levels of oxytocin, often referred to as the "love hormone."

Oxytocin is the neurotransmitter most closely associated with emotional bonding, trust, and attachment. It plays a crucial role in forming deep romantic connections and is released in significant quantities during intimate moments, such as cuddling, kissing, and even prolonged eye contact. For Omegas, this heightened sensitivity to oxytocin makes emotional intimacy a priority. They are wired to seek out relationships where feelings, connection, and trust are central components, and they are less likely to prioritize sex unless it serves to deepen the emotional bond they've already established.

Omega Males are often described as "romantic" or "emotionally available." They seek relationships where they can form deep, meaningful connections, and they are often more comfortable expressing their feelings than their Alpha or Beta counterparts. This doesn't mean that Omega Males lack sexual desire—rather, their primary focus is on the emotional aspects of the relationship. For them, physical intimacy is a byproduct of emotional closeness, not the primary driver.

Similarly, Omega females tend to place a higher value on emotional connection than on sexual satisfaction. They are often nurturing, empathetic, and deeply invested in their relationships, seeking partners who share their desire for emotional depth. While Omega Females are fully capable of enjoying and engaging in sexual intimacy, they are more likely to see sex as a way to enhance an already strong emotional bond rather than as an end. The release of oxytocin during moments of closeness reinforces their focus on romance, making emotional intimacy the cornerstone of their relationships.

Because Omegas are so strongly driven by oxytocin, they often find themselves less interested in casual sexual encounters. The lack of an emotional component can make purely physical relationships feel shallow or unfulfilling to them. They are more likely to invest time and energy in building long-term romantic connections, where trust, emotional support, and companionship are prioritized over sexual gratification.

Biological Drivers and Relationship Priorities

The biological underpinnings of these relationship priorities—testosterone for Alphas, a balance of both hormones for Betas, and oxytocin for Omegas—offer a clear explanation for why different people prioritize sex or romance. Alphas, with their elevated testosterone levels, are biologically predisposed to seek out sexual encounters as a form of validation and fulfillment. Their desire for physical intimacy often outpaces their need for emotional connection, especially in the early stages of a relationship.

Betas, with their more balanced hormone profiles, can prioritize both sex and romance, depending on the dynamics of the relationship. This adaptability allows them to shift their focus as needed, making them versatile partners who can navigate a variety of relationship dynamics.

Omegas, with their higher sensitivity to oxytocin, are more likely to prioritize romance, seeking deep emotional bonds over fleeting sexual satisfaction. For them, the emotional aspects of a relationship are far more fulfilling than the physical, and they are more likely to invest in long-term partnerships where trust and emotional intimacy are at the forefront.

Ultimately, the interplay between testosterone and oxytocin shapes our relationship priorities in profound ways. These hormones influence not only how we approach sex and romance but also how we perceive and engage with our partners. Understanding these biological drivers can shed light on why some people prioritize sex while others prioritize romance, offering valuable insights into the dynamics of human relationships.

Wired for Desire — How Biology and Culture Shape Sex Drive

Sexual desire doesn't come from just one place—it's a convergence of body chemistry, brain function, early life experiences, and social conditioning. Why one person feels an intense, persistent craving for sexual intimacy while another feels very little at all is not a mystery of willpower or personality—it's chemistry, wiring, and nurture at work.

Understanding sex drive requires peeling back layers of hormones, neurotransmitters, and life experiences. Some people are biologically primed to be more sexual; others are built for emotional connection, steadiness, or even disinterest. And while desire isn't a moral trait—neither high nor low libido makes someone better or worse—it does deeply influence how we connect, commit, and sustain relationships.

Let's explore a little further what actually causes a **high sex drive**, what contributes to a **low one**, and how these differences affect fidelity, emotional bonding, and long-term compatibility.

The Biological Blueprint of High Sex Drive

High libido often starts in the **body**, where certain chemicals and hormones amplify desire, arousal, and sexual motivation. Here are the key biological components associated with an elevated sex drive:

1. *Testosterone: The Accelerator*

Testosterone is the most influential sex hormone in both men and women. While men naturally produce much more, women also rely on testosterone for sexual desire. Higher testosterone levels are associated with:

- More frequent sexual thoughts
- Stronger pursuit of physical intimacy
- More persistent urges for sexual activity

- Increased risk-taking and sexual novelty-seeking
- Heightened confidence and assertiveness
- Higher sensitivity to visual and physical sexual stimuli

When testosterone is high, the brain is more sensitive to sexual cues, and desire often becomes harder to ignore or suppress. Individuals with high testosterone are typically more motivated by physical connection than emotional reassurance.

2. Dopamine: The Craving Chemical

Dopamine is the brain's reward molecule. It's released during pleasure, excitement, and novelty—and it plays a massive role in fueling desire. A high sex drive is often linked to:

- High baseline dopamine levels
- Greater reward sensitivity (wanting more stimulation)
- Enhanced sexual motivation and anticipation
- Stronger pleasure response to novelty and touch

People with naturally high dopamine activity often pursue sex not just for physical release, but for the psychological "high" it delivers.

3. Estrogen & Estradiol: The Feminine Flame

Estrogen, especially its potent form **estradiol**, is essential to female libido—but it also matters for men. High estradiol in women increases:

- Arousal and sensitivity during the ovulatory phase
- Sexual confidence and flirtatious behavior
- Emotional intensity connected to desire
- Heightened sexual responsiveness and desire
- Increased interest in romantic or sexual attention from others

- Emotional intensity in sexual experiences
- A greater pull toward connection, even outside of committed relationships

In men, estradiol is produced via conversion from testosterone and supports brain function, arousal, and balance. High estradiol in men, combined with high testosterone, can supercharge desire.

The Chemistry of Low Sex Drive

Just as some chemicals amplify desire, others naturally **dampen or regulate** it. These chemicals can slow down libido for biological or psychological reasons—and for some people, this is their baseline state.

1. Serotonin: The Brake Pedal

Serotonin is a mood stabilizer, and while it keeps us calm, too much serotonin can suppress sexual desire. Higher serotonin levels are associated with:

- Reduced sexual thoughts and cravings
- Less interest in novelty or risk
- Emotional stability, but decreased physical urgency

This is why some antidepressants (SSRIs) that boost serotonin can cause low libido as a side effect.

2. Progestogen (and Progesterone): The Cooling Hormone

Progesterone, a hormone related to fertility and pregnancy, often works in opposition to estrogen. When progesterone is high:

- Libido typically drops
- Emotional bonding may increase, but sexual energy decreases
- Physical readiness for sex diminishes

This is why women often feel less sexual in the second half of their menstrual cycle, during pregnancy, or while taking certain forms of birth control that elevate progesterone.

Oxytocin and Endorphins: The Feel-Good Factor

Oxytocin: The Bonding Hormone

Oxytocin is released during touch, cuddling, orgasm, and emotional intimacy. It doesn't create desire—but it **deepens emotional connection**. High oxytocin promotes:

- Attachment to a partner
- Trust and vulnerability
- The feeling of being "in love"
- A desire to emotionally connect before, during, and after sex

While it doesn't drive libido, oxytocin explains why sex can lead to attachment—or why someone with a high sex drive might still feel emotionally unsatisfied if bonding isn't present.

Endorphins: The Afterglow

Endorphins are natural painkillers and mood boosters. They're released after orgasm or physical closeness and bring a sense of:

- Relaxation and emotional satisfaction
- Safety and comfort
- Stress relief and emotional intimacy

High-endorphin individuals may feel more "rewarded" by connection and afterglow than the act itself, reinforcing affection-based sexuality.

Nature Meets Nurture: How Upbringing Shapes Desire

Biology isn't the only factor at play. While hormones set the foundation for libido, **nurturing and early life experiences** help shape how—and when—sexual desire shows up. Our environment influences how comfortable we feel expressing our desires, how we connect those desires to emotions, and whether we view sex as something empowering, shameful, pleasurable, or even dangerous.

Early Exposure to Sex

One of the biggest environmental influences on sex drive is **exposure to sexual content or behavior during childhood or adolescence**. People who were introduced to sexual concepts at an early age—through media, conversations, or direct experience—often show different patterns of sexual behavior later in life.

For some, early exposure may lead to **hypersexuality**, or a strong focus on sexual activity as a way to find comfort, validation, or stimulation. This doesn't always mean trauma was involved, though it can be. It might simply reflect that the person's neural circuits around desire were "turned on" earlier than average. As a result, these individuals may develop a **stronger sex drive** as they grow older, along with a need for more frequent or varied sexual expression.

Conversely, early exposure to sex in a **negative or traumatic** context can have the opposite effect. Some people respond to early sexualization by emotionally shutting down around intimacy, resulting in a **lower sex drive**, sexual aversion, or difficulty connecting physical intimacy to emotional fulfillment.

Cultural Conditioning and Parental Influence

Beyond early experiences, **parental attitudes** and **cultural messaging** also shape long-term libido. Children raised in environments that are open, sex-positive, and emotionally safe are more likely to develop a healthy, integrated sense of desire. They may feel confident in their sexual needs and more comfortable pursuing intimacy.

In contrast, those raised in sex-negative environments that emphasize shame, repression, or strict moral codes around sex may internalize guilt around their natural urges. This can cause a split between body and mind—where someone has a functioning libido but represses or denies it emotionally. Over time, this can dull sexual desire or cause it to emerge in distorted ways.

Long-Term Psychological Factors

Beyond childhood, various ongoing psychological factors influence sex drive. Chronic stress and mental health issues are big ones. High stress (say, from demanding work or life crises) often correlates with lower libido – the body's instinct is to prioritize survival issues over reproduction when under threat. Likewise, depression is notorious for reducing sex drive (and sometimes the medications for depression can too). Self-esteem and body image also play a role: someone who feels confident and attractive is generally more likely to feel sexual, whereas someone with poor self-image may experience less desire or be very inhibited. Past relationship experiences matter as well – e.g., someone who has been repeatedly betrayed or hurt might subconsciously lower their sex drive as a protective measure, since intimacy now equates to vulnerability. In contrast, a person who has had positive, loving sexual relationships may feel safe letting their libido flourish. All these environmental and psychological elements intertwine with biology. For instance, a man under chronic stress might have high testosterone on paper, but his cortisol (stress hormone) is high and mental state poor – thus, he experiences little libido. Or a woman who grew up being taught sex is "dirty" may have perfectly normal estradiol levels, yet she rarely feels "in the mood" because her mind puts on the brakes.

Commitment and Cheating: Hormones and the Struggle to Stay Monogamous

Now here's where things get especially interesting: Studies show that **individuals with high sex drives—driven by high testosterone or estradiol—are statistically more likely to cheat** or struggle with monogamy. It's not that they lack morals or love their partners less—it's that their **biological systems are wired for novelty and pursuit**, and that makes long-term sexual exclusivity more challenging.

High Sex Drive = Higher Risk of Infidelity

Research has found strong links between:

- **High testosterone in men** and increased likelihood of infidelity

- **High estradiol in women** and increased interest in new sexual or romantic partners

- Strong sex drive overall and greater difficulty maintaining long-term sexual satisfaction with a single partner

These individuals are not "bad" people—they're biologically primed to seek stimulation. Their brain chemistry is highly reward oriented. They often need higher doses of novelty, variation, or intensity to feel satisfied sexually. When those needs aren't met in a relationship, they may feel restless or tempted to explore outside connections—even when they love their partner.

Interestingly, the type of infidelity may differ by hormone:

- High-testosterone individuals may engage in **impulsive cheating** or casual flings

- High-estradiol individuals (especially women) are more prone to **emotional or serial monogamy**—moving from one committed relationship to another in search of a better match

In both cases, the underlying mechanism is the same: a **high-powered sexual system** that struggles with restriction and repetition.

Low Sex Drive = Lower Risk of Infidelity

On the flip side, individuals with **lower sex drives**—usually due to **lower testosterone and estradiol**—tend to report greater ease with long-term monogamy. Their systems don't require the same level of stimulation or novelty, and they are less driven by sexual urgency.

These individuals may form relationships based more on companionship, trust, and emotional closeness than on physical chemistry. Because their internal "pull" toward sex is milder, they're less likely to chase after external validation or pursue risky encounters. They often feel satisfied with a consistent, emotionally safe partner—and are statistically less likely to cheat.

Biology Doesn't Excuse Behavior—But It Helps Us Understand It

It's important to be clear: **biological tendencies don't justify cheating or deception.** Commitment is a choice, and plenty of high-libido individuals remain faithful because they value trust and connection. Likewise, some low-libido individuals may still cheat, for emotional or psychological reasons.

But understanding the **biological challenges behind monogamy** gives us a more compassionate and realistic view of human behavior. Someone with a strong sex drive—especially if shaped by early exposure, high hormone levels, or sexual reinforcement—may need to actively work to manage their impulses, communicate openly with their partner, or explore relationship structures that allow more expression. Meanwhile, someone with a lower drive might need to be mindful of staying engaged, attuned, and sexually present for their partner's needs.

Every person is different. And every relationship brings a unique balance of desire, intimacy, and challenge. But when we strip away the moral judgment and look at **what's really happening biologically and psychologically**, we begin to see the truth:

Sex drive isn't good or bad. It just is. The real power lies in knowing who you are—and owning it.

High sex drive does not mean someone is a cheater. Low sex drive does not make someone a better partner. But understanding the **biology, psychology, and upbringing** behind your libido—or your partner's—can prevent misunderstandings and mismatches.

We're all wired differently. Some of us burn hot. Others burn slow. Some people crave physical intimacy like oxygen. Others are fulfilled through touch, trust, or connection. None of it is wrong.

What matters most is that we stop judging ourselves or others for the type of desire we feel—and start being honest about it.

Embrace Who You Are: The Key to Authentic Relationships

One of the most fundamental truths about relationships—and life in general—is that authenticity is key to happiness and fulfillment. Yet, in the pursuit of love, companionship, or validation, many people struggle to align their true selves with the roles they take on in relationships. The pressure to conform to societal norms, partner expectations, or even personal insecurities can lead individuals to suppress their natural tendencies. This dissonance often results in heartbreak, frustration, and unbalanced dynamics.

If you are naturally a highly sexual person, that's okay. If you're deeply emotional and value romance above all else, that's okay too. The spectrum of human desires and priorities is vast, and there's no one-size-fits-all formula for what makes a person "right" or "worthy" in a relationship. The key is to understand who you are and to honor that truth, even when it feels challenging or countercultural.

The Harm of Pretending

One of the primary reasons people experience hurt or end up in one-sided relationships is a failure to be true to themselves. They may feel pressure to act in ways that don't align with their natural priorities, pretending to be more sexual when they're actually emotionally driven, or acting overly emotional when their true nature leans toward physical connection. This disconnect doesn't just strain their internal sense of self—it also creates a fragile foundation for the relationship.

When someone pretends to be something they're not, they may initially attract a partner who seems compatible with this false version of themselves. However, over time, the facade becomes harder to maintain, and the mismatch between their true desires and the relationship's dynamics becomes evident. For example:

- **The Emotional Pretender:** An emotionally driven person who tries to prioritize sex over romance may find themselves in a relationship where their deeper needs for emotional intimacy are unmet. They may feel lonely or undervalued because their partner doesn't see or respond to their true desires for connection and bonding.

- **The Sexual Pretender:** Conversely, a highly sexual person who suppresses their natural urges in favor of appearing more emotionally invested may feel stifled or resentful. They might struggle with unmet physical needs or feel like they are living inauthentically, leading to dissatisfaction or infidelity.

In both cases, the mismatch leads to frustration, resentment, and eventually, the erosion of trust and connection. When people are not true to themselves, they are more likely to enter relationships that cannot fully satisfy them—and they are less likely to attract partners who truly value and complement their authentic nature.

Different Approaches Work for Different Women—But Authenticity Always Wins

For example, some dating and relationship coaches encourage men to flirt, tease, and build sexual tension to win a woman's interest, while others emphasize being authentic, emotionally available, and getting to know her on a deeper level. The truth is, **either approach can work**, but it depends largely on the woman's natural priorities—**whether she's more sex-prioritizing or romance-prioritizing**. A woman driven by chemistry and physical connection may respond more to playful flirtation, while one who values emotional depth may be drawn to sincere conversation and bonding. In either case, the most important thing is that **a man stays true to himself**—because pretending to be someone you're not always backfires in the long run.

Why Authenticity Matters

Authenticity is the cornerstone of healthy relationships. When you embrace who you truly are—whether that means owning your sexual energy, celebrating your emotional depth, or navigating the fluidity of both—you create the conditions for genuine connection. Being true to yourself allows you to attract partners who align with your natural priorities and values, minimizing the risk of one-sided or unbalanced relationships.

1. **Self-Acceptance Creates Confidence:** When you are comfortable with your sexual or emotional nature, you exude confidence. Confidence is attractive because it signals to potential partners that you know who you are and what you want. This clarity helps filter out incompatible partners while drawing in those who resonate with your true self.

2. **True Connection Requires Vulnerability:** Pretending to be something you're not creates walls between you and your partner. True intimacy—whether emotional, physical, or both—requires vulnerability. Being open about your priorities,

desires, and boundaries fosters trust and sets the stage for a deeper, more fulfilling connection.

3. **Healthy Relationships Are Built on Honesty:** Honesty about your nature prevents misunderstandings and unmet expectations. If you are upfront about being a highly sexual person, for instance, your partner is less likely to expect you to conform to a more emotionally driven dynamic. Similarly, if you prioritize romance, expressing this early on helps ensure you attract a partner who values emotional intimacy.

4. **Alignment Reduces Resentment:** Relationships where both partners' priorities align are more harmonious. When you embrace your authentic self, you're more likely to enter relationships where your needs are met, and your partner's needs complement your own. This reduces the likelihood of resentment, which often arises when one or both partners feel their needs are ignored or misunderstood.

Embracing Your Natural Self

Accepting and embracing your natural tendencies—whether sexual, emotional, or somewhere in between—isn't always easy. Society often imposes rigid expectations about how people "should" behave in relationships. For example, men are often expected to prioritize sex, while women are often expected to prioritize romance. These stereotypes can create pressure to conform, even when they don't align with an individual's true nature. These societal expectations and stereotypes are not valid because being an Alpha is not exclusive to men, and being a Beta or an Omega is not exclusive to women, therefore, prioritizing sex over romance is not mandatory for all men, and prioritizing romance over sex is not mandatory for all women.

To counteract this pressure, it's important to engage in self-reflection and cultivate self-awareness. Ask yourself:

- Do I feel more fulfilled by physical connection or emotional intimacy?
- Have I ever pretended to prioritize one over the other to please a partner?
- What kind of relationships make me feel truly happy and satisfied?

The answers to these questions can help you better understand your natural inclinations and how they manifest in your relationships.

Accepting Others as They Are

Just as you should embrace your own nature, it's equally important to accept others for who they are. Not everyone will share your priorities, and that's okay. A highly sexual person might not be compatible with someone who prioritizes romance, and an emotionally driven individual may not thrive in a relationship with someone who values physical intimacy above all else. Compatibility is not about forcing alignment but about finding a partner whose nature complements your own.

When you accept yourself, you're better equipped to accept others without judgment. This mutual acceptance creates space for honest communication and respectful boundaries, even if a relationship doesn't ultimately work out. It also reduces the likelihood of resentment or blame, as both partners can acknowledge their differences without feeling pressured to change.

The Freedom of Authenticity

Being true to yourself is liberating. It allows you to approach relationships with clarity, confidence, and self-respect. Instead of molding yourself to fit someone else's expectations, you can focus on finding relationships that celebrate your natural priorities and align with your values. This authenticity doesn't just benefit you—it benefits your partners, who deserve to know and connect with the real you.

Whether you're a highly sexual Alpha, a balanced Beta, or an emotionally driven Omega, your nature is valid. Embrace it. Celebrate it. Be unapologetically true to yourself, and you'll find that the right relationships will follow.

Chapter 2

The Law of Relationship Formats

Relationships, much like the individuals who form them, are diverse in nature. Some grow from deep, mutual understanding and respect, while others are built on dynamics of domination, validation, or calculation. Every relationship has its unique flow of power, and these dynamics largely dictate the role each person plays within the relationship. The Law of Relationship Formats states that a relationship's dynamic and flow of power is arranged based on how both parties initiate contact, interact, and their motive for the relationship. In this chapter, we will explore what I call the four relationship formats: Dominated Relationships, Validated Relationships, Calculated Relationships, and Balanced Relationships. Each format offers a distinct way to understand how people manage power, affection, and emotional investment.

Dominated Relationships: The Man's Quest for Control

In a Dominated Relationship, the core dynamic revolves around the man's pursuit of control, both emotionally and relationally. These relationships are often driven by the imbalance of affection, where the woman is more invested in the relationship than the man. She works tirelessly to please him, sometimes sacrificing her own needs or desires in the process. Her actions are often motivated by a deep affection for him—she may find him irresistible, attractive, or embodying the qualities she values in a partner. But her investment doesn't match his. He, on the other hand, remains in the relationship primarily out of convenience, not a deep emotional attachment. A Dominated Relationship can easily form when an Alpha Male who prioritizes sex over romance and an Omega Female who prioritizes romance over sex gets together.

The man in a Dominated Relationship is typically an Alpha Male—dominant, confident, and accustomed to being in control. His sole quest is to gain and maintain power in the relationship, and he exercises this power through control. This control may manifest in subtle ways, such as being the decision-maker or the one whose emotional needs are always prioritized. In more overt instances, he may dictate what his partner should wear, how she should behave, or whom she can be friends with. Whether subtle or overt, the key to understanding Dominated Relationships is realizing that the man views his role as one of governance, and he often assumes this power because his partner allows it.

Why do some women find themselves in Dominated Relationships? In many cases, they are attracted to the Alpha Male's strength, decisiveness, and confidence. These qualities can be appealing, especially if she seeks a partner who can take the lead. However, over time, this dynamic can become lopsided. Her efforts to please him may intensify as his demands or expectations grow. It's not that the man dislikes her; he simply doesn't feel as emotionally tethered to the relationship as she does. She might stay because her attraction to him is strong, or because she hopes that, through her efforts, she can win more of his love and attention. But at its core, a Dominated Relationship is maintained by the woman's greater investment and the man's convenience-driven decision to stay. Although an Omega Female prioritizes romance over sex, her relational efforts tend to be sexual in order to meet his demands and please him. And since an Alpha Male prioritizes sex over romance, his reception of sexual gratification gives him more power, control, and dominance.

Validated Relationships: The Woman's Quest for Attention

On the flip side of the dynamic spectrum is the Validated Relationship, which revolves around the woman's desire for attention and validation. In these relationships, it is the man who is more invested, constantly seeking ways to please his partner and earn her approval. The woman, while receptive to his efforts, often maintains a certain emotional and sexual distance. She is less invested in him than he is in her, yet she remains in the relationship because it provides her with the attention, comfort, and validation she craves. A Validated Relationship can easily form when an Alpha Female who prioritizes sex over romance and an Omega Male who prioritizes romance over sex gets together.

Women who find themselves in Validated Relationships often fit the mold of the attractive, self-centered female. This does not necessarily mean that she is malicious or manipulative, but rather that she thrives on being admired, adored, and pursued. Her Relational Power comes from the attention she commands, and she exercises this power by being slightly detached or difficult to fully capture. She understands that the man is trying to win her affection, and she enjoys the process of being wooed. His efforts to please her often reinforce her sense of worth and desirability.

Why do some men end up in Validated Relationships? For many, the attraction to a beautiful or highly desirable woman can cause them to put her on a pedestal. They might see her as out of their league, or they may believe that by working hard enough, they can earn her full attention and affection. In reality, the dynamic often remains unbalanced. The man's need for her approval keeps him engaged, and the woman, while flattered, does not reciprocate his emotional depth. She stays because the relationship is comfortable and provides her with the validation she seeks, but she rarely invests more than she needs to in order to keep him around. Most importantly, since an Omega Male prioritizes romance over sex, his relational efforts tend to be more romantic, thus neglecting her sexual desires. And since an Alpha Female prioritizes sex over romance, his relational efforts are useless.

Calculated Relationships: The Game of Relational Strategy

Calculated Relationships differ significantly from the Dominated and Validated formats. Rather than being rooted in emotional attachment or a quest for power, these relationships are purely methodical and psychological. Both men and women can find themselves in this format, but the common denominator is that the person in control is a "player"—someone who views relationships as a game of strategy, carefully managing multiple partners without allowing themselves to become too attached to any one person.

In a Calculated Relationship, the person in power maintains a roster of romantic interests. Some partners may be more desirable or interesting than others, but none is allowed to dominate their emotional world. The key to the Calculated Relationship is maintaining equilibrium. No partner is given enough emotional or sexual leverage to tip the Balance of Power, and the person at the center of the rotation is careful to spread their attention and affections thinly enough that no one can claim too much of their time or energy. Their ultimate goal is not domination or validation but rather the ability to maintain as many relationships as possible for as long as possible.

Why do people gravitate toward Calculated Relationships? Often, it's a fear of vulnerability. By keeping multiple partners in play, the person avoids the risk of becoming too emotionally or sexually dependent on any one individual. They may enjoy the thrill of being chased, the excitement of variety, or the power that comes with being the one who never fully commits. Calculated Relationships thrive on ambiguity. Partners are left guessing about where they stand, and this uncertainty prevents any one person from gaining too much Relational Power.

Calculated Relationships can last for extended periods because the players involved are skilled at balancing their partners' emotional and sexual needs. They know when to give just enough attention to keep someone interested without letting things progress too far. The dynamic is coldly efficient, and while it may not provide deep emotional fulfillment, it offers a sense of emotional control and detachment that some people find preferable to the vulnerability of a more emotionally invested relationship.

Contrary to popular belief, it is very common for Beta Males and Beta Females to seek Calculated Relationships because of their fluidity of prioritization between sex and romance. They can pursue sexual desires and create sexual tension when needed and can express romantic desires and embrace romantic connections when needed. Because Betas have the toughest time finding their place in the dating market, they tend to pursue Alphas, but exude Omega-like behavior when dating Alphas, thus causing them to retaliate and practice Calculated Relationships.

Balanced Relationships: The Quest for Equality

The final format, and the most ideal in romantic narratives, is the Balanced Relationship. Unlike the previous formats, which are characterized by imbalances of power, Balanced Relationships are built on a foundation of mutual respect, love, and equality. Both partners in a Balanced Relationship are equally invested in each other, and neither has a significant advantage in terms of Relational Power. This balance is achieved because both individuals recognize each other's value and commit to maintaining that equilibrium over time.

In a Balanced Relationship, decisions are made together, and both partners' needs are considered equally important. There is no dominant partner who controls the relationship, nor is there a validation-seeker who relies on the other's affection to feel worthy. Instead, both individuals are emotionally secure and committed to building a partnership based on love, trust, and respect. This kind of relationship often requires significant emotional maturity and self-awareness, as both partners must be willing to compromise, communicate openly, and navigate challenges as equals.

Why do some people end up in Balanced Relationships while others fall into Dominated, Validated, or Calculated formats? Often, it comes down to personal growth and emotional availability. Individuals who are secure in themselves, who do not seek to control or be controlled, and who value mutual respect over power dynamics are more likely to gravitate towards Balanced Relationships. These individuals are not driven by the need to validate their self-worth through attention or control. Instead, they find fulfillment in the shared love and partnership that comes from being with someone who values them equally.

Balanced Relationships can be deeply rewarding because they offer stability, emotional safety, and a sense of partnership. Both partners are invested in each other's happiness, and the relationship is characterized by a sense of teamwork rather than competition or manipulation. However, achieving this balance is not always easy, and it often requires both individuals to do the personal work necessary to avoid falling into the more common power-imbalanced formats.

Why Do People Fall Into These Formats?

The reasons people end up in one relationship format over another are varied and complex, but certain patterns often emerge based on individual personality traits, emotional needs, and past experiences.

Dominated Relationships typically attract women who are drawn to the strength and decisiveness of a dominant partner. They may find security in having someone else take charge, but this often leads to an imbalance where they are more invested in pleasing their partner than in receiving equal affection. For men, the allure of maintaining control without deep emotional investment is convenient, and they may stay in such relationships because of the convenience, assertion of control, and reaffirmation of masculinity.

Validated Relationships appeal to women who seek validation through attention. They may enjoy being pursued and admired but are less interested in fully committing emotionally or sexually. Men who end up in these relationships often idolize their partner and are willing to make sacrifices in hopes of winning her full affection. This dynamic creates an imbalance where the man's efforts to please are met with only enough reciprocation to keep him engaged.

Calculated Relationships are often chosen by individuals who fear emotional vulnerability and prefer to maintain control through detachment. The person in power enjoys the game of managing multiple partners, avoiding deep attachment, and keeping others guessing. This format is appealing to those who prioritize emotional self-preservation over intimacy.

Balanced Relationships emerge when both individuals have done the emotional work to value each other equally. They seek a partnership based on love, respect, and mutual investment, and they are not interested in playing power games. People in Balanced Relationships are often those who have learned from past experiences and are ready for a balanced, committed partnership.

Ultimately, the relationship format someone gravitates toward is often a reflection of their emotional state and their approach to love and connection. Some people prefer the safety of control or validation, while others are willing to risk vulnerability for the sake of true equality and true love. Understanding these formats can help individuals recognize the dynamics at play in their own relationships and better understand the motivations behind their partner's behavior.

The Importance of Self-Awareness and Balance in Relationships

Attraction is a powerful force. It often dictates who we gravitate toward and how we navigate our romantic lives. However, relying solely on attraction as the foundation of a relationship can lead to imbalances, disappointment, and emotional exhaustion. A healthy relationship requires more than chemistry or infatuation—it demands mutual respect, effort, and a sense of equality. When people prioritize attraction above all else, they risk falling into one-sided dynamics, where one person invests far more than the other.

The Trap of Pursuing Alpha Males and Females

The allure of dominance, confidence, and beauty is undeniable. Many individuals—Beta and Omega Females, for example—are drawn to Alpha Males because of their masculinity and the seeming security that comes with their assertive nature. Similarly, Beta and Omega Males often find themselves pursuing Alpha Females because of their beauty, charm, and sex appeal. But while this attraction might feel compelling, it often leads to relational formats that are unbalanced and unfulfilling.

Alpha Males and Alpha Females tend to command Relational Power in ways that make them difficult to equalize with. The Alpha Male's focus on control and dominance can overshadow the needs and desires of his partner, creating a Dominated Relationship. Similarly, the Alpha Female's quest for validation through attention can place her partner in a position of constant striving, creating a Validated Relationship. Neither of these dynamics offers the mutual respect and balance that are essential for long-term happiness.

The truth is that attraction alone is not enough to sustain a healthy relationship. Pursuing someone solely because they embody qualities you find desirable—like dominance, beauty, or confidence—often leads to disappointment. Relationships are not about "leveling up" or seeking a partner who makes you feel better about yourself. Instead, they should be about finding someone who complements your strengths, respects your boundaries, and invests as much in you as you do in them.

Power, Pursuit, and the Illusion of "Leveling Up"

When people pursue someone who makes them feel like they are "leveling up," it's often driven by a desire to elevate their self-worth through association—seeking validation through someone perceived as more desirable, dominant, or attractive. Interestingly, **Alphas frequently accept these pursuits** not because they're emotionally invested, but because doing so reinforces their sense of **Relational Power**. For Alpha Males, being chased by emotionally invested Beta or Omega Females feeds their need for control. For Alpha Females, the constant admiration from Beta or Omega Males fuels their need for attention. In both cases, the imbalance is welcomed—not for connection, but for the **ego boost and power advantage** it creates.

Testosterone and the Desire for Power in Alpha Males

One of the defining traits of Alpha Males is their strong drive for dominance and control, and much of this can be traced to biological factors, specifically testosterone levels. Testosterone, a hormone present in both men and women but at significantly higher levels in men, plays a key role in influencing behavior. Among its effects, testosterone increases competitiveness, assertiveness, and the desire for power. These traits are often prominent in Alpha Males, contributing to their leadership tendencies and dominant personalities.

Why Alpha Males Gravitate Toward Dominated Relationships

Because testosterone fuels the drive for control, Alpha Males are naturally inclined to seek relationships where they can assert their dominance. A Dominated Relationship provides them with the Relational Power they desire. In this dynamic, the Alpha Male often assumes the role of decision-maker, the one who dictates the terms of the relationship. The woman in the relationship, who is usually more invested emotionally, works hard to please him, reinforcing his sense of control and superiority.

For Alpha Males, this type of relationship aligns with their intrinsic need to be in charge. The dominance they exhibit is not necessarily a conscious choice but rather a reflection of their hormonal and psychological makeup. They often thrive in situations where they hold the upper hand, as it satisfies their deep-seated need for authority and reinforces their self-perception as leaders.

Beta and Omega Males: A Different Approach

In contrast, Beta and Omega Males tend to have lower testosterone levels and, as a result, are less driven by the need for power and control. Their approach to relationships is often more collaborative and egalitarian. While Beta Males may still possess a desire to lead or protect, their actions are typically motivated by a sense of responsibility or partnership rather than a deep-seated drive for dominance. Omega Males, who are often more introspective and less concerned with societal hierarchies, may prioritize emotional connection and mutual understanding over Power Dynamics altogether.

Because they are not as driven by the need to assert control, Beta and Omega Males are less likely to pursue Dominated Relationships. Instead, they may find themselves in Balanced or Validated Relationships, where the Power Dynamics are either equal or skewed in favor of their partner. This difference highlights how hormonal and personality traits influence the type of relationships people seek.

Testosterone's Role in Power Dynamics

It's important to understand that testosterone doesn't just influence the Alpha Male's desire for control within romantic relationships—it also affects how they navigate the world in general. Men with higher testosterone levels often exhibit greater confidence, risk-taking behavior, and a willingness to assert themselves in various situations. These traits can make them attractive to partners who are drawn to strength and decisiveness, but they can also contribute to Imbalanced Relational Dynamics if not tempered by emotional intelligence and self-awareness.

In a relationship, this drive for dominance can manifest in various ways, from decision-making and setting the pace of the relationship to establishing the rules of engagement. For Alpha Males, maintaining control is not just a preference—it is often a deeply ingrained part of their personality. This makes it more likely for them to gravitate toward Dominated Relationships, where they can assert their authority and feel secure in their role as the dominant partner.

Balancing the Alpha Drive

While the tendency for Alpha Males to seek Dominated Relationships is rooted in their biology and personality, it doesn't mean they are incapable of achieving Balanced Relationships. With self-awareness and a willingness to grow, Alpha Males can learn to temper their drive for control and foster a partnership where both individuals are equal contributors. However, this requires conscious effort and a commitment to understanding and respecting their partner's needs.

For those who are attracted to Alpha Males, it's crucial to recognize this inherent drive for dominance and assess whether it aligns with their own desires and boundaries. Relationships with Alpha Males can be rewarding, but they also require navigating the Power Dynamics carefully to ensure that both partners feel valued and respected.

The influence of testosterone on Alpha Males plays a significant role in their preference for Dominated Relationships. This biological drive, combined with their natural confidence and assertiveness, makes them more likely to seek Relational Power. Understanding these dynamics can help individuals make informed choices about the types of relationships they enter and the partners they pursue.

The Hormonal Blueprint of Alpha Females: Estrogen, Dopamine, and the Drive for Attention

Just as testosterone plays a significant role in shaping the behavior of Alpha Males, the combination of estrogen and dopamine heavily influences the motivations and relationship patterns of Alpha Females. These hormonal drivers not only affect emotional expression and sensitivity but also regulate reward systems in the brain—especially those linked to social validation, admiration, and power through attention. Understanding how these hormones interact gives insight into why Alpha Females are more inclined to seek **Validated Relationships**, as opposed to the relational preferences typically seen in Beta and Omega Females.

Estrogen and the Social Influence Drive

Estrogen, the primary female sex hormone, plays a critical role in shaping emotional intelligence, social awareness, and interpersonal sensitivity. But more than that, estrogen enhances a woman's responsiveness to social cues and approval. In Alpha Females, who often have naturally higher or more dominant expressions of this hormone, there is an amplified awareness of how they are perceived—particularly in social and romantic environments.

Alpha Females are often hyper-attuned to admiration, praise, and recognition. This isn't vanity in the shallow sense—it's a neurochemical loop created by hormonal activity. Estrogen increases the brain's receptivity to the emotional highs that come from social engagement and external validation. In turn, these highs create a feedback loop: the more attention and admiration they receive, the more emotionally fulfilled and powerful they feel.

Because of this, Alpha Females are often drawn to **Validated Relationships**, where the man is highly invested and constantly working to win her approval. This kind of relationship dynamic allows her to maintain Relational Power through attention, admiration, and emotional leverage.

Dopamine and the Reward of Being Desired

Dopamine, the brain's "reward" chemical, works in tandem with estrogen to reinforce attention-seeking behavior. For Alpha Females, receiving attention and admiration doesn't just make them feel good—it creates a surge of dopamine, reinforcing the behavior and motivating them to seek it again and again.

This is why Alpha Females often gravitate toward Romantic Dynamics where they are chased, praised, and pedestalized. The more a man tries to win her over, the more dopamine she experiences, which affirms her value and sense of power. This dopamine-driven motivation is a key reason why Alpha Females may stay in relationships where they're not emotionally attached, but where the attention flow remains constant.

In other words, while a man in a Validated Relationship may be emotionally invested and aiming for love, the Alpha Female is often emotionally detached—but neurologically invested. The attention feeds her reward system, making her feel powerful and desired even if she doesn't return the same level of affection.

Beta and Omega Females: Different Hormonal Profiles, Different Motivations

In contrast, **Beta and Omega females** typically have different hormonal responses and relational needs. While they too have estrogen and dopamine responses, they tend to be more emotionally relational than socially strategic. Beta Females often seek security, emotional reciprocity, and stability in relationships. They may be feminine, nurturing, and even socially active, but they're less driven by the thrill of attention and more motivated by emotional closeness and consistency.

Omega Females, on the other hand, are often introspective, independent, and emotionally self-contained. They are the least socially dependent and are more likely to value authenticity over validation. Their hormonal responses tend to be less centered around external attention and more around internal emotional balance. As a result, Omega Females are rarely drawn to relationships where they are being chased purely for their looks or status. They typically avoid highly performative or status-based Relationship Dynamics altogether.

Because of these differences, Beta and Omega Females are less likely to pursue or maintain Validated Relationships. They're not energized by the constant attention of a highly invested partner unless there is genuine emotional compatibility. They may even find such behavior excessive or overwhelming if it isn't grounded in mutual emotional interest.

The Alpha Female's Power Strategy: Attention Over Emotion

For the Alpha Female, the Validated Relationship is more than just a romantic connection—it's center stage. She becomes the center of emotional effort, the object of admiration, and the controller of the emotional pace. Her power is in how much someone desires her, how far they're willing to go to win her over, and how much attention she can command without fully giving herself in return.

Her hormonal wiring—estrogen enhancing her social sensitivity and dopamine rewarding her for every like, compliment, or gesture—pushes her toward dynamics where her value is constantly reaffirmed. She may not consciously seek to manipulate, but her biology motivates her to remain in relationships where she receives far more attention than she gives.

This doesn't make Alpha Females incapable of love or deep connection, but it does mean that without self-awareness and maturity, they may unintentionally or intentionally structure their relationships around **validation** rather than reciprocity. The pursuit of power through attention becomes a natural extension of their hormonal drives.

The Root of Toxic Relationship Dynamics: Selfishness, Self-Centeredness, and Extreme Ideologies

When relationships become toxic, the breakdown is rarely about surface-level disagreements. Toxicity is almost always rooted in deeper issues—unresolved emotional wounds, Imbalanced Relational Dynamics, and, in many cases, unchecked **ideological extremism**. At the core of these unhealthy patterns lie two major human flaws: **male**

selfishness and **female self-centeredness**. These traits are often amplified by **extreme masculine** and **extreme feminine ideologies**, which distort the way men and women view themselves, their roles in relationships, and what they believe they are entitled to.

These internal belief systems can feed narcissism in both men and women and are often the driving forces behind **Dominated Relationships** and **Validated Relationships**. When narcissism merges with ideological extremism, relationships cease to be mutual and instead become arenas for control, exploitation, and emotional neglect.

Male Selfishness and the Narcissistic Pursuit of Dominated Relationships

Men who are deeply narcissistic often fall into a mindset of **selfish entitlement**. This is where **extreme masculine ideology** plays a dangerous role. In this belief system, the world is viewed as a hierarchical structure where **men rule, dominate, and own**. The belief is not just that men *should* lead—but that they inherently *deserve* to, by virtue of being male. The unspoken message is:

"Men rule the world. The world is owned by men. Therefore, I rule this relationship—and I own the woman I'm with."

This ideology shapes how narcissistic men engage with relationships. Their selfishness is not just personal—it's ideological. They will **know** when they are hurting their partner. They will see the emotional damage. But they won't care—not because they are unaware, but because they believe it is their right to behave that way. Their emotional detachment is powered by the belief that **her pain is secondary to his comfort, his desires, and his dominance**.

This is why so many narcissistic men naturally gravitate toward **Dominated Relationships**. In such dynamics, they are able to maintain total control. The woman is often more emotionally invested, more willing to please, and more desperate to hold onto the connection. This gives the narcissistic man the power he craves. He sees her as a possession, not a partner. He feels no obligation to reciprocate love or kindness because, in his mind, **she exists to serve and satisfy him.**

Female Self-Centeredness and the Narcissistic Pursuit of Validated Relationships

On the other side of the spectrum, narcissistic women are often guided by **self-centered entitlement,** which is heavily influenced by **extreme feminine ideology.** In this belief system, the world is not just for women—it is **owed** to them. The message embedded in this mindset is:

"Women run the world. The world is owed to women. Therefore, men exist to serve, praise, and reward me simply for being a woman."

This belief distorts how narcissistic women view relationships. Instead of seeking connection, partnership, or love, they seek **validation and worship.** They often expect men to chase, provide, perform, and sacrifice without ever feeling obligated to reciprocate. If the man is hurt, overlooked, or emotionally drained, it doesn't register—**not because she can't see it, but because she doesn't care to.** In her mind, **his emotional suffering is irrelevant because he "owes" her for being in his life.**

This self-centeredness makes **Validated Relationships** the perfect setup for narcissistic women. In these dynamics, the man is constantly trying to win her over, working tirelessly to make her happy. She, in turn, gives just enough attention to keep him invested but never enough to balance the scales. It becomes a cycle of emotional extraction—**he gives, she takes, and she feels justified in taking more.** Her beauty, her femininity, and her presence are seen as sufficient payment for his effort.

The Role of Ideology in Justifying Toxic Behavior

Both male selfishness and female self-centeredness become toxic when backed by **ideological justification**. These extreme ideologies allow people to commit emotional harm without guilt or accountability.

- A **man with extreme masculine ideology** may cheat, manipulate, or emotionally neglect his partner, and instead of feeling remorse, he'll rationalize it: *"She's lucky to be with me. I'm the man. I run things."*

- A **woman with extreme feminine ideology** may ignore her partner's needs, manipulate him emotionally, or keep him in a one-sided relationship, and justify it by thinking: *"He's a man. He can handle it. If he wants me, he has to earn me every day."*

In both cases, empathy is absent. Accountability is absent. And equality—the heart of any truly healthy relationship—is completely missing.

Why This Creates a Cycle of Narcissism and Imbalance

When these traits go unchecked, they don't just affect one relationship—they create patterns. A man who views women as possessions will likely bounce from one Dominated Relationship to another, seeking women who are more emotionally invested than he is. A woman who sees men as emotional ATM machines will rotate from one Validated Relationship to the next, collecting attention and admiration while offering little emotional reciprocity in return.

In these cycles, narcissism flourishes because each new partner unknowingly feeds it. And unless there is self-awareness and emotional growth, both the selfish man and the self-centered woman will continue hurting others under the belief that **they are entitled to do so.**

The Antidote: Rejecting Extremes, Embracing Balance

The only way to break free from these toxic patterns is to **let go of extreme ideologies** and the entitlements they create. No one "owns" their partner. No one is owed anything simply for existing as a man or a woman. Relationships are not about dominance, nor are they about being worshiped. They are about **connection, effort, respect, and mutual investment.**

- A man must recognize that being male does not give him authority over his partner. Control is not intimacy. Obedience is not love.

- A woman must recognize that being female does not entitle her to endless praise and effort without reciprocity. Attention is not affection. Worship is not love.

The key is to seek **Balanced Relationships**, where both partners are equals—emotionally, psychologically, and energetically. In a Balanced Relationship, **there is no entitlement, only effort**. No one sees themselves as superior, and no one is made to feel inferior. Both people give, both receive, and both grow together.

Healing and Self-Awareness: Keys to Avoiding Calculated Relationships

Another critical step in building healthy relationships is cultivating self-awareness and addressing past wounds. Many people are drawn to Calculated Relationships because they lack the emotional tools to recognize manipulative or detached behavior. If you are not emotionally healed, you may find yourself competing for the attention of someone who is unwilling—or unable—to offer genuine intimacy. This dynamic can leave you feeling unfulfilled and undervalued, trapped in a cycle of pursuing someone who only sees you as one of many options.

Healing involves taking the time to understand your emotional needs, boundaries, and patterns. It means asking yourself why you are drawn to certain types of people and whether those attractions are serving your long-term happiness. For example, if you find yourself repeatedly drawn to partners who are unavailable or emotionally detached, it might be worth exploring whether this reflects an unmet need for validation or a fear of intimacy.

Self-awareness also helps you recognize when you are giving more than you are receiving. A healthy relationship is not about sacrificing your well-being to make someone else happy. It is about finding a partner who is willing to meet you halfway, who values your effort and reciprocates it in kind. If you find yourself consistently over-investing while your partner gives little in return, it may be time to reassess whether the relationship is truly serving your needs.

Pursuing the Balanced Relationship

The ultimate goal in any romantic endeavor should be to find a Balanced Relationship. This is the only format where both partners are equally invested, and neither feels superior or inferior to the other. In a Balanced Relationship, there is no competition, no struggle for Power, and no need to prove your worth. Instead, both individuals see each other as equals and are committed to building a partnership that is based on love, respect, and shared effort.

Balanced Relationships require emotional maturity and a willingness to prioritize the relationship over ego or personal agendas. Both partners must be willing to communicate openly, address challenges together, and make compromises when necessary. This doesn't mean that the relationship is free from conflict, but it does mean that both individuals are committed to resolving issues in a way that respects each other's needs and feelings.

The beauty of a Balanced Relationship is that it allows both partners to thrive. Because neither person feels undervalued or overburdened, the relationship becomes a source of support and growth. Both individuals can be themselves without fear of judgment or rejection, and the dynamic remains stable because both are putting in equal effort.

Avoiding Relationship Pitfalls

Relationships are complex, and there is no one-size-fits-all approach to finding happiness. However, certain principles remain universal. Attraction may spark a connection, but it cannot sustain a relationship on its own. Pursuing someone solely because of their dominance, confidence, beauty, or appeal often leads to one-sided dynamics that leave you feeling unfulfilled. Instead of striving to "level up" or "date out of your league," focus on building connections that are rooted in mutual respect and balanced effort.

Healing and self-awareness are critical steps in avoiding the pitfalls of unbalanced relationships. By understanding your needs, setting healthy boundaries, and recognizing your own worth, you can make better choices about who you allow into your life. Most importantly, remember that the only relationship format worth pursuing is one where both partners see each other as equals and are equally committed to making the relationship work.

Ultimately, relationships are not about winning or losing, domination or validation. They are about partnership, connection, and shared growth. When both individuals bring their best selves to the table and are willing to invest equally in the relationship, the result is a bond that is not only fulfilling but enduring.

Chapter 3

The Law of Dating Scarcity

The dating landscape is often compared to a pool, a figurative space where singles mingle, connect, and explore potential romantic relationships. While the water may seem equally distributed on the surface, this pool has unexpected depths and currents that create vastly different experiences for individuals depending on where they find themselves swimming. The Law of Dating Scarcity states that one's positive or negative dating experiences are largely dependent upon the abundance or shortage of available romantic and or sexual options, or perception thereof. Just as the water in a real pool varies in temperature and depth depending on which end you're in, the Dating Pool has sides that seem to benefit different groups—one end feels decidedly Male-Benefitting, and the other, Female-Benefitting.

To illustrate this dynamic, imagine a Dating Pool with 200 singles: 100 men and 100 women. You might assume that, given equal numbers, the dating experiences would be relatively balanced. Yet, within this same pool, there are unique areas where the Balance of Relational Power shifts dramatically, and the experiences become skewed. On one side of the pool, you find 80 women vying for the attention of only 20 men; this is the Male-Benefitting side. On the opposite side, you have 80 men pursuing only 20 women; this is the Female-Benefitting side.

At first glance, it might seem as though the population is unbalanced, but globally speaking, men do not outnumber women, nor do women outnumber men. The male-to-female ratio may vary from country to country but remains fairly equal on a larger global scale. Yet, depending on which end of the pool you're navigating in, it may feel as though one gender holds an overwhelming majority. This imbalance is less about sheer numbers and more about perceived availability and competition. Where there is scarcity, there is a shift in Power Dynamics, and this scarcity is felt more keenly on whichever side of the pool you're navigating in.

Understanding the dynamics of these different ends of the dating pool is essential to understanding how relationships form, thrive, or struggle within them. Let's take a closer look at each side of the pool and how the interplay of numbers impacts Relationship Dynamics.

The Male-Benefitting Side of the Pool

The Male-Benefitting side of the dating pool is where men are a rarity, and women outnumber them significantly. In our earlier example, this side would feature 20 men and 80 women. In this environment, the men, because of their relative scarcity, hold a distinct advantage in Relational Power. This imbalance creates a dynamic where women are competing more intensely for male attention, giving men the upper hand when it comes to choosing their partners and dictating the terms of relationships.

Because men are in demand in this area, they have more opportunities to engage in what we have described as "Dominated Relationships" or "Calculated Relationships." In a Dominated Relationship, the man may hold significant control over the relationship's trajectory, including its pace, level of emotional investment, and commitment. The competition among women can lead to situations where women might feel pressured to settle for less than they want or accept dynamics that benefit the man more than themselves, (such as infidelity), simply because they don't want to lose their chance with what they believe to be one of the few available men.

Similarly, men in this side of the pool can approach relationships with a calculated mindset. They can evaluate their options, knowing that they are in high demand and can afford to be selective. These "Calculated Relationships" allow men to weigh their choices, perhaps keeping multiple options open before deciding if and when to commit. Women, meanwhile, may feel the need to work harder to prove their worth, and this dynamic shifts the power in favor of the men, often at the cost of emotional balance in the relationship.

This Power Imbalance does not inherently mean that men in this part of the pool are intentionally manipulative or that women are less capable of asserting themselves. Rather, the scarcity of men amplifies the pressure on women, making it more likely that men will unconsciously or consciously adopt behaviors that reflect their favorable position. As a result, it's much easier for men in this scenario to structure relationships that cater to their desires, sometimes to the detriment of their partner's needs. The competition among women creates a kind of relational leverage for men that might not exist in a more evenly balanced environment.

The Female-Benefitting Side of the Pool

On the opposite side of the pool, the situation is reversed. Here, women are in short supply, and men outnumber them by a wide margin—20 women and 80 men (as an example). In this Female-Benefitting space, the dynamics shift dramatically. Just as men held the upper hand in the Male-Benefitting side, women now have more Relational Power. They have the luxury of choice, with men competing for their attention and investment.

In this scenario, women are far more likely to find themselves in what we have termed "Validated Relationships" or "Calculated Relationships." In a Validated Relationship, the woman's needs, desires, and emotional fulfillment take center stage. Men, understanding that women are a rarity in this side of the pool, are more willing to put in the effort to win their affection and keep the relationship thriving. This dynamic often results in women feeling more empowered, with their standards and expectations being more likely to be met, as men must work harder to secure and maintain a relationship.

The Relational Power in this side of the pool allows women to be more discerning and deliberate in their choices, which naturally leads to a form of "Calculated Relationships" for women as well. However, unlike in the Male-Benefitting side, where men calculate based on abundance, women calculate based on scarcity. They can assess their suitors more critically, knowing that they have many options. This creates a dynamic where women can afford to hold out for the kind of relationship they desire without feeling pressured to settle. The scarcity of available women forces men to compete by offering more of what women value in a relationship, whether that's emotional investment, financial stability, or a shared vision of the future. ☐

Men, on the other hand, may find themselves feeling the pressure of competition in this part of the pool. The sheer number of men vying for the attention of a smaller group of women creates a competitive environment where they must differentiate themselves from one another. In this environment, men may feel they have less control over the direction of the relationship. They may also experience a sense of frustration or dissatisfaction, as their chances of securing a partner are lower due to the numbers game. The imbalance forces them to put more effort into their relationships and may make them feel less secure in their role within the relationship.

When the Dating Pool Favors the Worst in People

Because the Dating Pool is split into a **Male-Benefitting side** and a **Female-Benefitting side**, certain individuals naturally hold more Relational Power depending on their environment. When this advantage is combined with unhealthy beliefs or behaviors—such as narcissism, entitlement, or extreme gender ideologies—it can lead to highly toxic dynamics. Those who already benefit from the numbers game may begin to exploit others emotionally, using their position not to build connection, but to feed ego and control.

When Power Corrupts: The Dark Side of Dating Pool Advantage

A man in a **Male-Benefitting Dating Pool** who holds extreme masculine ideology (believing *"men own the world"*), is narcissistic, and practices **male selfishness** can become dangerously exploitative in relationships. With women outnumbering men in his environment, he may feel no urgency to commit or consider a partner's emotional needs. Instead, he may rotate partners, withhold affection, and use his dating advantage to reinforce toxic behaviors. This combination of power and selfish ideology can lead to manipulative or dismissive relational patterns, where women are seen as disposable or only valued for what they provide.

Likewise, a woman in a **Female-Benefitting Dating Pool** who holds extreme feminine ideology (believing *"the world owes women everything"*), is narcissistic, and practices **female self-centeredness** can also be deeply problematic. With men competing for her attention, she may use validation as currency, stringing along multiple suitors without reciprocating interest. In this environment, a self-centered woman can exploit her position to gain attention, resources, or emotional leverage without ever investing authentically. Just like her male counterpart, she may never build genuine connections because her advantage reinforces ego, not empathy.

Overlooking What's Right in Front of You

While the dark side of Dating Pool advantage reveals how power can corrupt, there's another major problem that stems from it: the **illusion of scarcity**. Even in an environment where one gender has the upper hand, people often convince themselves that suitable partners are hard to find. This illusion doesn't come from an actual lack of options—it comes from fixating on high-demand individuals, ignoring viable matches, and chasing perceived value instead of real compatibility.

The Illusion of Scarcity and Power Shifts

It's important to remember that the Male-Benefitting and Female-Benefitting sides of the Dating Pool are not about actual population imbalances but about perceived scarcity. In the real world, the male-to-female ratio remains relatively equal across most societies, yet the experience within the dating pool can feel vastly different based on where you find yourself swimming. These perceptions shape behavior, attitudes, and Relational Dynamics in profound ways.

When individuals feel as though they are swimming in the side of the pool where they outnumber the opposite sex, they may unconsciously adopt strategies that reflect this scarcity. On the Male-Benefitting side, women may lower their standards, compete more intensely, or tolerate behaviors they wouldn't normally accept. On the Female-Benefitting side, men may overextend themselves, compromise more readily, or settle into roles they don't feel comfortable in, simply to avoid losing out on a relationship.

It's also worth noting that while these Power Shifts can create distinct advantages for one gender or the other, they are not inherently stable or permanent. As people move through the dating pool—whether due to changing social circles, geographic moves, or evolving life stages—they may find themselves in different parts of the pool at different times, experiencing shifts in Power Dynamics as they go. A man who once thrived in a Male-Benefitting environment may later find himself in a Female-Benefitting space, and vice versa. The dating pool is fluid, and the dynamics are ever-changing.

Navigating the Depths

The depth of the dating pool is determined not just by numbers but by how those numbers create perceptions of scarcity and abundance, and how those perceptions influence Relational Power. Whether you're swimming in the Male-Benefitting or Female-Benefitting side of the pool, the Power Dynamics are shaped by the competition—or lack thereof—between genders. In the Male-Benefitting side, men enjoy the advantage of choice, allowing them to shape relationships that often cater more to their needs and desires. In the Female-Benefitting side, women hold the upper hand, empowering them to pursue relationships that validate their worth and give them greater control over relational dynamics.

Men who prioritize sex over romance tend to have an easier time navigating the Male-Benefitting side of the dating pool. With a multitude of options, a man can exercise those options by engaging in multiple sexual escapades. There is no need for this small minority of men to express romantic interest or pursue deep emotional connection because women will compete regardless because of the scarcity of men. However, on the other hand, women who prioritize romance over sex tend to have an easier time navigating the Female-Benefitting side of the dating pool. With a multitude of options, a woman can refrain from sexual activities. There is no need for this small minority of women to explore sexual desires because men will compete and work hard for their love and affection regardless.

Understanding the shifting dynamics of the dating pool can help singles recognize the subtle forces at play in their own relationships. Relational Power is not static, and neither is the dating pool. The key to navigating it successfully lies in understanding where you are, what the dynamics are in that space, and how those dynamics affect your experience in forming and maintaining relationships. While the Balance of Power may tilt in favor of one gender or the other depending on where you swim, recognizing the flow of these dynamics allows individuals to make more conscious choices about the kinds of relationships they engage in and how they approach them.

By diving deeper into the dating pool's currents, we gain a clearer understanding of the forces that influence our relationships. This knowledge can empower singles to navigate the complexities of the dating world with greater awareness and intention, and to form connections that reflect their true desires rather than the pressures of scarcity or competition.

Balancing the Dating Pool: Moving Beyond the Competitive Mindset

While the dating pool can feel unbalanced, leading to Power Dynamics shaped by scarcity and competition, the key to achieving balance isn't necessarily found in shifting the numbers. It starts with shifting your mindset. The first step toward creating a healthier dating environment is to remove the competitive mindset that often arises in these scenarios. When singles view dating as a competition, they lose sight of what truly matters: compatibility, shared values, and mutual respect.

You should never want to date someone simply because they're in high demand. If you're drawn to someone primarily because others are chasing after them, that's a sign that the competitive mindset has taken hold. Likewise, no one should feel resigned to scarcity as an unchangeable reality. While the numbers in a given setting might create the perception of scarcity, the truth is that solutions are within reach—both on a local and larger scale.

The Psychology of Scarcity: Why We Want What's Rare

Scarcity isn't just a marketing trick or a fluke of the dating world—it's deeply embedded in human psychology. The moment something becomes limited, exclusive, or hard to get, we tend to want it more. This isn't just about attraction; it's about how our minds are wired to respond to supply and demand, perceived value, and competition.

Understanding the psychology of scarcity—alongside basic economic principles like supply and demand—helps explain why people often chase the unattainable, overlook viable options, and perceive imbalances in places where abundance might actually exist.

1. Scarcity Feels More Valuable

When something seems rare, we think it's more special. If someone is in high demand or hard to get, they seem more attractive—not always because of who they are, but because they're harder to access. This is called the **scarcity effect**.

2. Supply and Demand

It's just like economics: When **supply is low** and **demand is high**, value goes up. In dating, if someone is being chased by a lot of people, they seem more "valuable," even if there are plenty of other good matches out there.

3. We Want What Others Want

If a person is popular, it triggers something called **social proof**—we assume they must be worth wanting. This makes people overlook great options who aren't in the spotlight or being pursued by many.

4. The Ego Loves a Challenge

Chasing someone hard to get can feel like a personal win. It boosts the ego. But many people ignore emotionally available, compatible partners because they don't come with the same "chase."

5. The Truth? You're Not Out of Options

Men and women in unbalanced dating pools often **ignore viable partners** who are "in their league" and claim there's no one available. The problem isn't scarcity—it's preference. They're often chasing the most desired people instead of the best fit.

Perceived Scarcity: The Allure of the Unattainable

While the imbalance in the dating pool may feel very real to those navigating it, the scarcity of available partners is often more about perception than reality. This perception arises when people ignore, disregard, or avoid viable romantic options in favor of chasing after highly sought-after individuals. The allure of someone who appears to be in high demand—whether due to their social status, physical attractiveness, or other desirable traits—can overshadow the reality that there are plenty of suitable partners available within one's "league."

Why People Avoid Viable Options

There are several reasons people might ignore or avoid viable romantic options in favor of pursuing highly sought-after individuals:

1. **The Thrill of the Chase**: Some people find the pursuit of a hard-to-get partner exhilarating. The effort involved can make the potential reward feel more significant, even if it's not ultimately fulfilling.

2. **Social Validation**: Being with someone who is widely perceived as desirable can provide a sense of status or validation. This can drive individuals to prioritize appearances over genuine compatibility.

3. **Fear of Missing Out**: People may fear they're "settling" if they pursue someone who isn't widely sought after, even if that person is a better match for them in terms of values, goals, and personality.

4. **Unrealistic Standards**: Media, social influences, and personal insecurities can lead to inflated or unrealistic standards, causing people to overlook perfectly good matches in favor of an idealized partner.

5. **Internalized Competition**: Some individuals equate romantic success with "winning" over others, prioritizing partners who are in high demand rather than focusing on what truly matters in a relationship.

The Influence of Perceived Competition

In both Male-Benefitting and Female-Benefitting dating pools, individuals can fall into the trap of perceiving scarcity because they are drawn to the thrill of competition. When someone is highly sought after, they can appear more valuable simply because others want them. This creates an artificial sense of scarcity, leading people to believe their dating pool is smaller or less viable than it truly is.

For instance:

- **Men in a Female-Benefitting Pool**: Men in an environment where they outnumber women may perceive scarcity if they focus exclusively on women who are being heavily pursued by other men. These men may ignore or avoid women who are more compatible or more interested in them because they're fixated on "winning" the attention of a highly sought-after woman. This focus can lead them to believe that there aren't enough women available when in reality, there are plenty of viable options if they broaden their perspective.

- **Women in a Male-Benefitting Pool**: Women in a setting where they outnumber men may also perceive scarcity when they focus on men who are particularly attractive, socially dominant, or otherwise in high demand. These women may disregard men who are genuinely interested in them or more compatible, creating the illusion that there aren't enough men available. This misperception can lead to feelings of frustration and resignation when, in reality, they have options—they're just choosing not to explore them.

The Hidden Influence: Why We Want Who Others Want (Mate Choice Copying)

In addition to people placing more value on what seems scarce, overlooking viable options, and competing unnecessarily in the dating pool, there's also a fascinating psychological and scientific phenomenon at play: **Mate Choice Copying.** This concept helps explain why people—especially women—tend to be more attracted to someone if they see that others are also interested in that person. It's not just about ego or status; it's a subconscious behavior rooted in evolutionary psychology. When someone appears to be desired by others, our brains interpret that as a sign of value, making us more likely to pursue them ourselves—even if they're not the best match for us personally.

What Is Mate Choice Copying?

Mate choice copying (also known as Preselection)**,** is a behavior seen in both animals and humans, where individuals are more likely to choose a mate if they see that other individuals are also interested in that mate.

In simple terms:

We're more likely to be attracted to someone if we see that other people are attracted to them.

The Evolutionary Background

In evolutionary terms, this behavior likely developed as a shortcut to identifying high-quality mates. Early humans, like many animals, didn't always have the luxury of time or experience to evaluate every potential partner's health, status, or fertility. So instead, they could **observe the choices of others as a signal**.

If several women were interested in the same man, it suggested he had desirable traits—maybe strength, status, resources, or good genes. Rather than starting from scratch, other women might copy that interest, assuming he's a safe bet. This **social learning strategy** helped people make quicker and possibly better mating decisions.

Real-Life Examples

In modern dating, mate choice copying shows up all the time:

- **Attractiveness increases with attention**: A man who is ignored may seem average—but if women start showing interest in him, others may see him as more attractive, even if nothing about him has changed.

- **Popularity signals value**: A woman with a lot of male attention is often seen as more desirable, not just because of her looks, but because people assume she must have something special.

- **Ex-partner interest**: People often become more desirable to others after they enter a relationship. Sometimes, even people who previously overlooked them become interested. This is known as the *"taken effect."*

Why We Do It

Mate choice copying is driven by a few key psychological principles:

1. **Social Proof** – We naturally trust the opinions of others. If others find someone attractive, we take that as "proof" they have value.

2. **Risk Reduction** – Choosing a mate is a high-stakes decision in evolutionary terms. Copying others' choices can reduce the chance of picking a poor-quality partner.

3. **Scarcity Effect** – The more in-demand someone is, the more scarce (and therefore valuable) they seem. This scarcity increases their perceived worth.

The Catch

While mate choice copying made sense for survival in ancestral environments, in modern dating it can create some problems:

- **Overhyped Attraction**: People may become obsessed with someone not because of true compatibility, but because of their perceived popularity.

- **Overlooked Potential**: Many great, compatible partners are ignored simply because they aren't being actively pursued or don't have a crowd around them.

- **Toxic Competition**: Mate choice copying can increase rivalry and competition, especially in dating environments where people focus on the same "high demand" individuals.

Dating Out of Your League: When Desire Meets Reality

Sometimes, the person we want may seem more valuable because of a **scarcity mindset**, the thrill of **competition**, or simply because others seem to want them too—a result of **mate choice copying**. In the process, we may overlook great, compatible people who are right in front of us, choosing instead to chase someone who appears more "valuable" or "in demand." But in many cases, that person may be **unattainable**, not because we're not worthy of love, but because we're trying to **date out of our league**—pursuing someone whose lifestyle, looks, social status, or values don't realistically align with ours. This can lead to cycles of frustration, missed connections, and feelings of rejection, all fueled by distorted perceptions rather than genuine compatibility.

Why "Dating Out of Your League" Is Misguided

The concept of "dating out of your league" is often seen as aspirational, a way of proving your worth by securing a partner who is perceived as more attractive, successful, or desirable. However, this mindset is inherently problematic. It places relationships in a framework of competition and hierarchy, where the goal is not connection but "cool points." When one person views their partner as being "out of their league," it creates an immediate imbalance. The person who feels "less than" is likely to overcompensate, while the person on the pedestal may feel less motivated to invest equally.

This dynamic is a recipe for an Unbalanced Relationship. When one partner is constantly striving to prove their worth, they often neglect their own needs and desires. Meanwhile, the partner who is being pursued may take their attention for granted or fail to reciprocate the same level of effort. Over time, this creates resentment, dissatisfaction, and an unhealthy dynamic where one person is always giving, and the other is always taking. Rather than aiming to "date out of your league," it's far more rewarding to seek a relationship where both partners see each other as equals. This doesn't mean settling or lowering your standards; it means recognizing that mutual respect, shared values, and balanced effort are far more important than external markers of desirability.

Societal Acceptance of the Term "Dating Out of Your League."

On the contrary, some people see the term "Dating Out of Your League" as derogatory and disrespectful. It's seen as placing more value on one individual over another. But as for anything else in life, there are levels. Someone who has more sexual or romantic experience than someone else is out of their league.

When you date someone in your league, you date someone on your relational level. By default, Alphas, both Males and Females will typically have more dating experience than Betas and Omegas. That is not something to feel insecure about or shame someone for.

As a society, we need to stop being sensitive about logical dating levels and experience. Telling someone to not date someone out of their league is not downplaying them as an individual. But instead, it's protecting them from the pitfalls of one-sided relationships.

Overcoming The "In Your League" Concept

The concept of someone being "in your league" often gets dismissed in favor of the idea that love knows no boundaries. While it's true that attraction and compatibility can transcend conventional standards, the reality is that shared values, mutual interest, and comparable life experiences are foundational to successful relationships. People who are perceived as being "out of one's league" often attract significant competition because they are seen as highly desirable by a wide range of people. Choosing to focus on individuals who are more aligned with your own personality, lifestyle, and goals—people who are truly compatible—can help eliminate unnecessary competition and reduce the perception of scarcity. This doesn't mean settling for less than you deserve; it means valuing connection and compatibility over societal or superficial metrics of desirability.

How to Break the Cycle

- Don't assume someone is better just because others want them.
- Stop chasing based on competition—focus on connection.
- Give real chances to people who show up, care, and are aligned with your values.

Shifting Focus to Avoid Perceived Scarcity

To overcome the illusion of scarcity, it's important to adjust how you view the dating pool. Here's how both men and women can shift their focus:

For Men in a Female-Benefitting Pool

- **Reevaluate What You're Seeking**: Rather than competing for the attention of women who are highly pursued, take a step back and consider whether they truly align with your values, interests, and long-term goals.

- **Appreciate Genuine Interest**: Focus on women who show genuine interest in you. These connections are more likely to lead to fulfilling relationships than those built on competition or superficial attraction.

- **Let Go of the Competition**: Remind yourself that dating isn't about "winning" or proving your worth by being chosen by someone who is in high demand. It's about finding someone who appreciates and complements you.

For Women in a Male-Benefitting Pool

- **Expand Your Options**: Avoid fixating on men who are seen as the most desirable in your social circle or community. Look for men who are genuinely interested in building a meaningful connection.

- **Prioritize Compatibility Over Status**: Ask yourself if the qualities you're drawn to in a man are truly important for a long-term relationship, or if they're influenced by societal expectations or competition.

- **Recognize the Value of Mutual Effort**: A man who values you and puts in effort to build a connection is far more likely to lead to a successful relationship than one who is simply in high demand.

Embracing Abundance Through a Balanced Mindset

The scarcity in the dating pool often exists only in our minds. By focusing on compatibility, authenticity, and mutual interest, you can shift your perspective from one of scarcity to one of abundance. There are countless viable options out there—people who may not be in the spotlight but who are ready to form meaningful connections. Rather than chasing after the unattainable or allowing the competitive mindset to cloud your judgment, take a step back. Look around at the people who may not immediately capture your attention but who possess the qualities that truly matter in a partner. When you remove the pressure of competition and embrace the possibilities within reach, you may find that the dating pool is deeper and more fulfilling than you ever imagined. Here's how to break free from the competitive mindset and rebalance the dating pool:

1. Shift Your Perspective on Scarcity

The first step to rebalancing the dating pool is to challenge the idea that scarcity is something you have to accept. Just because you live in a place where there seems to be a shortage of available partners doesn't mean you're stuck. Instead, see scarcity as an invitation to explore new opportunities and broaden your horizons.

- **Don't Settle for Scarcity**: Avoid making choices out of fear that there are no other options. If you're on the male-benefitting side of the dating pool as a woman or the female-benefitting side as a man, recognize that you deserve a relationship where you're valued for who you are, not where you are.

- **Focus on Quality, Not Quantity**: True compatibility isn't about finding someone quickly because options feel limited; it's about taking the time to build a connection with someone who aligns with your values and desires.

2. Consider Relocation as an Option, Not an Obligation

Sometimes, the imbalance in the dating pool is tied to geographic factors. Certain cities or regions may have skewed gender ratios, which can impact your experience. If you're finding it challenging to meet compatible partners where you currently live, relocating to a different city or region can be a viable solution—but only if it aligns with your personal and professional goals.

- **Men in Majority-Male Cities**: If you're a man living in a city where men outnumber women, consider exploring opportunities in cities where the opposite is true. This can provide a fresh perspective and increase your chances of meeting women in a more balanced environment.

- **Women in Majority-Female Cities**: If you're a woman living in a city where women outnumber men, moving to a city with a higher male population could offer a similar benefit.

However, relocation should never feel like a forced choice. If you're in a city with a strong career path or deep personal roots, it's important to weigh these factors carefully. A good career, supportive community, and personal happiness are just as important as romantic prospects.

3. Create Local Opportunities for Connection

Relocation isn't the only way to rebalance the dating pool. You can take proactive steps in your current environment to surround yourself with more members of the opposite sex. By intentionally putting yourself in settings where you're likely to encounter potential partners, you can create opportunities to meet people without the pressures of scarcity.

For Women: Find Men in Male-Dominated Spaces

Men often gravitate toward activities and environments that reflect their interests. By engaging with these spaces, women can position themselves in settings where they're more likely to meet single men.

- **Attend Sports Events**: Professional sports games are a hub for male attendance, offering a fun and social environment where women can meet potential love interests.

- **Join Hobby Groups**: Consider joining clubs or groups that align with male-dominated interests, such as hiking clubs, gaming groups, or car enthusiast meetups.

For Men: Find Women in Female-Dominated Spaces

Women often gather in spaces that reflect their interests and activities. By frequenting these spaces, men can increase their chances of meeting single women.

- **Work in Retail or Fashion**: Malls and retail environments are popular places for women, and men who work in these spaces can naturally meet and interact with potential partners.

- **Attend Cultural Events**: Book clubs, art exhibits, or dance classes are often female-dominated spaces where men can connect with women in a relaxed and creative setting.

4. Emphasize Authenticity Over Strategy

Ultimately, the goal of balancing the dating pool is to foster genuine, meaningful connections—not to game the system. The key is to approach dating with authenticity, focusing on finding someone who truly complements your life rather than viewing it as a numbers game.

- **Don't Chase for the Sake of Competition**: The value of a partner lies in their compatibility with you, not in how many others want them. Resist the urge to pursue someone simply because they're in high demand.

- **Be Yourself in Every Setting**: Whether you're attending a sports game, working at the mall, or volunteering at an event, being authentic is the most attractive quality you can bring to any interaction.

Finding Balance Within Yourself

Balancing the Dating Pool isn't just about shifting the external circumstances—it's about finding balance within yourself. By stepping away from the competitive mindset, embracing opportunities to meet others authentically, and exploring options like relocation or local engagement, you can create an environment where meaningful connections are possible. Remember, the dating pool is what you make of it. By focusing on compatibility, shared values, and mutual respect, you can transform the dating experience from one of scarcity and competition into one of abundance and possibility.

Chapter 4

The Law of Relational Modes

In the complex world of human relationships, where emotions, biology, and personal experiences collide, it's crucial to understand the dynamics that drive our behaviors and desires. The Law of Relational Modes states that individuals tend to behave romantically or erotically depending on the phase, stage, era, or season that they are in, and will base their relationship or lack thereof on their current phase, stage, era, or season. Relationships can take many forms, but at the core of Relational Dynamics lie two fundamental modes which I call: **Romantic Mode** and **Erotic Mode**. Each mode is a lens through which people view, engage, and experience connection with others, whether seeking love or physical intimacy.

These two modes—Romantic and Erotic—aren't merely preferences or personality traits. They are deeply tied to both biological makeup and psychological conditioning. Some individuals are predisposed to spend most of their time in one mode, while others fluctuate between the two, depending on circumstances. This chapter delves into these two modes, their differences, and how they shape the relational landscape for those who embody them.

Romantic Mode: The Quest for Connection

Romantic Mode is centered on emotional bonding and the pursuit of love. When someone is in this mode, they prioritize deep, meaningful connections, often looking for relationships that have the potential to evolve into long-term commitments. People in Romantic Mode are not simply seeking a partner for casual enjoyment or fleeting satisfaction; they are searching for something more enduring—love, emotional safety, and companionship. Needless to say, men and women who prioritize romance over sex tend to be in Romantic Mode more often than not.

For many, Romantic Mode can be seen as the idealized approach to relationships. It emphasizes mutual respect, emotional vulnerability, and a desire to grow together. It is often characterized by gestures of affection, emotional support, and a sense of shared purpose.

Omegas and Some Betas in Romantic Mode

Interestingly, people who predominantly operate in Romantic Mode tend to be **Omegas** and some **Betas**. As previously mentioned, these individuals often find fulfillment in emotional connection and personal attachment, as they tend to have more **oxytocin receptors** in their brains. Oxytocin, often referred to as the "love hormone" or "bonding hormone," plays a significant role in creating feelings of attachment and affection. When oxytocin levels rise, particularly during moments of intimacy, it enhances feelings of trust, emotional closeness, and long-term bonding.

For Omegas, this hormonal influence is powerful, shaping their Relational Priorities. They often "catch feelings" more easily because their biological makeup predisposes them to seek security and intimacy rather than brief encounters or short-term flings. Omegas may be seen as those who prefer love stories over casual entanglements, finding emotional satisfaction in nurturing and caring relationships.

Similarly, many Betas, though often more versatile in their relationship dynamics, also lean toward Romantic Mode. These individuals value harmony and connection and often seek relationships where emotional stability and support are front and center. Betas in Romantic Mode may not always seek the all-consuming passion that characterizes some relationships, but they do prioritize emotional connection and reliability.

It is important to understand that for those in Romantic Mode, **romance tends to be more important than sex**. This is a key distinction. While physical intimacy is certainly a part of their relationships, it is often seen as secondary to emotional intimacy. This emphasis on connection is a direct result of the abundance of oxytocin receptors, which leads to an increased sensitivity to emotional bonding. For Omegas and Betas, relationships are a way to build a secure, loving environment that fosters mutual growth and emotional support.

Erotic Mode: The Pursuit of Pleasure

In contrast to Romantic Mode, **Erotic Mode** is focused on physical desire, sexual exploration, and casual encounters. People operating in this mode prioritize passion, novelty, and the thrill of attraction. Erotic Mode is often associated with a focus on sex, physical satisfaction, and short-term gratification rather than long-term emotional commitment. When someone is in Erotic Mode, they are not necessarily seeking emotional depth; instead, they are driven by sexual desire, excitement, and the pleasures of the body. Needless to say, men and women who prioritize sex over romance tend to be in Erotic Mode more often than not.

Erotic Mode can be seen as the more primal and instinctual side of human relationships, where the focus is on fulfilling immediate sexual needs. It values passion and intensity but often lacks the emotional investment that characterizes Romantic Mode. For some, this mode is liberating and empowering, as it allows individuals to explore their sexual desires without the expectations or constraints of a committed relationship.

Alphas and Some Betas in Erotic Mode

Those who spend most of their time in Erotic Mode tend to be **Alphas** and certain **Betas**. Alphas, in particular, are more likely to prioritize sex over emotional connection. As mentioned before, this is largely due to their higher levels of **testosterone**, the hormone that drives sexual desire and competitive behavior. Testosterone not only increases libido but also heightens the desire for sexual dominance and conquest, making Alphas more inclined to seek casual relationships or partners who fulfill their sexual needs.

For Alpha Males and Alpha Females, relationships in Erotic Mode are often driven by a desire for physical pleasure and adventure. They may enjoy the excitement of new sexual experiences and the validation that comes from being desired by multiple partners. Rather than seeking long-term emotional bonds, they often thrive on the dynamics of attraction and sexual chemistry.

Some Betas, while more adaptable than Alphas, also spend a significant amount of time in Erotic Mode. These individuals may fluctuate between Romantic and Erotic Modes depending on their needs or the context of a relationship. However, when in Erotic Mode, they share similar desires for physical intimacy and sexual exploration as their Alpha counterparts.

It's crucial to recognize that for people in Erotic Mode, **sex is prioritized over romance**. While emotional intimacy may eventually develop, the primary focus is on sexual satisfaction and the freedom that comes with non-committed relationships. Erotic Mode allows for a more flexible and less emotionally demanding approach to relationships, where pleasure and excitement take precedence over long-term bonding.

The Power Dynamics of Erotic Mode

For those who operate predominantly in Erotic Mode, the dating pool often presents opportunities for Power Dynamics that favor their approach to relationships. **Alpha Males** and **Alpha Females**—who prioritize sex and are in Erotic Mode—can easily benefit from the nature of casual dating, where sexual attraction and desirability are key. They are often able to leverage their physical appeal, confidence, and assertiveness to attract multiple partners and maintain control over their relationships.

In Erotic Mode, Alphas often find themselves engaging in relationships that can be categorized as **Dominated Relationships**, **Validated Relationships**, or **Calculated Relationships,** as previously discussed. These relationship types reflect the transactional nature of Erotic Mode, where sexual or personal benefits are prioritized over emotional connection.

- **Dominated Relationships** occur when one partner exercises control or influence over the other, often through sexual dominance or assertiveness. In Erotic Mode, Alpha Males may take on the dominant role, using their sexual appeal to attract and maintain partners who are drawn to their power and confidence.

- **Validated Relationships** are driven by the desire for approval or validation through sexual conquest. In Erotic Mode, Alpha Females may seek out partners to affirm their desirability and status, deriving satisfaction from being wanted by others. These relationships often lack emotional depth but provide a sense of affirmation for the Alpha Female's sexual prowess.

- **Calculated Relationships** are characterized by a strategic approach to dating, where one or both partners engage in the relationship for personal gain—whether it be sexual, financial, or social. In Erotic Mode, Alphas may use their charm and attractiveness to form relationships that serve specific purposes, without the need for long-term emotional commitment.

Why Erotic Mode Thrives in the Modern Dating Pool

In the contemporary dating landscape, where apps, social media, and the casual dating culture prevail, those in Erotic Mode often find themselves at an advantage. Alpha Males and Alpha Females, with their high testosterone levels and sexual assertiveness, can easily navigate the realm of short-term relationships and casual encounters. Their focus on sex and physical attraction aligns well with the current dating trends, where instant gratification and surface-level connections are often prioritized.

In this environment, individuals who embody Erotic Mode have a relatively easier time finding partners who share similar desires for casual, non-committed relationships. Whether through dating apps, nightlife, or social circles, Alphas are able to capitalize on their sexual confidence and charisma to create opportunities for Erotic Mode relationships.

In addition, men in the Male-Benefitting side of the dating pool tend to be in Erotic Mode more often than Romantic Mode because their lustful appetite is always satisfied. However, women in Erotic Mode are at a disadvantage because they are more likely to get heartbroken because they are being exercised as options since there are a plethora of women to choose from in the Male-Benefitting side of the dating pool. Nonetheless, women in the Female-Benefitting side of the dating pool who are in Erotic Mode can take advantage of their scarcity by leveraging sex and male loneliness.

The Tension Between Romantic and Erotic Modes

While Romantic Mode and Erotic Mode represent two distinct approaches to relationships, the reality is that most people move between these modes at different times in their lives. The tension between the desire for emotional connection and the pursuit of physical pleasure is a common experience for many and understanding how these modes operate is key to navigating relationships.

For those who primarily live in Romantic Mode, it can be difficult to understand or connect with someone who spends most of their time in Erotic Mode. Similarly, those in Erotic Mode may find it challenging to engage in relationships that require deep emotional investment. This tension often leads to misunderstandings, mismatched expectations, and, in some cases, heartache.

At the same time, both modes offer their own set of advantages and challenges. Romantic Mode fosters emotional security and long-term fulfillment, while Erotic Mode offers freedom, excitement, and sexual exploration. Neither mode is inherently better than the other; they simply reflect different aspects of human relational needs.

In the following chapters, we will explore how individuals can manage these modes and the Power Dynamics that come with them, but for now, it is important to simply recognize the existence of these modes and how they shape the way people interact with one another in the ever-evolving world of relationships.

Knowing Your Relational Mode: A Key to Authentic Connections

Navigating relationships requires a deep understanding of oneself and a willingness to be honest about personal desires. One of the most fundamental steps in building authentic connections is identifying which Relational Mode you are currently operating in: **Romantic Mode** or **Erotic Mode**. Are you seeking a deep emotional connection that can blossom into a long-term relationship, or are you looking for instant physical satisfaction and casual encounters? Understanding your intentions is the first step but communicating them to potential partners is equally critical.

In a world that is increasingly connected yet emotionally complex, being clear about your Relational Mode can help you avoid misunderstandings, mismatched expectations, and unnecessary heartbreak.

Why Self-Awareness in Relational Modes Matters

It is not uncommon for people to enter the dating scene without fully understanding their own desires. This lack of clarity often leads to confusion—not just for the individual but for their potential partners as well. If you're in Romantic Mode, hoping for love and emotional intimacy, you may feel hurt or rejected if you become involved with someone who is operating in Erotic Mode, prioritizing casual flings and sexual gratification. Similarly, if you're in Erotic Mode, seeking fun and physical satisfaction, you may feel trapped or misunderstood if someone you're dating expects emotional depth and commitment.

To avoid these pitfalls, it's essential to ask yourself a simple but revealing question: **What am I looking for right now?**

- Are you ready to invest emotionally and build a long-term partnership?

- Or are you looking to explore physical intimacy and enjoy the thrill of short-term connections?

Neither choice is wrong, but failing to recognize and articulate your current mode can lead to complications. **Knowing your mode is an act of self-awareness. Communicating it is an act of respect.**

The Importance of Communication

Once you've identified your relational mode, the next step is to communicate it honestly and directly with any potential partners. This transparency is not just considerate—it is essential. Being upfront about your desires and expectations helps to:

- **Prevent Mismatched Expectations**: If both you and your partner are in Romantic Mode, you can explore a connection with mutual understanding. If both are in Erotic Mode, you can enjoy the relationship for what it is. But if one person is seeking love and the other is seeking casual intimacy, acknowledging this difference early can save both parties from frustration or disappointment.

- **Establish Boundaries**: Clear communication helps establish the boundaries of the relationship. When both partners know the mode the other is operating in, they can decide whether they want to move forward, adjust expectations, or part ways.

- **Build Trust and Respect**: Being honest about your intentions creates a foundation of trust, even in casual or short-term relationships. Transparency shows that you respect not only yourself but also your partner's time and emotional well-being.

For example, if you're in Romantic Mode, you might say, *"I'm looking for something serious and long-term. I want to build a meaningful connection with someone."* If you're in Erotic Mode, you might say, *"I'm not looking for anything serious right now. I want to enjoy meeting new people and exploring connections without any long-term commitments."*

While these conversations may feel awkward at first, they are crucial for fostering clarity and ensuring that both partners are on the same page.

Accepting Differences in Relational Modes

Another important aspect of Relational Dynamics is **acceptance**. Sometimes, you may meet someone whose Relational Mode does not align with yours. Perhaps you're in Romantic Mode, hoping for emotional connection, while they're in Erotic Mode, seeking physical satisfaction. Or vice versa. In these situations, it's essential to accept the differences without judgment or frustration.

Here's why acceptance matters:

1. **Avoiding Pressure**: Trying to convince someone to change their Relational Mode rarely works and can damage the potential for any kind of relationship. Forcing someone in Erotic Mode to pursue a romantic commitment—or pressuring someone in Romantic Mode to engage in a purely physical relationship—often leads to resentment and hurt.

2. **Embracing Individuality**: People's desires and priorities evolve over time. Just because someone is in Erotic Mode now doesn't mean they will always be. Similarly, someone in Romantic Mode may later choose to explore a more casual

approach. Respecting where someone is in their relational journey is an act of empathy.

3. **Saving Time and Energy**: Accepting differences allows you to move on gracefully if the alignment isn't there, freeing you to find someone whose Relational Mode matches your own.

The Role of Dating Apps and Real-World Interactions

In the modern dating landscape, there are countless tools designed to help people find connections, whether for love or physical intimacy. Many dating apps explicitly ask users to specify their intentions: Are you looking for a long-term relationship? Something casual? Just exploring? This isn't a trivial question—it's a way to help people align their Relational Modes from the outset.

Dating Apps for Romantic Mode

For those in Romantic Mode, seeking meaningful connections and emotional intimacy, certain apps cater to this desire. These platforms are designed to foster long-term relationships, with questions and algorithms tailored to help people find compatible partners based on shared values, goals, and emotional readiness. These apps often encourage users to take the time to build a connection, emphasizing communication and compatibility over instant gratification.

Dating Apps for Erotic Mode

On the other hand, if you're in Erotic Mode, there are apps that cater to casual encounters and physical connections. Adult-oriented platforms often attract individuals seeking short-term flings or no-strings-attached relationships. These apps prioritize immediacy and physical attraction, making them a good fit for those in Erotic Mode.

Transparency in the Real World

The principles that apply to dating apps are equally relevant in real-world interactions. Whether meeting someone at a bar, a social event, or through mutual friends, being transparent about your Relational Mode is just as important. While you may not have a profile to fill out in person, a simple conversation can achieve the same clarity.

For example, if you're meeting someone in a casual setting and feel a connection, you might say, *"I had a great time talking with you. Just so you know, I'm not looking for anything serious right now, but I'd love to get to know you better."* Or *"I'm at a point in my life where I want to focus on finding someone for a long-term relationship. Is that something you're open to?"*

This kind of honesty can set the tone for a relationship that is respectful and mutually beneficial, regardless of the outcome.

Romantic Desires and Sexual Urges: Both Are Natural

One of the most pervasive societal myths is that certain Relational Modes are inherently "better" or more acceptable than others. Traditionally, men have been expected to be in Erotic Mode, seeking casual sex and prioritizing physical satisfaction, while women have been expected to be in Romantic Mode, looking for love and emotional connection. These stereotypes are not only outdated—they're also harmful.

In truth, **romantic desires and sexual urges are both natural and valid aspects of being human.** There is nothing wrong with a man seeking a deep, committed relationship, just as there is nothing wrong with a woman seeking a short-term fling. Both Romantic Mode and Erotic Mode are legitimate expressions of human needs and desires.

Logically thinking, if only men were in Erotic Mode, and women weren't, then men wouldn't have any women to be erotic with. And if only women were in Romantic Mode, and men weren't, then women wouldn't have any men to be romantic with. This outdated way of thinking is what makes men think they have to lie about just wanting something casual, and what makes women think they won't be able to find love.

Society is evolving, and with it, our understanding of relationships. Breaking free from stereotypes and embracing the diversity of human connection allows for more authentic and fulfilling interactions. Whether you're a man in Romantic Mode or a woman in Erotic Mode—or any other combination—it's important to honor your truth and pursue relationships in a way that feels right for you.

The Fluidity of Relational Modes: Seasons of Change

In addition to understanding that Human Relational Modes aren't gender specific and understanding the importance of being transparent about your Relational Mode, it's also important to understand that relationships are rarely static. Just as people evolve over time—shaped by their experiences, environments, and choices—so too do their Relational Modes. Romantic Mode and Erotic Mode are not fixed states; they are fluid, capable of shifting depending on the phase, stage, era, or season of life a person is in. Understanding this fluidity allows us to approach relationships with greater empathy for ourselves and others, recognizing that change is not only natural but also deeply personal.

From Erotic Mode to Romantic Mode

It's common for individuals who spent their younger years in Erotic Mode, prioritizing physical satisfaction and short-term flings, to transition into Romantic Mode later in life. This shift often aligns with personal growth, changing priorities, or biological and societal factors.

For example, someone who spent their teens or 20s exploring casual relationships and sexual freedom may find that, by their 30s or 40s, their desires have evolved. They might now yearn for emotional intimacy, stability, and the kind of connection that can support long-term commitments like starting a family.

This transition can be influenced by:

- **Aging and Maturity**: With age often comes a deeper understanding of oneself and a greater appreciation for emotional depth.

- **Desire for Legacy**: The biological drive to create a family or form lasting bonds often becomes more pronounced with time.

- **Burnout from Casual Relationships**: After years of casual dating, some may feel a longing for the emotional security and mutual growth that Romantic Mode offers.

In such cases, the shift from Erotic Mode to Romantic Mode isn't a rejection of the past but a natural progression into a new chapter of life.

From Romantic Mode to Erotic Mode

Conversely, someone who spent their youth in Romantic Mode—wearing their heart on their sleeve, seeking love, and prioritizing emotional intimacy—may find themselves transitioning into Erotic Mode later in life. This shift is often triggered by personal experiences or changing circumstances.

For instance, a person who experienced heartbreak or disappointment in love during their younger years might feel a need to step away from the vulnerability of Romantic Mode. They may turn to Erotic Mode to focus on personal pleasure, freedom, and self-discovery.

Other factors that can lead to this transition include:

- **A Desire for Exploration**: Someone who felt they never got the chance to fully explore their sexual freedom may embrace Erotic Mode later in life.

- **Healing Through Independence**: After repeated heartbreaks, some may choose to prioritize their own needs and desires, finding empowerment in casual connections.

- **Shifting Priorities**: For those who have fulfilled their long-term goals, such as raising a family or achieving career stability, the later stages of life may bring an opportunity to rediscover and prioritize their own pleasure and enjoyment.

How Environment Shapes Relational Modes

A person's Relational Mode can not only be determined by biology, personality, and their life stage, but it can also be deeply influenced by their environment. The culture, social circles, and opportunities around an individual play a significant role in shaping how they approach relationships.

Relocation and Cultural Shifts

Moving to a new city or country with a vastly different cultural attitude toward relationships and sexuality can lead to a shift in Relational Mode. For instance:

- Someone who moves to a more **sexually accepting culture** may feel liberated to explore Erotic Mode, free from the societal constraints or stigmas they faced before.

- Conversely, someone who moves to a more **conservative culture** might find themselves embracing Romantic Mode, as societal norms encourage deeper emotional connections over casual flings.

Changing Social Circles

The people we surround ourselves with can also impact our Relational Modes. A shift in friend groups or social environments might expose someone to new perspectives on relationships and intimacy:

- Joining a group that values casual, open relationships may encourage a move toward Erotic Mode.

- Becoming part of a community that emphasizes emotional intimacy, and long-term partnerships might foster a shift toward Romantic Mode.

Social settings provide both the freedom and the context to explore different aspects of ourselves, including how we relate to others.

The Role of Experiences in Relational Modes

Life experiences—positive and negative—are some of the most powerful influences on Relational Modes. While **biology and nature** often set the baseline, experiences add depth, color, and complexity to how we approach relationships.

- **Alphas Predominantly in Erotic Mode**: While Alphas are often biologically predisposed to Erotic Mode due to higher testosterone levels, life experiences—such as meeting a partner who challenges their emotional depth—can inspire a shift toward Romantic Mode.

- **Omegas Predominantly in Romantic Mode**: Similarly, Omegas who naturally prioritize love and connection might explore Erotic Mode after a series of heartbreaks or a life event that reshapes their priorities.

Your relational mode is not just a reflection of your biology—it is also a reflection of your **life story**.

It is also important to note that someone who prioritizes sex over romance might logically engage in Romantic Mode just because of age or decline in attraction level. But that doesn't mean that infidelity down the line isn't a possibility. The need for novelty can return, as this "newfound" Romantic Mode can be only a phase.

Likewise, someone who prioritizes romance over sex might logically engage in Erotic Mode because of numerous heartbreaks or the fear of missing out can possibly return to being the "helpless romantic" that they are. Everyone is different and there is no "one size fits all" in everyone's life story, experiences, and romantic decisions.

Why Do We Have Two Relational Modes? Introducing the Dual Mating Strategy

Why do humans even have two Relational Modes—Romantic and Erotic—in the first place? Why not just one clear, consistent approach to love and connection? The answer lies deep in human evolution. Our biology, shaped over thousands of years, has wired us to pursue **two different but equally important relational goals**: one focused on **long-term bonding and emotional security**, and the other driven by **short-term attraction and sexual desire**. This internal divide is known as the **Dual Mating Strategy (also known as Strategic Pluralism)**, and it helps explain why so many people feel pulled between the desire for love and the urge for lust—sometimes at the exact same time.

Understanding the Dual Mating Strategy

To fully grasp the complexities of human relationship dynamics, it's essential to explore the concept of the **Dual Mating Strategy**—a theory rooted in evolutionary biology and psychology. This strategy helps explain why people often experience internal tension or seemingly contradictory desires when it comes to love, sex, and partnership.

In its simplest form, the **Dual Mating Strategy** suggests that humans—particularly women, but also men to some degree—are biologically wired to pursue **two different types of partners** for two different evolutionary purposes: one for **genetic advantage** and the other for **emotional stability and resource security.**

This dual strategy isn't inherently manipulative or deceptive; rather, it's a subconscious biological impulse that can heavily influence romantic and sexual behavior, especially when someone is unaware that this split in desire even exists.

The Two Sides of the Strategy

1. Short-Term Mating: The Erotic Impulse

The short-term component of the dual mating strategy aligns closely with **Erotic Mode**. It involves the pursuit of partners with strong physical traits, charisma, confidence, and dominant energy—traits often associated with **Alpha Males or Females**. These traits are subconsciously interpreted as signs of **high genetic fitness**, and historically, selecting such partners would have increased the likelihood of producing strong, healthy offspring. Short-term mating is fueled by high testosterone attraction, passion and novelty, risk-taking behaviors, physical chemistry, and excitement. This side of the strategy often manifests during peak fertility, under the influence of ovulation cycles, hormonal surges, or even in high-stimulation environments like nightlife, festivals, or adventurous travel. In modern terms, short-term mating can take the form of fling relationships, one-night stands, secret affairs, and emotionally unavailable but sexually desirable partners.

2. Long-Term Mating: The Romantic Impulse

The long-term component of the strategy mirrors **Romantic Mode**. This involves seeking out partners who are emotionally reliable, nurturing, protective, and resource-stable—traits associated with **Betas or Omegas**. These partners are seen as safe, loyal, and capable of investing in a long-term bond, providing emotional security, care, and support. Long-term mating is fueled by oxytocin bonding, trust, emotional compatibility, security and stability, shared values, and long-term goals. In contemporary life, long-term mating is seen in marriage or committed partnerships, co-parenting dynamics, relationships built on trust and mutual growth, and emotional best friends who become life partners.

Why Dual Mating Strategy Creates Internal Conflict

The challenge with the dual mating strategy is that it **pulls people in two directions**. One part of a person might crave the safety and emotional depth of a Romantic Mode partner, while another part longs for the excitement and physical thrill of an Erotic Mode connection. This internal split can lead to:

- **Romantic dissatisfaction**: A person in a committed relationship may feel emotionally secure but sexually bored or unstimulated.

- **Sexual infidelity or temptation**: Someone might deeply love their partner yet feel drawn to a more physically alluring, dominant individual.

- **Decision paralysis**: When choosing a partner, people may struggle between the one who "feels right" for the future and the one who "turns them on" right now.

- **Post-relationship regret**: After settling down with the stable choice, one may wonder what could have been with the exciting, wild option—or vice versa.

This tension doesn't mean someone is unfaithful or flawed. It simply means they're human—and are navigating the natural biological impulse to **balance survival with desire**.

Evolution's Role in Dual Mating

From an evolutionary standpoint, the dual mating strategy made perfect sense:

- The **"wild" genetic partner** (often in Erotic Mode) would provide strong genes, immunity, and physical prowess.

- The **"safe" emotional partner** (often in Romantic Mode) would help raise the offspring, provide resources, and offer social bonding and protection.

This strategy **maximized reproductive success**—passing on the best genes while ensuring that offspring had the highest chances of survival through nurturing and support.

In ancient times, this might have been played out more instinctively. In modern relationships, however, the Dual Mating Strategy often plays out subconsciously in romantic and sexual decisions, sometimes causing confusion, guilt, or shame—especially when societal expectations demand monogamy, purity, or commitment.

Men and the Dual Mating Strategy

While the concept is often discussed in relation to female mating psychology, **men also experience a form of the dual strategy**, though typically in a more outwardly behavioral way. Men may seek long-term partners who are nurturing, emotionally intelligent, and loyal—qualities ideal for family-building—while also being drawn to physically attractive or sexually adventurous partners for short-term flings.

This, again, is rooted in evolutionary wiring: spreading one's genes while also securing a nurturing environment for those offspring to thrive in. Today, it can be seen in the disparity between the partner a man wants to "settle down" with versus the kind of partner he is drawn to in the heat of the moment.

Your Mating Strategy Is Still *Your* Strategy

The dual mating strategy is not destiny—it's data. It gives us insight into **why we feel pulled in multiple directions**, but it doesn't dictate what we must do. We are not slaves to biology. We have the power of **conscious choice**.

The key is to be aware of these instincts—not to shame them, suppress them, or blindly follow them—but to **understand** them. You get to decide how you want to move forward in your relationships, who you want to be with, and what kind of intimacy fulfills you—physically, emotionally, and psychologically.

No One Gets to Decide Your Path But You

Whether you choose to follow your Romantic Mode, Erotic Mode, or both at different times, **no one has the right to define what your journey should look like**. Your relational desires, sexual needs, and emotional goals are valid—whether they align with tradition, challenge cultural expectations, or fall somewhere entirely unique.

The Dual Mating Strategy explains how human desire evolved. But your story is still being written—by you.

In the end, your relational path is yours to walk. Whether you're chasing love, exploring sex, or seeking both in your own way and time, you owe no one an explanation—only honesty with yourself and the people you engage with.

Your Relational Mode Is Your Decision

In a world that often imposes societal norms and expectations, it's important to remember that **your relational mode is your choice**. No one has the right to dictate how you pursue love, sex, or connection. Whether you find fulfillment in long-term emotional bonds or casual, physical relationships—or move between the two at different times in your life—your desires and decisions are valid.

Breaking Free from Stereotypes

Contrary to traditional gender roles and societal norms:

- There is **nothing wrong with a man** prioritizing Romantic Mode, seeking love, and desiring a committed relationship.

- There is **nothing wrong with a woman** embracing Erotic Mode, exploring her sexuality, and seeking short-term flings.

As mentioned before, both romantic desires and sexual urges are natural parts of being human. They are neither inherently good nor bad—they simply reflect different aspects of the human experience.

Owning Your Journey

Whether your Relational Mode is influenced by biology, experience, environment, or personal choice, it belongs to you. It is your life story, shaped by the phases, stages, and seasons you've lived through. There is no single "correct" way to approach relationships—only the way that feels right for you in the moment.

Embracing your Relational Mode as a reflection of your unique journey empowers you to pursue relationships with authenticity and confidence. It allows you to navigate the complexities of connection while staying true to yourself, respecting the paths of others, and finding fulfillment in the relationships that align with your needs and desires.

Ultimately, the key is to honor your personal evolution, communicate your intentions openly, and embrace the beauty of change. Life is fluid, and so are relationships. Whatever mode you find yourself in, it is a valid and valuable part of your human experience.

Authenticity as the Foundation

Understanding your Relational Mode, communicating it openly, and accepting differences in others are the keys to building healthy, fulfilling relationships. Whether you're in Romantic Mode, seeking love and commitment, or in Erotic Mode, exploring physical satisfaction and freedom, your desires are valid. The journey begins with self-awareness and continues with transparency and respect.

By recognizing the diversity of Human Relational Modes and embracing them without judgment, we can navigate the complexities of relationships with honesty and empathy—creating space for connections that honor the truth of who we are.

SECTION 2

THE PRINCIPLES

Chapter 5

The Law of Leading and Resulting

The delicate dance between power and connection within a relationship often revolves around how each partner approaches intimacy, affection, and ultimately, power. At the core of this dynamic is the understanding of how a relationship might flow on the front end is not necessarily how it will flow on the back end. The Law of Leading and Resulting states that a relationship that begins mutually romantic in nature will eventually require erotic energy by one or both parties, and a relationship that begins mutually erotic in nature will eventually require romantic energy by one or both parties. This law governs the cyclical and predictable patterns of emotional and sexual desires, which in turn shape the Balance of Power between partners.

In relationships, particularly intersexual dynamics, two primary forces influence behavior and decisions: sex and emotions. These two forces are often prioritized differently by individuals, particularly across the spectrum of Alpha, Beta, and Omega personalities. For women, these priorities are further complicated by the natural flow of their emotions and hormones, which fluctuate as part of their menstrual cycles. Men, however, do not experience these same physiological shifts, which can create a profound asymmetry in relationship dynamics. This chapter explores these differences, laying the groundwork for deeper discussions on maintaining and navigating power balances.

The Female Dynamic: The Shift Between Erotic and Romantic Modes

For women, their approach to relationships often starts with a clear priority—either sex or love. Whether a woman identifies as an Alpha Female, Beta Female, or Omega Female, her personal orientation towards these two key aspects of intimacy will shape how she initiates and navigates her relationships. However, despite these priorities, women are subject to a constant, natural shift between Erotic Mode (desiring sex) and Romantic Mode (desiring love). This shift is driven largely by hormonal fluctuations linked to the menstrual cycle, which causes not only emotional shifts but also a change in relational needs and desires.

Alpha Females and Beta Females: Leading with Sex

Alpha Females, who are typically assertive and confident in their personal and sexual power, often lead with the desire for sex. In relationships, sex is often a primary tool for them to assert control, dominance, and intimacy. Similarly, Beta Females who prioritize sex over romance may not have the overt assertiveness of the Alpha, but they still lead with sex as a key component in their Relational Dynamic.

As mentioned before, this prioritization of sex creates what is called "Erotic Mode." When a woman is in Erotic Mode, her immediate goal is to satisfy physical and sexual desires. Her attention is focused on passion, physical connection, and often a sense of control through sexuality. But because of the constant shifts in a woman's emotional and hormonal state, this Erotic Mode rarely remains static. Over time, the Alpha Female or Beta Female, no matter how sexually driven she may be at the outset, will often find herself transitioning toward Romantic Mode.

Erotic Mode cannot remain the dominant state for most women because the natural oscillations of their hormonal cycles tend to result in a deeper emotional craving. This craving is rooted in the need for affection, commitment, and security—hallmarks of love and romance. Thus, even a woman who initially prioritizes sex will often find herself desiring emotional intimacy, turning from a purely physical connection to one that is rooted in love.

Beta Females and Omega Females: Leading with Love

Conversely, women who prioritize love over sex—such as Beta Females who are emotionally driven or Omega Females who are nurturing and passive in relationships—lead with their desire for a romantic connection. In their Romantic Mode, the focus is on emotional bonding, stability, and love. They seek partners who can provide them with security, trust, and affection before sexual desires come to the forefront.

For these women, Romantic Mode governs their relational interactions, often compelling them to pursue emotional closeness before physical intimacy. However, just as Erotic Mode leads to an eventual shift into Romantic Mode, the reverse is also true. Women who begin relationships with a focus on love will frequently find themselves transitioning into Erotic Mode.

Over time, the emotional closeness and security these women seek through love will give way to a natural desire for physical intimacy. The progression from an emotionally rooted connection to one that seeks sexual fulfillment is not unusual; in fact, it is a predictable result of the constant interplay of emotions and hormones. Thus, women who lead with love often find themselves desiring the very thing they initially placed second - sex.

The Constant Oscillation

The Law of Leading and Resulting for women can be summarized by this oscillation between Erotic Mode and Romantic Mode. Whether a woman begins by leading with sex or with love, the natural rhythm of her emotions and hormonal cycles almost ensures that she will switch modes at some point. The Alpha Female or Beta Female who leads with sex will almost inevitably find herself craving romance as her emotional state shifts. Likewise, the Beta Female or Omega Female who leads with love will find herself desiring sex as the emotional security she gains transitions into the need for physical satisfaction.

The reason for this oscillation is because sexual intercourse causes women to release the "love hormone" oxytocin. Frequent sex, especially with the same partner results in an escalation of oxytocin levels. This is why although a relationship may start off as just casual, most of the time the woman will begin to "catch feelings" and believe that the relationship is a committed and monogamous relationship. On the other hand, a woman who began a relationship in Romantic Mode will often times result in her having a desire for a casual or sexually exciting relationship because when a woman falls in love, her testosterone levels increase. This is why it's not uncommon for women in committed relationships, to get bored with their partners and feel as though they're unsatisfied because something is "missing."

This oscillation can make maintaining power in a relationship more challenging for women. Because their desires and Relational Priorities are constantly in flux, they may struggle to maintain the same level of control or influence they initially established. One moment they may feel dominant and in control through their sexuality, and the next, they may find themselves emotionally vulnerable, seeking validation through love.

The Male Dynamic: Stability in Relational Modes

In contrast to women, men do not experience the same natural oscillation between Erotic Mode and Romantic Mode. Their emotional and hormonal states remain relatively stable throughout a relationship, which means that once they prioritize either sex or love, they are more likely to remain consistent in that mode.

Alpha Males and Beta Males: Leading with Sex

Alpha Males, who often prioritize sex as a form of dominance and control, lead with Erotic Mode. For them, sex is not only a source of physical pleasure but also a means of establishing power in the relationship. Beta Males who prioritize sex, while less aggressive than their Alpha counterparts, still lead with Erotic Mode as their primary relational drive.

Because men do not experience the same cyclical shifts as women, an Alpha or Beta Male who begins a relationship by leading with sex is more likely to remain in Erotic Mode. His priorities do not change as dramatically or as frequently as those of a woman. As a result, men who lead with sex tend to remain focused on physical intimacy and dominance, rarely transitioning into a Romantic Mode in the same way that women do.

Beta Males and Omega Males: Leading with Love

Beta Males and Omega Males who prioritize love over sex typically enter relationships with a focus on emotional connection. These men are often nurturing, seeking companionship and validation through emotional bonding rather than physical intimacy. For them, Romantic Mode governs their relationships, and they are less likely to shift into Erotic Mode unless prompted by external factors, such as their partner's desires. Even then, it will be extremely difficult to do so.

Like their Erotic counterparts, men who lead with love tend to remain in Romantic Mode. Their emotional and hormonal stability means that they do not experience the same internal push to transition into Erotic Mode that women do. As a result, men who prioritize love over sex tend to remain focused on emotional intimacy, providing stability in their relationships that contrasts with the natural oscillations experienced by women.

Dominated, Validated, and Calculated Relationships

The Law of Leading and Resulting also plays a critical role in different types of relationship dynamics. In this framework, relationships can be categorized into three main types, as mentioned before: Dominated Relationships, Validated Relationships, and

Calculated Relationships. Each type of relationship is influenced by how the partners lead with either sex or love, and how their Relational Modes shift (or do not shift) over time.

Dominated Relationships

In a Dominated Relationship, the man maintains control over the woman, often through the consistent prioritization of sex instead of romance. For men, this is particularly straightforward because their emotional and hormonal stability allows them to remain in Erotic Mode without much fluctuation. As a result, a man who leads with sex instead of romance is able to maintain a steady source of power in the relationship, exploiting his partner's natural oscillations to remain in control.

For women in Dominated Relationships, the challenge lies in their constant shifts between Erotic Mode and Romantic Mode. Because their desires and priorities change over time, they may find themselves relinquishing control to their partner, who remains steady in his Relational Mode. This dynamic reinforces the Imbalance of Power, as the man is able to maintain his dominance while the woman's shifting desires make it difficult for her to establish consistent control. When a woman enters a Dominated Relationship leading with sex, it will result in her falling deeper into the Dominated Relationship because she will "catch feelings" once all the oxytocin starts "kicking in," causing her to fight harder for the man's love. And when a woman enters a Dominated Relationship leading with love, it will also result in her falling deeper into the Dominated Relationship because she will become more erotic once the testosterone elevates, causing her to oblige to a relationship that is more sexual in nature, hence the Dominant Male succeeds in his quest.

Validated Relationships

In a Validated Relationship, the woman maintains control over the man through the constant attention he gives her. For women, the constant oscillation between Erotic Mode and Romantic Mode can make this dynamic more complex. When she's in Romantic Mode, she'll be more receptive of the man's affection and admiration. But when she's in Erotic Mode she'll be resistant of his affection and admiration, causing him to fight harder for her approval, thus pushing him farther into the Validated Relationship. This is because when a man falls in love, his testosterone levels decrease, causing him to become more agreeable and compliant.

Because men do not experience the same shifts in Relational Priorities, how he starts the relationship is how he'll proceed. If a man enters a Validated Relationship in Romantic Mode, he'll remain in Romantic Mode even if the woman shifts from Romantic Mode to Erotic Mode. However, it's very unlikely for a man to enter a Validated Relationship in Erotic Mode because the sole purpose of a Validated Relationship is for the woman to gain affection and admiration, not sexual satisfaction. It's also less likely for a Validated Relationship to begin in Erotic Mode because Alphas Males who prioritize sex over romance and lead with Erotic Mode will avoid Validated Relationships all together, because these types of relationships don't benefit them in any way, shape, or form.

Calculated Relationships

In Calculated Relationships, one or both partners exploit the natural shifts in Relational Priorities to their advantage. For men, this means capitalizing on their partner's oscillation between Erotic Mode and Romantic Mode to maintain control or achieve specific goals within the relationship. Women, too, can engage in Calculated Relationships, using their understanding of their own emotional and hormonal shifts to navigate Power Dynamics and achieve relational goals.

In this type of relationship, the oscillations of the female partner and the stability of the male partner are not seen as liabilities but as opportunities. By understanding and anticipating the shifts in Relational Modes, the partners in a Calculated Relationship can maintain a careful Balance of Power, using each other's strengths and weaknesses to their advantage.

Swimming In The Dating Pool

Whether a man or woman leads with sex or leads with love is also determined by their position in the Dating Pool. A man in the Male-Benefitting side of the Dating Pool can lead with sex and start off in Erotic Mode because he has more leverage since he's in demand. However, a man in the Female-Benefitting side of the dating pool must lead with love because he doesn't have leverage. On the contrary, a woman in the Female-Benefitting side of the dating pool can lead with love and start off in Romantic Mode because she has more leverage since she's in demand. And a woman in the Male-Benefitting side of the dating pool has to lead with sex and start off in Erotic Mode because she doesn't have leverage.

But since a woman's Erotic Mode results in Romantic Mode, women in the Male-Benefitting side of the dating pool tend to remain in that side of the pool because of the oxytocin that is accumulating and causing them to compete and "fight harder." And since a woman's Romantic Mode results in Erotic Mode, women in the Female-Benefitting side of the dating pool will either remain there just for relational control, or they'll shift to the Male-Benefitting side of the dating pool in search of a more masculine man to meet her erotic needs.

However, since a Man's Erotic Mode remains in Erotic Mode, men in the Male-Benefitting side of the dating pool will also remain there because of the luxury of having a plethora of sexual options. Lastly, since a Man's Romantic Mode remains in Romantic Mode, men in the Female-Benefitting side of the dating pool will also remain there because their drop in testosterone makes them less competitive and more eager for the romance that is depleting and women's interest levels that are diminishing.

Understanding the Law of Leading and Resulting

The Law of Leading and Resulting is a powerful force in relationships, particularly when it comes to understanding the dynamics between men and women. For women, the constant oscillation between Erotic Mode and Romantic Mode presents unique challenges, as their Relational Priorities shift in response to hormonal and emotional fluctuations. It's important to remember that how women lead the priority in a relationship will most likely result in them prioritizing the opposite.

Understanding the Interplay of Personalities, Desires, and the Menstrual Cycle

Relationships are complex, influenced not only by personalities and desires but also by the natural rhythms of the human body. One of the most profound yet often misunderstood influences on Relationship Dynamics is the menstrual cycle. Understanding the biological and emotional shifts women experience during their cycle can provide greater insight into how and why they approach relationships with varying priorities—be it romance or physical intimacy.

The menstrual cycle is a biological process with a profound impact on a woman's mood, energy levels, and desires. While every woman is unique, certain patterns are universal due to hormonal changes. These shifts often explain why some women may lead relationships with the desire for sex, while others may lead with the desire for love—and how these priorities might change over time.

This is known in science as **Ovulatory Shift Hypothesis,** a theory in evolutionary psychology that explains how a woman's preferences, desires, and behaviors subtly shift around the time of **ovulation**—the peak of her fertility cycle.

Ovulation: Nature's Peak for Desire

One of the most critical phases of the menstrual cycle is **ovulation**, a time when a mature egg is released from an ovary and travels down a fallopian tube. During this phase, a woman is at her most fertile, meaning she is biologically primed to conceive. Nature has designed this phase to encourage reproduction, and as a result, many women experience a significant increase in sexual desire.

This heightened sex drive during ovulation is not only natural but also serves an evolutionary purpose. A stronger desire for physical intimacy increases the likelihood of reproduction, ensuring the continuation of the species. For women who lead with sex, this period amplifies their Erotic Mode, making them more likely to prioritize physical connection in their relationships. Even women who typically lead with love may find themselves shifting into Erotic Mode during ovulation, driven by the biological imperative to reproduce.

Luteal Phase: The Shift to Motherly Priorities

After ovulation, the menstrual cycle transitions into the **luteal phase**, the final stage before menstruation. During this phase, the body prepares the uterus for a potential pregnancy. Hormone levels, particularly progesterone, rise, leading to physical and emotional changes that reflect a "motherly" state.

For many women, the luteal phase is marked by a decrease in sexual desire and an increase in behaviors that promote pregnancy and nurturing. Women in this phase may prioritize rest, emotional bonding, and stability—qualities associated with Romantic Mode. If a woman meets a partner during this time, she may lead with love rather than sex, as her focus shifts toward creating a safe, stable environment that supports potential reproduction.

This natural shift explains the **Law of Love Leading Sex Resulting** and the **Law of Sex Leading Love Resulting**. Depending on where a woman is in her menstrual cycle, her initial Relational

Priorities may vary. If she meets a partner during ovulation, she may be drawn to them sexually, leading with Erotic Mode. Over time, this physical connection may transition into an emotional bond, resulting in Romantic Mode. Conversely, if she meets someone during the luteal phase, she may prioritize emotional connection first, with physical intimacy developing later.

Individual Variations and Societal Perceptions

While these patterns are biologically rooted, it is important to recognize that every woman is different. Some women naturally have higher sex drives than others, regardless of where they are in their menstrual cycle. This variation is influenced by a combination of genetics, personality, environment, and life experiences. Society must embrace and normalize these differences, understanding that a high sex drive in women is completely natural and should not be stigmatized.

Just as some women lead with sex and others with love, some women experience a stronger Erotic Mode throughout their cycle, while others are more consistently in Romantic Mode. Neither approach is better or worse; they simply reflect individual differences that deserve respect and acceptance.

Timing Matters: The Role of the Menstrual Cycle in Relationship Dynamics

As previously mentioned, one of the most intriguing aspects of the Law of Leading and Resulting is the role timing plays in relationship formation. When a woman meets a potential partner during her menstrual cycle can have a significant impact on her initial priorities.

- **During Ovulation:** A woman's heightened sex drive may lead her to prioritize physical attraction and intimacy. She may find herself drawn to confident, assertive partners who exude sexual energy, as these traits align with her Erotic Mode. Thus, she may be more receptive of Alpha Males and even Bad Boys (if they are Alpha Males).

- **During the Luteal Phase:** A woman's focus shifts toward emotional connection and stability. She may prioritize nurturing and romantic qualities in a partner, leading with love and seeking someone who can provide security and care. Thus, she may be more receptive of Beta Males (Average Joes), or even Omega Males (Nice Guys).

This timing creates a fascinating interplay between biology and Relational Dynamics. For example, a relationship that begins during ovulation may start with a strong physical connection but evolve into the need for a deeper emotional bond as the woman transitions into Romantic Mode. Conversely, a relationship that begins during the luteal phase may start with love and emotional connection but later develop into a need for a passionate, physical aspect as the woman moves into Erotic Mode during her next ovulation.

Implications for Understanding Relationship Dynamics

Recognizing the influence of the menstrual cycle on Relational Priorities can help both men and women navigate relationships with greater empathy and awareness. For women, understanding their own natural rhythms can empower them to make choices that align with their desires and priorities at any given time. For men, acknowledging these biological shifts can foster patience, understanding, and support, creating a foundation for healthier and more Balanced Relationships.

Moreover, this knowledge underscores the importance of communication. By openly discussing desires, priorities, and emotions, partners can bridge the gaps created by these natural fluctuations, ensuring that both parties feel seen, heard, and valued.

Expanding The Law of Leading and Resulting Beyond the Menstrual Cycle

While the menstrual cycle provides an illuminating lens to understand shifts in Relational Priorities and dynamics, **The Law of Leading and Resulting** is not exclusively governed by biology. As previously mentioned, human relationships are influenced by a wide array of factors, including life stages, environmental changes, and personal development. These shifts can alter a person's Relational Mode, transforming their priorities and ultimately tilting the Balance of Power within the relationship.

Understanding how life circumstances impact Relational Dynamics is critical for fostering long-term connections. This is particularly true when partners have different ways of leading and responding in relationships. The interplay of these factors often explains why once-balanced dynamics can feel misaligned over time and why navigating these changes can be challenging, particularly for men who lack the biological cues that women experience.

Transitioning from Romantic Mode to Erotic Mode

Consider a woman who begins a relationship in Romantic Mode, leading with love and prioritizing emotional connection and stability. Over time, changes in her environment or life stage—such as personal growth, career achievements, or a desire for excitement—might prompt her to seek more sexual stimulation. She may now crave an Erotically charged relationship that aligns with her newfound priorities, even if it contrasts with her initial Relational Mode.

For instance, a woman in a long-term relationship with a Beta Male (Average Joe) or an Omega Male (Nice Guy) may have initially been drawn to his nurturing and stable nature. However, as her priorities shift, she may begin to expect more excitement, dominance, or sexual energy from her partner. If he is unable to adapt and align with her current Erotic Mode, the Relationship Dynamic can become strained, tilting the Balance of Power away from harmony.

Transitioning from Erotic Mode to Romantic Mode

On the other hand, a woman who leads with sex and thrives in an Erotically charged relationship may find her priorities shifting toward emotional connection and stability as she progresses through life. This could occur due to external factors such as wanting to settle down, having children, or simply growing tired of surface-level intimacy. She may now expect her partner to exhibit greater emotional sensitivity and align with her Romantic Mode.

For example, a woman in a relationship with an Alpha Male (Bad Boy) may have been initially attracted to his confidence, dominance, and sexual energy. However, as her needs evolve, she might begin expecting him to become more emotionally available, empathetic, or nurturing to satisfy her new desire for a deeper emotional connection. If he remains steadfast in his Erotic Mode and does not adapt, the dynamic becomes misaligned, creating tension and potentially undermining the relationship.

How These Shifts Tilt the Balance of Power

When one partner's Relational Mode shifts and the other's does not, it creates a misalignment that drastically alters the **Balance of Power** in the relationship. The partner experiencing the shift at times gains leverage, as they are now seeking something their counterpart may not be equipped to provide. This dynamic can lead to frustration, unmet expectations, and even power struggles if not properly addressed. In other instances, the partner experiencing the shift may lose leverage because they are now fighting to convince their partner to align with them.

The Core of Relational Desire: Happiness vs. Satisfaction

As we continue to explore the deeper layers of **The Law of Leading and Resulting**, we must draw attention to a crucial but often misunderstood distinction: the difference between **happiness** and

satisfaction—and how these emotional states align with **Romantic Mode** and **Erotic Mode**, respectively.

Understanding this distinction helps illuminate many of the confusing and contradictory behaviors that occur in relationships. It reveals why partners can feel emotionally disconnected despite "getting along," why relationships that appear stable can still feel unfulfilling, and why people stay in or leave relationships that seem, from the outside, to be working. This clarity also helps decode two of the most culturally persistent relationship archetypes: why *nice guys finish last* and why *bad boys don't commit*.

Let's break it down.

Romantic Mode = Pursuit of Happiness. Erotic Mode = Pursuit of Satisfaction

When someone is in **Romantic Mode**, they are primarily looking for **happiness**. This involves emotional intimacy, companionship, nurturing, trust, and security. Romantic Mode is tied to long-term bonding, peace, stability, and future-building. The person in this mode often evaluates the relationship in terms of emotional well-being and whether their life feels *happy* and emotionally supported.

In contrast, when someone is in **Erotic Mode**, they are not seeking happiness—they are seeking **satisfaction**. Erotic Mode is fueled by sexual chemistry, intensity, physical desire, and the thrill of attraction. It's about presence, passion, and stimulation in the *now*, rather than peace and stability in the long-term future. Satisfaction is rooted in physical fulfillment and emotional arousal—not emotional calm.

Why the Confusion Happens

The confusion between these two modes is one of the biggest sources of misalignment in relationships. Many people assume that if they're happy, they'll be satisfied—or that if they're satisfied, they'll be happy. But the truth is: **happiness and satisfaction are not interchangeable.** In fact, they often exist in tension with each other.

Example 1: Happy, But Not Satisfied

A woman may be in a loving relationship with a kind, stable man. He listens. He's supportive. He provides safety and emotional connection. On paper, she's "happy." But inside, something feels missing—there's no spark, no fire. That feeling of boredom creeps in. She might not even fully understand it at first. It's because she's now in **Erotic Mode**—her body and subconscious are seeking passion and physical stimulation, but her partner is stuck in **Romantic Mode**, focusing only on happiness, peace, and emotional closeness. This is when women say: "I love him, but I'm not in love with him." "I feel like something is missing." "We get along great, but I don't feel the spark."

She's happy, but **she's not satisfied**. And that dissatisfaction grows, eventually pulling her away—physically, mentally, or emotionally. Just as the Law of Leading and Resulting states, a relationship that begins mutually romantic in nature will eventually require erotic energy by one or both parties (usually the woman). This is non-negotiable and inevitable, and this shift will occur either early in the relationship or further down the line.

Example 2: Satisfied, But Not Happy

Now flip the script. A woman may be in a sexually electric relationship with an exciting, dominant partner—someone who knows how to satisfy her body and keep her in constant suspense. But the relationship is chaotic. There's emotional distance, instability, or drama. She's **satisfied**, but she's not **happy**. This is when women say: "I can't stop thinking about him, but I know he's bad for me." "I wish he would just open up and commit." "The sex is great, but I feel emotionally exhausted."

When she tries to stabilize the relationship and pull her partner into **Romantic Mode**, she may be met with resistance. That's when she tries to "force" connection—asking for deeper conversations, demanding commitment, or setting expectations for emotional bonding. Often, this backfires. Her partner resists because he leads with satisfaction, not happiness. And now, she's torn: her body is satisfied, but her heart feels starved. And just as the Law of Leading and Resulting states, a relationship that begins erotic in nature will eventually require romantic energy by one or both parties (usually the woman). This is also non-negotiable and inevitable, and this shift will also occur either early in the relationship or further down the line.

Women Create Happiness from Satisfaction

Here's where it gets even more interesting: **women, generally speaking, pursue satisfaction first and then try to create happiness from that satisfaction.** They are biologically and psychologically inclined to seek excitement, desire, and passion. Once that's in place, they attempt to build an emotional connection *on top of it*.

This explains two things perfectly:

- **Why nice guys finish last:** Nice guys often lead with love, emotional safety, and consistency—Romantic Mode from the start. But if a woman is in Erotic Mode or seeking satisfaction first, she won't feel the chemistry. She'll interpret his emotional presence as "nice" but not "exciting." He leads with happiness, and she's looking for satisfaction. And women do not create satisfaction from happiness, therefore she will not try to "convince" him to satisfy her.

- **Why bad boys don't commit:** Bad boys tend to lead with sex, excitement, and unpredictability—Erotic Mode. They satisfy a woman's need for passion, especially in earlier life stages or during emotionally charged periods. But when a woman transitions into Romantic Mode, she begins to want *more*—emotional safety, vulnerability, and consistency. She expects the bad boy to switch modes with her. But he usually doesn't or can't. His consistency lies in Erotic Mode, and that's where the relationship fractures. And since women try to create happiness from satisfaction, she will continue to try to "convince" him to make her happy.

Men Pursue Happiness, Not Satisfaction

Now let's turn the focus to men. Generally speaking, **men prioritize happiness over satisfaction**. They are more inclined to value peace, emotional ease, and loyalty in relationships. Their natural desire is to create a safe, drama-free space where they feel appreciated, respected, and comfortable. This is why many men lead with Romantic Mode and remain in it.

When a man finds emotional peace with a woman—especially one who doesn't stress or pressure him—he will most likely stay with her, even if the sex isn't always intense. Because for him, **happiness produces long-term satisfaction.**

This also explains why:

- **A man will leave a toxic woman, no matter how good the sex is.** If she constantly disrupts his peace—even if she satisfies him sexually—he will eventually feel drained. Satisfaction without happiness is not sustainable for him.

- **A man will stay with a woman who is his peace.** She may not satisfy him in wild, unpredictable ways—but her presence brings calm. Her love brings consistency. Her energy supports him. He feels **happy**, and that's the base from which he creates his own satisfaction.

Dual Mating Strategy and the Pursuit of Happiness vs. Satisfaction

To fully understand modern relationship dynamics, we must bridge two powerful frameworks: **Dual Mating Strategy** and the **Happiness vs. Satisfaction Paradigm**. These two concepts—one biological, the other psychological—are often treated separately, but in truth, they are deeply interconnected. When aligned, they reveal exactly *why* people behave the way they do in relationships, and *why* so many relational misfires occur despite the presence of love, attraction, or commitment.

Revisiting Dual Mating Strategy

As previously mentioned, in evolutionary psychology, **Dual Mating Strategy** suggests that women have evolved to pursue two different types of partners for two different biological purposes:

1. **Short-Term Strategy:** Driven by the desire for strong genetics—typically during peak fertility phases (like ovulation)—this strategy favors men with traits like dominance, physical strength, confidence, charisma, and sexual magnetism. These men are often referred to in cultural terms as **Alpha Males** or "Bad Boys." This pursuit is primarily **Erotic** and seeks **satisfaction** in the form of sexual chemistry, thrill, and intensity.

2. **Long-Term Strategy:** This strategy is about securing resources, emotional stability, and long-term support—especially important during child-rearing phases. Here, women seek men who are reliable, nurturing, emotionally available, and consistent. These are often **Beta Males** or **Omega Males**, culturally framed as "Nice Guys" or "Average Joes." This pursuit is primarily **Romantic** and seeks **happiness** in the form of peace, safety, and bonding.

Why This Knowledge Matters

Understanding how **Dual Mating Strategy** aligns with **Happiness vs. Satisfaction** gives us the clearest explanation yet for: Why women get "the ick" in Romantic Mode when Erotic Mode needs aren't met. Why women lose emotional control in Erotic Mode but can't feel stable love in that same state. Why men "check out" of relationships that become emotionally unstable even if they're sexually satisfying. Why relational misalignment often feels like a betrayal—even though no one did anything wrong.

It also shows **why relationship longevity** depends on both partners being able to **switch modes and respond to the other's dominant desire** at the right time. This ability to shift relational priority consciously—between Erotic Mode and Romantic Mode, between satisfaction and happiness—is the true art of relational mastery. Because once you understand the deeper operating system behind attraction, love, and commitment, **you stop reacting and start leading.**

How Biology Drives Desire: Linking Dual Mating Strategy, Ovulatory Shift, and The Law of Leading and Resulting

The **Dual Mating Strategy** and **Ovulatory Shift Hypothesis** seamlessly align with **The Law of Leading and Resulting** and the **Happiness vs. Satisfaction Paradigm** by illustrating how a woman's shifting biological states directly influence her relational priorities. During ovulation, when fertility peaks, the body favors short-term mating strategies—driving women into **Erotic Mode**, where they lead with sexual desire in pursuit of **satisfaction** (aligned with the desire for genetically ideal partners). As hormone levels shift post-ovulation, women naturally transition into **Romantic Mode**, seeking emotional connection and stability in pursuit of **happiness**. This cyclical shift mirrors the Law of Leading and Resulting, where initial desires (sex or love) often evolve into the opposite mode, creating a dynamic interplay between biology and emotional needs. Together, these frameworks reveal that a woman's internal rhythm governs not only who she's attracted to, but also how and why her relationship priorities evolve over time.

The Challenge for Men

For men, these shifts in Relational Dynamics can be particularly challenging to navigate. Unlike women, whose biological cycles naturally promote oscillations between Erotic and Romantic Modes, men tend to remain consistent in their leading priority. An Alpha Male who leads with sex, for example, is likely to remain in Erotic Mode, while a Beta or Omega Male who leads with love is more likely to remain in Romantic Mode.

This consistency, while often a source of relational stability, can also become a limitation. A man whose partner undergoes a significant Relational Mode shift may struggle to adapt because he lacks the hormonal or biological cues that facilitate such transitions. Instead, his ability to navigate these changes must come purely from **experience, emotional intelligence, and personal development**. This can be a steep learning curve, especially for men who are less attuned to Relational Dynamics or have not prioritized growth in this area.

The Need for Adaptability

The only way to overcome this misalignment is for men to develop the ability to **navigate Relational Mode switches**. This involves recognizing when their partner's priorities have shifted and learning how to adapt their behavior to meet these new needs. This can be short term in conjunction with his partners menstrual cycle, or long term with a change in environment or life stage. For an Alpha Male in an Erotically charged relationship, this might mean cultivating greater emotional sensitivity to align with his partner's Romantic Mode. For a Beta or Omega Male in a Romantically charged relationship, it might mean stepping into a more confident, assertive role to align with his partner's Erotic Mode.

Adaptability requires self-awareness, communication, and a willingness to grow. Men who can successfully navigate these shifts not only strengthen their relationships but also gain the ability to maintain balance and harmony even as Relational Dynamics evolve.

Embracing Complexity

The interplay between personalities, desires, and the menstrual cycle is a testament to the complexity of human relationships. While biology plays a significant role, it is only one piece of the puzzle. Everyone brings their unique personality, history, and experiences to the table, creating a rich tapestry of relational dynamics. By understanding the natural rhythms of the body—such as the heightened sex drive during ovulation and the nurturing focus during the luteal phase—individuals can better navigate the Law of Leading and Resulting. Whether a woman leads with sex or love, her natural shifts between Erotic and Romantic Modes are not flaws or inconsistencies but rather reflections of her biology and humanity. As we continue to explore these dynamics in the chapters ahead, it is important to approach these discussions with curiosity and compassion. Relationships are not static; they are living, evolving connections shaped by the interplay of biology, emotion, and choice. Embracing this complexity allows us to better understand ourselves and our partners, fostering deeper connections and more fulfilling relationships.

Embracing Change and Growth

The Law of Leading and Resulting is a dynamic framework that reflects the evolving nature of human relationships. While biological factors such as the menstrual cycle play a significant role in shaping relational priorities, life stages, environment, and personal growth are equally impactful. Recognizing these shifts—and understanding how they influence Relational Modes—is essential for maintaining balance and connection. For women, these changes are often accompanied by natural biological cues, but for men, they require intentional effort and development. The ability to adapt to a partner's shifting priorities is a skill that can be cultivated, enabling both partners to navigate the complexities of relationships with empathy and understanding. As relationships evolve, the Balance of Power will inevitably shift. Embracing these changes as opportunities for growth rather than threats to stability can transform challenges into steppingstones for deeper connection and fulfillment.

CHAPTER 6

The Law of Progressing and Regressing

In any relationship, the interplay of emotions between two people can be understood as a form of dynamic energy exchange. That energy, however, is not always constant or predictable. The Law of Progressing and Regressing states that Relationships of all sorts, casual or committed, will go through periods where closeness is required and periods where distance is required, and the failure to adhere to what is required, closeness or distance, will cause a disruption in the overall dynamic of the relationship. The human heart doesn't follow a linear path, and emotions are far from consistent or static. Instead, they can be thought of as "mood temperatures" that influence how we relate to one another, how power shifts within a relationship, and how it ultimately evolves—or devolves—over time.

When two people connect, they bring their own emotional states, needs, and desires into the equation. These emotional states are in constant flux, particularly for women due to hormonal shifts that occur with the menstrual cycle. While men may largely remain stable in their emotional temperature throughout a relationship, women's moods and needs may change rapidly, altering the Balance of Power, affection, and dynamics within the relationship. This shifting of temperatures is the key to understanding what I call the *Psychological Mathematics of Mood Temperatures*.

Mood Temperatures: A Fundamental Concept

Mood temperatures describe the varying states of emotional need or distance that a person may experience at any given time. Simply put, someone can be "hot" when they desire connection, intimacy, and attention, or "cold" when they need space, distance, or independence. Understanding this binary framework can help us break down how two individuals affect each other in a relationship and how power shifts based on these emotional states.

Hot: The Need for Affection and Intimacy

When a person is emotionally "hot," they crave connection. This state often signals a need for affection, attention, or closeness—whether romantic, sexual, or emotional. Someone who is hot is actively seeking heat from their partner, reaching out for affection or intimacy. In relationships, when one partner is hot, they may prioritize closeness over anything else, creating a dynamic where their emotions drive the relationship forward.

Cold: The Need for Space and Distance

On the other side of the spectrum, being "cold" represents a desire for distance. A cold partner is withdrawn, perhaps emotionally unavailable, seeking space for themselves rather than closeness with their partner. Coldness can manifest as detachment, a lack of effort, a lack of interest, or even outright avoidance. Coldness doesn't always mean indifference, though; it simply indicates that a person needs something different from their partner—whether it's time alone, emotional independence, or respite from the intensity of the relationship.

Menstrual Cycles and Female Mood Variability

One of the most important aspects of mood temperatures is how they fluctuate, particularly in women. Due to hormonal changes throughout the menstrual cycle, a woman can move from hot to cold—or from cold to hot—more abruptly than a man typically would. These shifts can happen with little warning and can sometimes be misunderstood by their partners. When a woman's mood temperature shifts rapidly, the Balance of Power in the relationship can change just as quickly.

Men, on the other hand, tend to maintain a more stable emotional temperature. If a man starts a relationship feeling "hot," he is likely to stay hot, investing consistently in the relationship. On the flip side, if he begins in a "cold" state—uninterested or emotionally distant—he is likely to remain cold, continuing to invest little effort or attention.

The Psychological Mathematics of Mood Temperatures

Understanding the Psychological Mathematics of Mood Temperatures involves more than just recognizing mood temperatures; it requires acknowledging how these temperatures interact with each other to affect the relationship's dynamic. Just like in mathematics, emotional states follow certain rules of interaction. Let's consider the most relevant mathematical principle to this analogy: the multiplication of positive and negative numbers.

In this context, a positive number represents heat or emotional investment, while a negative number represents coldness or emotional distance. The formula works as follows:

- **A positive multiplied by a positive equals a positive**: If both partners are emotionally hot, the relationship stays warm and progresses, with both people pouring energy and affection into one another.

- **A negative multiplied by a positive equals a negative**: If one partner is hot while the other is cold, the emotional temperature often balances toward coldness. The partner seeking distance (cold) may find the other's emotional intensity (hot) overwhelming, causing them to withdraw even more.

- **A negative multiplied by a negative equals a positive**: Surprisingly, when both partners are cold—emotionally distant—there is potential for one or both to heat up over time.

Coldness breeds a sort of balance that can eventually ignite a renewed interest or desire. For instance, when a woman is emotionally distant and the man is equally distant, her desire for affection may reignite, causing her to become "hot."

Examples of Temperature Dynamics in Action

Consider a relationship where the woman begins emotionally distant—cold. If the man, too, is emotionally distant, they may initially drift apart. But in some cases, the woman's emotional state will change, often because she notices the man is not overly needy or demanding. This emotional coldness from both sides can lead to a positive turn, where the woman, recognizing the man's independence, becomes more interested or invested in him. Mathematically, this is the negative multiplied by the negative, yielding a positive outcome—her emotional temperature heats up.

Conversely, if a woman starts cold and the man is hot—seeking affection, intimacy, and closeness—her emotional distance may deepen. The more he pushes for connection, the more she feels the need to pull away, further cooling her mood temperature. In this case, a negative (her emotional coldness) is multiplied by a positive (his emotional heat), leading to a negative outcome—the relationship cools down overall.

A caveat to keep in mind is that just because both a man and a woman are hot, and the relationship is hot because a positive number multiplied by a positive number equals a positive number, the woman can abruptly go cold, but the man will remain hot, and a positive number multiplied by a negative number equals a negative number. This is why men often find themselves in a situation where everything was "lovey-dovey" one minute and the next minute he finds himself fighting for her love. Once this happens, it's next to impossible to shift the dynamic in his favor because men generally do not change mood temperatures.

On the flipside, if a woman is hot and a man is cold, it's easier for a woman to also go cold and switch the dynamic in her favor because she naturally will eventually go cold anyway. Nonetheless, if a woman is cold and a man is cold, she will eventually go hot, tilting the balance in his favor. And since men tend to stay at the same mood temperature, he will remain cold for the most part.

Progression and Regression Periods in Relationships

Just as temperatures rise and fall, relationships experience cycles of progression and regression. Progression occurs when emotional investment builds over time, heating the relationship and pushing it toward deeper intimacy or commitment. Regression happens when emotional distance expands, cooling the relationship and pushing the partners further apart.

Progression Periods

A relationship progresses when one partner's emotional heat encourages the other to respond in kind. For example, if a woman starts in a hot emotional state, craving affection and intimacy, and her partner responds with equal heat, the relationship moves forward. As her emotional temperature heats up, she may require more closeness from her partner. If he meets this need, the relationship progresses further. Her emotional heat, multiplied by his emotional heat, creates an upward trajectory of connection.

Regression Periods

Conversely, a relationship regresses when one partner's emotional heat is met with coldness, or when both partners remain emotionally distant. If a woman is cold, and her partner's constant emotional heat makes her withdraw even more, the relationship regresses. The more one partner pushes for closeness, the more the other retreats. Over time, this dynamic can lead to an emotional distance that is difficult to close. Her emotional coldness, multiplied by his emotional heat, results in a negative number—a colder and more distant relationship.

Dominated Relationships

A Dominated Relationship may occur when the man's emotional coldness is met with equal emotional coldness from the woman. Initially, both partners may seem disinterested or emotionally distant, but over time, the relationship may shift in the man's favor. This happens because the woman, recognizing that her partner is not needy or demanding, begins to feel a sense of intrigue or desire. The negative multiplied by the negative—her coldness and his coldness—equals a positive outcome, igniting her interest.

In this case, the man holds the power in the relationship. His emotional distance keeps the woman from gaining too much control, causing her to become completely powerless. Over time, this dynamic leaves the man in a position of dominance, as the woman's emotional temperature heats up in response to his continued coldness. Dominated Relationships can also occur when the man's emotional coldness is met with emotional heat from the woman from the beginning of the relationship. She will find herself fighting to gain attention and attraction from the man right from the start. But since he will never get hot, she will find herself in an endless battle of fighting for his love, which will leave her completely Relationally Powerless.

Validated Relationships

In a Validated Relationship, the emotional power shifts to the woman. This occurs when her emotional coldness is met by the man's consistent emotional heat. In this dynamic, the more distant she becomes, the more effort the man puts into the relationship, seeking affection and giving her validation. Her emotional coldness, multiplied by his emotional heat, creates a negative cycle where she holds the upper hand. This type of relationship can be emotionally draining for the man, who continuously invests in someone who remains emotionally distant. Over time, the woman gains more control over the relationship, as her partner's consistent heat keeps her in a position of emotional power.

Validated Relationships can also occur when a woman's emotional heat has shifted to emotional coldness and a man's emotional heat has remained hot. This overwhelms the Psychological Mathematics of Mood Temperatures because the man is unable to cool off due to men's lack of biological and physiological factors to swing from one mood temperature to another. Therefore, once a relationship has evolved into a Validated Relationship, it is highly unlikely for the Balance of Power to tilt in favor of the man.

Calculated Relationships

In a Calculated Relationship, a man uses his heat on his partner or partners who are also hot. However, once the natural shift in mood temperature occurs, he will use his heat on another partner or other partners who are also hot. If men don't have a way to cool off from emotional heat, and since a positive number multiplied by a negative equal a negative number, the only way certain men see possible to avoid overheating and overwhelming his cold partner or partners is to use his heat on someone else who is also hot or other people who are also hot. Hence, he will never turn anyone off, push anyone away, or make anyone loose interest. This is why "Players" can keep partners around for prolonged periods of time.

Women can also use mood temperature switching in Calculated Relationships. Although it is biologically easier for women to shift from cold to hot and from hot to cold, women may use the tactic of Calculated Relationships when they switch Relational Modes. Meaning, when she needs emotional fulfillment, she can receive it from one of her options, and when she needs sexual fulfillment, she can also receive it from one of her options, ultimately never overheating or overwhelming the Psychological Mathematics of Mood Temperatures.

Hot Temperatures: Romantic Mode vs. Erotic Mode

When a person is hot, they can either be in Romantic Mode or Erotic Mode. Let's call Romantic Mode "Dry Heat" and call Erotic

Mode "Humidity." When a woman is cold, then goes hot, she can experience Dry Heat or Humidity depending on whether she's leans more towards sex or leans more towards romance in the Sex vs Romance Priority Meter. As previously mentioned, Alphas and some Betas tend to prioritize sex over romance, therefore, when an Alpha Female and when some Beta Females are hot, their heat will most likely be Humidity – Erotic Mode. And when some Beta Females and Omega Females are hot, their heat will most likely be Dry Heat – Romantic Mode.

The Evolution of Hot Temperatures: Shifting Between Leading and Resulting

As previously mentioned, interplay between Romantic Mode and Erotic Mode is not static, and an individual's primary Relational Mode can evolve throughout the course of a relationship. This shift often occurs in individuals who start hot in either Romantic Mode or Erotic Mode and transition to the opposite result while remaining hot in their mood temperature. Here's how these shifts typically occur:

Love-Leading to Sex-Resulting

When someone begins hot in Romantic Mode, they may initially prioritize emotional closeness, seeking companionship, deep conversation, and shared experiences. Over time, however, this emotional closeness can lead to a desire for physical intimacy as an outcome of their emotional attachment. This shift results in a transition from Love-Leading to Sex-Resulting; the person remains hot in their emotional state but begins expressing their heat through Humidity (Erotic Mode), moving from prioritizing connection to seeking physical intimacy. Keep in mind that when a woman falls in love, her testosterone levels rise, and testosterone increases sex drive.

For example, a Beta Female who initially seeks closeness may, after establishing an emotional attachment, transition to seeking physical connection as a natural progression. While they started in a Love-

Leading state, they eventually move toward a Sex-Resulting state, where physical closeness becomes a primary goal once the emotional attachment is secured. But since the Psychological Mathematics of Mood Temperatures are at play, her rise in temperature, which is humid and in an erotic state, will cause her to fight for his love in a more sexual demeaner. Her strategy for "winning the man over" will be sexual in nature and she will attempt to satisfy him sexually, giving him more control and more power.

Sex-Leading to Love-Resulting

In contrast, someone who begins hot in Erotic Mode may prioritize physical intimacy at the onset, using chemistry and physical attraction to drive connection. However, as the relationship progresses, they may shift toward a deeper emotional connection, evolving from Sex-Leading to Love-Resulting. The physical bond becomes a catalyst for developing Romantic Mode, where emotional connection is sought as an outcome of the initial physical connection. Keep in mind that women experience a surge in oxytocin through sexual intercourse, and oxytocin, also known as the "love-hormone," is the hormone that makes someone feel attached to someone else.

For instance, an Alpha Female may initially seek physical intimacy as the primary means of connection. But as the relationship grows, they may find themselves wanting emotional closeness, evolving from an Erotic Mode focus to a Romantic Mode focus. Here, the relationship remains hot, but the motivating need shifts from physical intimacy to emotional depth. But once again, since the Psychological Mathematics of Mood Temperatures are at play, her rise in temperature, which is dry heat and in a romantic state, will cause her to fight for his love in a more romantic demeaner. Her strategy for "winning the man over" will be more romantic in nature and she will attempt to satisfy him romantically, causing him to lose interest and potentially "dump" her because he was only interested in a sexual relationship. Or he will keep her around for convenience since she will support him and nurture him in an attempt to make him fall in love with her.

The Role of Dating Pool Dynamics in Mood Temperature Expression

Mood Temperatures don't exist in a vacuum; they're significantly influenced by the social dynamics of the Dating Pool. The environment in which a person operates—their relative standing within the Dating Market—affects how freely they can express their Mood Temperature and whether their heat or coldness ultimately influences the Power Dynamics within their relationships.

The Impact of Overheating on Power Dynamics

The ability to manage or distribute one's emotional heat plays a significant role in determining the Balance of Power within a relationship. Overheating, whether romantic or erotic, can shift the dynamics of power, dependency, and influence between partners, often giving the partner who remains emotionally balanced an advantage.

- **For Men in the Male-Benefitting Pool:** Since these men can express their heat across multiple connections, they avoid placing all their emotional or sexual energy in one relationship. This approach helps them maintain Relational Control, as their partners are less likely to feel needed or overwhelmed by the man's emotional or sexual heat. This keeps the Balance of Power in the man's favor, as he can strategically regulate his heat without losing his emotional or sexual center.

- **For Women in the Male-Benefitting Pool:** When women overheat in this scenario, it often results in an Imbalance of Power. The man, who maintains the ability to distribute his heat elsewhere, gains a Relational Advantage, as the woman's heightened need intensifies her dependence on him. Her overheating serves to increase his control over the relationship, as her emotional or physical reliance creates an unequal dynamic where he is less emotionally invested.

- **For Men in the Female-Benefitting Pool:** Men in this position are more likely to become dependent on a single connection due to their limited dating options. As they overheat—whether in Romantic Mode or Erotic Mode—their increased emotional or sexual reliance gives the woman greater control over the relationship. This can lead to a situation where the man's intense need for connection makes him vulnerable to imbalances, as he lacks alternative options to temper his emotional investment or sexual needs.

- **For Women in the Female-Benefitting Pool:** With ample options at their disposal, women in this position can manage their emotional heat without overheating, preventing them from becoming overly reliant on any single partner. This variety ensures that they maintain Relational Control, as they can distribute their emotional or physical investment in ways that prevent excessive dependency. Their ability to avoid overheating enables them to maintain power within the relationship, as they are less emotionally invested in any one connection.

The Mathematical Outcome of Emotional States

The Psychological Mathematics of Mood Temperatures shows us that relationships are far from simple. Mood Temperatures interact in ways that can either push partners closer together or drive them apart. When two people come together, their emotional and or sexual states—whether hot or cold—determine the trajectory of their relationship. By understanding how these Mood Temperatures interact, we can begin to see the hidden forces at play in our relationships.

Relationships are not stagnant; they progress, regress, and shift based on these emotional and sexual interactions. The Balance of Power, attention, and control are constantly in flux, and each partner's

Mood Temperature plays a key role in determining whether the relationship moves forward or falls apart.

Navigating the Complexity of Mood Temperatures

The Psychological Mathematics of Mood Temperatures within relationships is a complex formula that combines Mood Temperatures with Relational Modes, personality types, and Dating Pool Dynamics. The result is an intricate web of interdependencies and imbalances that shape the flow of power, connection, and attachment. Mood Temperatures alone do not dictate the outcome of a relationship; they work in tandem with Relational Priorities (Romantic or Erotic) and environmental factors (Male- or Female-Benefitting Dating Pool) to create a constantly shifting emotional and sexual landscape. By understanding how these variables interact, one can gain deeper insight into the subtle forces at play in relationships and the Power Dynamics that stem from our emotional and sexual needs, expectations, and behaviors.

The Root of Imbalances

The Imbalances of Power in relationships often arise from the misuse of nature and the misunderstanding of how Relational Dynamics are meant to operate. At its core, relationships are about the exchange of emotional, physical, and psychological resources. This exchange requires balance for the relationship to flourish, but when one party withholds or overdraws, it leads to instability and dissatisfaction. Let's explore this concept through the metaphor of power as currency and how its distribution defines the dynamics of different types of relationships.

The Nature of Power Exchange in Relationships

There's an old saying that encapsulates the vulnerability and empowerment inherent in relationships:

- *"When a man loves a woman, she becomes his weakness, and when a woman loves a man, he becomes her strength."*

This highlights the inherent Exchange of Power that occurs when two people connect. For a relationship to work, this exchange must be reciprocal and balanced. When a man falls in love with a woman, he inherently gives her his power—his emotional energy, attention, and resources—because she becomes his emotional vulnerability. In return, she is supposed to act as his backbone and support system, providing him with emotional stability, encouragement, and strength.

If she reciprocates appropriately, they create a balanced and mutually beneficial relationship. But if she withholds, or if he gives too much without ensuring reciprocity, the relationship becomes unbalanced, leading to various forms of relational dysfunction.

Relational Power as Currency

Let's conceptualize Relational Power as currency—units of love, attention, and effort. Imagine a scenario where a man's love and power are symbolized by monetary amounts, and how he gives or withholds this currency determines the relationship's dynamics.

1. The Ideal Exchange: Balanced Relationships

- A man gives a woman $100 of his love and power. This signifies full emotional investment—he is open, vulnerable, and committed.

- The woman, strengthened by this investment, gives him back $50 in the form of emotional support, encouragement, and care.

- This creates a Balanced Relationship: he ends up with $50 (replenishing some of his initial power), and she has $50, symbolizing her strength from his investment.

This reciprocity keeps both partners emotionally secure and invested. The man's initial gift of power is respected and returned in a way that allows him to maintain balance while enabling the woman to feel loved and supported.

2. The Validated Relationship: Power Hoarding

- A man gives a woman $100 of love and power, leaving himself with $0.

- Instead of reciprocating $50 to balance the exchange, the woman gives him *nothing (no emotional support or encouragement)*. She keeps the full $100, leaving her enriched but him depleted.

In this scenario, the woman becomes dependent on the man's continual investment to maintain her own sense of security and validation. She expects him to keep giving her $50 or $100 repeatedly, but without offering anything in return. Over time, this causes the man to become needy and clingy, as he keeps giving without receiving the support he needs to replenish his emotional energy. The Imbalance of Power leaves him at a disadvantage, creating the dynamics of a **Validated Relationship** where she holds all the power.

3. The Calculated Relationship: Partial or No Reciprocity

- A man gives a woman $50 of love and power—an incomplete emotional investment.

- The woman, in turn, gives him back $25, very little emotional support and encouragement, leaving her with $25 and him with $75.

- A woman receives $100 of love and power from a man—complete emotional investment.

- The man is given back $25, very little emotional support and encouragement, leaving him with $25 and her with $75.

This exchange often occurs when the man is only partially invested in the relationship or views the woman as expendable. By withholding his full $100 of love and power, he signals that he doesn't truly want her or value the connection. Although she gives back some of what she's received, the relationship lacks depth and commitment. Alternatively, the woman who received full emotional investment only returned partial emotional support, which creates a one-sided dynamic where neither party is fully happy, and the dynamics are not balanced. These are **Calculated Relationships**, defined by transactional rather than emotional exchanges.

4. The Dominated Relationship: Overdrawn Resources

- A man gives a woman $0 of love and power—he offers no emotional investment or vulnerability.

- Despite his lack of giving, the woman provides him with $100 of love and power, leaving her at -$100 and him at $100.

In this scenario, the man maintains all his emotional resources while continually drawing from the woman's. He becomes the relational "creditor," repeatedly expecting her to provide love, support, and sexual satisfaction while he offers nothing in return. Over time, the woman becomes emotionally bankrupt, drained by the constant demands of the relationship. This is a **Dominated Relationship**, where the power remains entirely in the man's hands, and the woman is left overdrawn and dependent.

The Problem with Power Imbalances

The fundamental issue in all these scenarios is the lack of balance in power exchange. Nature dictates that when a man gives a woman his love and power, she should respond by returning enough support to maintain equilibrium. However, many relationships falter because:

- **Women fail to reciprocate appropriately**: A woman who hoards the man's emotional investment without offering anything in return creates a dynamic where he is perpetually depleted.

- **Men give too little**: A man who only offers partial investment signals that he isn't fully committed, which destabilizes the relationship and leaves the woman feeling undervalued.

- **Men give without ensuring reciprocity**: When a man gives endlessly without requiring balance, he becomes needy and emotionally dependent, which undermines his strength and value in the relationship.

- **Women invest in men who offer nothing**: Women who give to men who haven't proven their commitment end up in Dominated Dynamics where their resources are drained without replenishment.

The Rules for Healthy Power Exchange

To create balanced relationships, both men and women must adhere to the following principles:

For Women:

- Only exchange power with a man who has given power first. This ensures he is fully invested in the relationship.

- Only invest in men who give $100 of love and power. A man who gives less isn't truly committed, and reciprocating his partial effort leaves you undervalued.

- Avoid over-investing in men who offer nothing. If he hasn't given power, don't drain your own resources trying to prove your worth to him.

For Men:

- Stop giving power to women who don't reciprocate. If she isn't giving back $50 of support, you're overinvesting and depleting yourself.

- Only give $100 of love and power to women you truly want. Partial investments signal ambivalence and lead to unstable dynamics.

- Avoid giving endlessly without boundaries. Require balance in the exchange to maintain your own emotional health and strength.

Balancing the Books

A healthy relationship is built on the principle of a Balanced Power Exchange. When a man gives love and power to a woman, she should respond by offering support and strength in return. This exchange ensures that both partners remain emotionally replenished and equally invested. By adhering to these principles, individuals can avoid the pitfalls of Imbalanced Dynamics, fostering relationships that are not only functional but also deeply fulfilling.

The Correlation Between Power Exchange, Relational Currency, Progression and Regression, and Mood Temperatures

To maintain balance in any relationship, it's not enough to simply give love, affection, and effort freely. Timing is everything. And that timing is determined by two key principles: the **Law of Progressing and Regressing** and the **Psychological Mathematics of Mood Temperatures**.

Together, they explain *when* you should exchange power and Relational Currency and *when* you should withhold it to protect yourself from emotional depletion, imbalance, and one-sided attachment.

Power and Relational Currency

Power in a relationship isn't just control or dominance. It's emotional currency. When you invest your time, attention, love, and effort into someone, you're giving them power—relational value they can either return or withhold.

But giving power isn't always the problem. The real issue arises when you give it during the wrong emotional climate. That's where the Law of Progressing and Regressing and Mood Temperatures come into play.

When to Exchange Power and Relational Currency: During Progression and Heating Up

The best time to give power and Relational Currency is when the relationship is progressing and both mood temperatures are rising. In other words, when there's clear forward motion and both people are emotionally warming up.

Why?

Because emotional momentum is in your favor. The other person is open, available, and responding to you. You're not forcing connection—they're meeting you halfway or even leading. When you give power during this phase, it often gets returned, multiplied, or built upon.

This is when love, intimacy, support, and affection can deepen without imbalance. Both partners are making relational deposits, and both are emotionally profitable from the exchange.

If you feel your partner is investing—showing effort, initiating contact, returning affection—then it's safe to give power. Give it in measured doses and watch how they respond. A healthy progressing relationship doesn't drain you—it fills you.

When to Withhold Power and Relational Currency: During Regression and Cooling Down

Giving power and Relational Currency during regression is what creates most of the emotional imbalance in relationships.

If your relationship is regressing—meaning one or both of you is pulling away—it is not the time to give more. If your partner is cold, distant, inconsistent, avoidant, or emotionally unavailable, giving them love, effort, and attention will only increase your loss. The more power you give to someone who is pulling back, the more you deplete yourself and reinforce the imbalance.

This is especially true when you're emotionally hot, but your partner is cold. You will feel the urge to "fix it" by giving more: more validation, more attention, more patience. But giving more during this period only makes you more dependent, while they become more distant. Power should not be given to someone who is showing you they don't want it.

During regression and cooling, the wise move is to stop investing. Let your partner feel the absence of your energy. Let them decide if they want to move forward again. This protects your emotional reserves and prevents a Validated or Dominated dynamic from forming, where one person does all the giving and the other does all the receiving.

The Risk of Mistimed Power Exchange

Giving power at the wrong time creates dysfunction. It leads to one-sided emotional debt, clinginess and neediness, resentment and burnout, loss of self-worth, and loss of respect from the other person.

When you invest during regression, you set yourself up to be taken for granted. When you give during progression, you give from a place of power, not weakness.

Relational timing is not about being manipulative—it's about being intelligent with your emotional energy. Not every connection deserves full investment. And even good connections need good timing.

Let the Emotional Climate Guide You

The emotional weather in your relationship will always tell you what to do. If things are warming up, let your guard down, and exchange power wisely. But if things are cooling down, conserve your emotional energy.

Don't fall into the trap of thinking that more giving leads to more love. Giving leads to love only when both people are open to it. Power must be exchanged, not drained. And timing is the difference between a thriving relationship and an emotional deficit.

You don't need to chase. You don't need to overcompensate. You just need to pay attention to the emotional season you're in. Give during progression. Protect during regression. That's how you master the mathematics of emotional power.

The Number One Rule: Overcome Regression by Breaking Codependency

If there's one rule that stands above all others when facing regression periods and emotional coldness in a relationship, it's this: **do not become codependent.**

Codependency is the trap of tying your self-worth, happiness, and emotional stability entirely to your partner. It's the belief—conscious or unconscious—that your value is defined by their approval, affection, or attention. And when your partner begins to pull away or grow cold, this mindset causes panic. That panic turns into over-giving, chasing, and emotional desperation, which only deepens and accelerates the regression.

Where Codependency Comes From

Many people fall into codependency due to **low self-esteem or a lack of self-worth.** They give power as a way to feel valuable, believing that if they love hard enough, they'll finally be enough. But the truth is, no amount of love from you can force someone to warm up to you. And no healthy relationship can thrive when one person is giving from emptiness instead of abundance.

You may love your partner—but they cannot be your *everything*. They are not your emotional sun, and they are not the center of your universe. The more you orbit around them, the more you abandon yourself. And the more you abandon yourself, the more emotionally powerless you become.

Why Men Struggle More With Emotional Coldness

This challenge is especially difficult for **men,** who typically don't experience the same biological or hormonal mood shifts that women do. Once emotionally hot, men tend to *stay* hot—remaining attached, invested, and focused, even as their partner pulls away. Without the built-in emotional flexibility that women naturally experience, men often struggle with emotional self-regulation and end up overwhelming their partner by continuing to give, push, or pursue during a regression phase.

That's why **men must work even harder to develop emotional self-control.** Not every pullback from your partner is rejection. Not every cold period is permanent. And not every instinct to give more should be followed. Emotional discipline is key.

The Long Game: Let Experience Teach You

The good news is **experience is a powerful teacher.** Over time, you begin to recognize patterns. You learn when to give and when to step back. You learn that silence doesn't always mean abandonment. You discover that loving someone deeply doesn't mean abandoning yourself. And you come to understand that relationships are emotional roller coasters—and it's your responsibility to stay strapped in without losing yourself every time the ride dips. You learn when to **give power**, and when to **reclaim it**. You learn how to **ride the emotional roller coaster** without losing your center. You develop the ability to let the relationship breathe without suffocating it with need.

Your Emotional Temperature Is Your Responsibility

The ultimate skill is knowing **when to invest**, and when to **let emotional space do the work for you**. When you're no longer driven by fear, panic, or neediness, you reclaim your power. You become the thermostat—not the thermometer.

At the end of the day, the most valuable skill is the ability to **regulate your own emotional state**, no matter what your partner is doing. You cannot control their mood temperature, their interest level, or their investment. But you can control your own. When you stop chasing, stop pleading, and stop measuring your worth by how much someone else loves you, you step back into your own power.

Progression happens not just through love, but through wisdom. And wisdom begins the moment you stop making someone else responsible for your emotional temperature. That's the key to surviving regression, avoiding codependency, and mastering the exchange of relational power.

Chapter 7

The Law of Running and Chasing

In every relationship, there exists an inherent dynamic of power and desire. This dynamic, whether overt or subtle, dictates how partners interact with one another and ultimately shapes the relationship's trajectory. The Law of Running and Chasing states that at every moment of a relationship, there is always one party who has more interest, passion and desire than the other party, and said party tends to make more of an effort and has more invested into the relationship than the other party, however, the roles are reversed if and when the pursuant begins to flee. This chapter delves into this timeless interplay, explaining the roles of dominance and pursuit that govern human connections.

Understanding the Runner and the Chaser

In nature, dominance exists in nearly every relationship, whether among animals or humans. This dominance manifests in various ways, from who leads the group to who sets the tone in a relationship. In romantic and sexual relationships, this dynamic can be described through the archetypes of the Runner and the Chaser.

The Runner is the individual who holds the upper hand, often perceived as the less invested party. They are the ones who keep an emotional or physical distance, intentionally or unintentionally creating a sense of intrigue and challenge. On the other hand, the Chaser is the one who desires the Runner more, seeking their acceptance, affection, or approval. This person is more vulnerable and emotionally invested, and their actions often revolve around winning over the Runner.

Preference in Roles: The Desire to Run or Chase

It's important to recognize that some individuals naturally prefer the role of the Runner, while others are more inclined to be Chasers. These preferences often reflect deeper emotional patterns, personal values, and beliefs about love and vulnerability.

Controversially, there are people who consciously prefer to be Chasers. For them, the emotional intensity, passion, and longing that comes with the pursuit of love is deeply meaningful. It is believed by some that Chasers, despite their vulnerability, get to experience what it truly means to love someone with full emotional investment. The joy, heartbreak, and growth that come from loving deeply are profound experiences Runners often avoid due to emotional detachment or fear of vulnerability.

While Runners may enjoy the comfort of control and emotional safety, Chasers embrace the uncertainty of desire. This willingness to risk, to feel deeply, and to act on love rather than avoid it, is seen by some as the truest form of emotional courage—and, ultimately, a fuller experience of what it means to love.

Healthy vs. Unhealthy Pursuits

Pursuing someone is a natural and necessary part of forming a connection, but there is a healthy way to pursue and an unhealthy way to chase. Traditionally, someone—often the man—needs to make the first move and put in effort to initiate the relationship. This initial effort sets the foundation for mutual interest.

However, a healthy pursuit requires reciprocation. If your efforts are met with equal or increasing interest from the other person, it signifies a Balanced Dynamic. On the other hand, if your actions are not quickly or eventually reciprocated, the pursuit shifts into an unhealthy chase. Continuing to invest energy in someone who does not return it creates imbalance and emotional strain, leading to feelings of frustration and rejection. Recognizing this shift early is critical to maintaining your emotional well-being and avoiding unnecessary heartache.

Making a Love Life Decision

Naturally, in any relationship, one person will have more feelings for their partner than their partner has for them. Ultimately, one must decide, do you want to pursue someone and date someone you like, or pursue someone and date someone who likes you? Logically it makes more sense for someone to only date someone or people who have an interest in them, however, there are psychological reasons for the allure of pursuing someone you have interest in regardless of their interest in you.

The Psychology of Pursuing

The mind is extremely powerful, and if someone can tap into someone's mind, there are very strong and sometimes harmful consequences. The person who has a mental hold on the other person has a great deal of Relational Power. Sometimes it can be malicious and on purpose, but other times it's covert and subconscious. However, the question remains, why do people chase those who seem unattainable? The answer lies in fundamental psychological principles.

The 5 C's Mind States

The phenomenon of pursuing people who don't reciprocate your feelings as much—or at all—can be explained by psychological triggers that activate specific mental and emotional states. These mind states, I call the **5 C's**, offer insight into why individuals often chase the unattainable, even when it might not be in their best interest. These mind states—*Chase, Competitive, Confused, Curious,* and *Challenge*—reveal the intricate workings of the human mind when navigating desire, rejection, and pursuit.

1. Chase Mind State

The Chase Mind State is the primal drive activated when someone feels the thrill of pursuit. Humans are wired to value things that seem elusive or scarce. When a person withholds love, attention, or intimacy, it can create a psychological reward system: the harder something is to get, the more valuable it seems.

In this state, the Chaser derives meaning and validation from the act of chasing itself. The more effort they put in, the more invested they feel, regardless of whether the other person is reciprocating. The Chase Mind State often leads people to overlook red flags or mismatches in compatibility because the act of pursuit becomes a means to an end.

2. Competitive Mind State

Humans are inherently competitive creatures. The Competitive Mind State is triggered when a person perceives a rival or feels that their desired partner is highly sought after. This can create a scarcity illusion, making the person more desirable simply because they seem to be in demand.

In this state, the Chaser becomes preoccupied with "winning" the affections of the Runner, often as a way to affirm their own self-worth. The competition can be with others or even with the idea of rejection itself. This mind state is not about love or connection but about proving something—to themselves, to others, or to the object of their pursuit.

3. Confused Mind State

Confusion is a powerful emotional trigger. The Confused Mind State arises when the Chaser receives mixed signals from the Runner. Hot-and-cold behavior, inconsistent communication, or withholding intimacy can create an emotional push-and-pull that keeps the Chaser hooked.

In this state, the Chaser spends mental and emotional energy trying to decipher the Runner's intentions. This confusion heightens their emotional investment because the uncertainty creates a sense of urgency and importance. Paradoxically, the lack of clarity often strengthens their desire to "solve" the Relationship Dynamic.

4. Curious Mind State

Curiosity is another potent motivator in human behavior. The Curious Mind State is triggered when a person encounters someone who is enigmatic, unpredictable, or withholding in some way. The mystery of the Runner's emotions or intentions compels the Chaser to dig deeper, often mistaking intrigue for genuine emotional connection.

This mind state is often fueled by the desire to understand the "why" behind the Runner's behavior. Why are they distant? Why don't they want me as much as I want them? The pursuit becomes about unraveling the mystery, which can make the Runner appear more complex and attractive than they might actually be.

5. Challenge Mind State

The Challenge Mind State is driven by the human desire for growth and achievement. When someone seems difficult to attain, it creates the illusion that they are a "prize" worth working for. This state thrives on the belief that overcoming obstacles or "winning" the Runner's love is a sign of personal accomplishment.

In this state, the Chaser sees rejection or resistance not as a dealbreaker, but as a challenge to overcome. They interpret the Runner's disinterest as a temporary barrier rather than a definitive no. This mindset can lead to prolonged chasing behaviors, as the Chaser focuses on proving their value rather than considering whether the Runner is truly a good match.

Why Do People Pursue Those Who Don't Want Them?

The 5 C's Mind States—*Chase, Competitive, Confused, Curious, and Challenge*—highlight the psychological mechanisms that make the unattainable so appealing. Here's why these states often lead people to pursue those who don't reciprocate:

1. **Scarcity Increases Perceived Value:**

   When someone is emotionally or physically unavailable, their perceived worth increases. The mind equates difficulty with desirability.

2. **Emotional Activation Feels Addictive:**

   The ups and downs of chasing someone who doesn't fully reciprocate create an emotional rollercoaster. This unpredictability releases dopamine, which can make the pursuit feel addictive.

3. **Validation Through Winning:**

   Securing the affection of someone who initially seemed disinterested can feel like a powerful affirmation of self-worth. This drives the Chaser to persist, even in the face of rejection.

4. **The Illusion of Depth:**

   When someone is hard to figure out, they often appear more complex or deep than they really are. The Chaser projects qualities onto the Runner that may not exist, fueling their desire to "unlock" them.

5. **Self-Reflection Through Challenge:**

   Pursuing someone difficult to attain often becomes a personal challenge, reflecting the Chaser's own insecurities or unresolved issues. It's less about the Runner and more about proving something to themselves.

Breaking Free from the 5 C's

Understanding the 5 C's Mind States is the first step in breaking free from the cycle of chasing those who don't reciprocate. Recognizing these psychological triggers can help individuals reflect on their motivations and make healthier choices in relationships. Instead of being driven by scarcity, competition, or confusion, the goal should be to seek balanced connections where mutual interest and respect form the foundation. The question isn't whether the chase is worth it—but whether the person being pursued truly aligns with your values, needs, and emotional well-being.

The Logic Behind The Desire To Be Chased

Not only are there psychological reasons as to why people tend to chase after unattainability and scarcity, there are also psychological reasons as to why "Runners enjoy running." In relationships where there is a significant Imbalance of Power, the Runner and Chaser dynamic becomes deeply ingrained, often leading to prolonged cycles of pursuit. The motivations that keep Runners and Chasers locked in these roles are based on different forms of relational "currency"—the exchange of convenience or comfort in return for stability in the relationship. Runners in these relationships find incentive in their partner's continuous effort to chase, as it guarantees certain benefits. Meanwhile, the Chaser, despite being in a less powerful position, continues to pursue because they hold onto the hope of achieving a sense of acceptance, affection, or approval.

Why People Like Being Chased

Being chased in a romantic context can be an exhilarating experience, and it's not just about ego. There are deep psychological and emotional reasons why people enjoy being chased. When someone actively seeks your approval or affection, it can trigger feelings of validation, desirability, and control, which are often linked to self-worth and interpersonal dynamics. Here's a breakdown of the key reasons why people like being chased:

1. Validation and Affirmation

At its core, being chased is an external affirmation of one's value. When someone pursues you, it can feel like confirmation that you are attractive, interesting, and worth investing effort in. This sense of validation is especially potent in a world where people often seek reassurance of their worth through relationships and external recognition.

- **Emotional Enhancement:** The attention and effort from a Chaser can provide a powerful emotional high, reinforcing the idea that you are special or unique.

- **Ego Boost:** It's natural to feel flattered when someone prioritizes you, making you the center of their attention and effort.

2. The Feeling of Control and Power

Being chased often places you in the position of the Runner, where you hold the emotional upper hand. This dynamic allows you to dictate the pace and terms of the relationship, giving you a sense of control.

- **Decision-Making Power:** As the Runner, you decide whether to reciprocate, how much to invest, and how the relationship unfolds.

- **Emotional Leverage:** When someone is chasing you, they're often more emotionally invested, giving you the ability to set boundaries or assert your needs without fear of losing the connection.

3. Desire for Scarcity and Exclusivity

People are naturally drawn to things that seem scarce or in high demand. When you're being chased, it creates the illusion of your own "scarcity" and desirability. The Chaser's pursuit reinforces the idea that you are a valuable and exclusive "prize" that not everyone can attain.

- **Perception of Worth:** The effort someone puts into chasing you can make you feel more valuable because humans tend to equate effort with importance.

- **Sense of Uniqueness:** Being the object of someone's desire can make you feel like one-of-a-kind, as though you have qualities that set you apart.

4. The Thrill of the Game

For some, the dynamics of running and chasing can feel like an exciting, emotional game. Being chased can be thrilling because it activates feelings of intrigue, mystery, and anticipation.

- **Emotional Activation:** Knowing someone is actively trying to win your attention can create a sense of excitement and drama, keeping things interesting.

- **Sense of Adventure:** The chase can feel like a journey or story, where you are the protagonist being pursued by someone eager to win your heart.

5. Safety in Emotional Distance

For individuals who are hesitant to open up or commit, being chased offers a layer of emotional safety. As the Runner, you maintain distance and control, avoiding vulnerability while still enjoying the benefits of attention and affection.

- **Low Risk:** The Chaser is doing the emotional labor, so you can engage at your own pace without the fear of rejection.

- **Maintaining Boundaries:** Being chased allows you to explore interest without feeling obligated to fully invest until you're ready.

6. Confirmation of Attractiveness and Social Status

On a broader scale, being chased can also serve as a signal of social desirability. If someone is pursuing you, it suggests that you're seen as attractive, likable, or high-status, which can boost your confidence.

- **Social Proof:** Knowing that someone values you can enhance how you perceive yourself and how others view you.
- **Desirability Amplification:** The fact that you are being chased can even attract more admirers, as people often gravitate toward those who are already desired.

7. The Allure of Control Without Commitment

Some people enjoy being chased because it allows them to engage in the dynamics of romance without committing to a relationship. This can be especially appealing for those who aren't ready for emotional investment but still enjoy the attention and validation.

- **Freedom Without Obligation:** The Runner gets the benefits of admiration and affection without having to fully reciprocate or take on the responsibilities of a relationship.
- **Emotional Exploration:** Being chased can help people test their own feelings, exploring what they want in a partner without making definitive choices.

The Psychological Impact of Being Chased

While being chased can feel empowering and affirming, it's important to recognize the potential downsides. If the pursuit is one-sided or prolonged, it can lead to imbalances in the Relationship Dynamic. It's also possible for someone to become too reliant on external validation, which can be damaging in the long term.

The enjoyment of being chased ultimately stems from deeply rooted human needs: the need for connection and recognition. When balanced with mutual interest and respect, the dynamic can be exciting and rewarding. However, the healthiest relationships are built on mutual desire and effort—not solely on the thrill of pursuit.

Regression Periods and Emotional Vulnerability

The Chaser is most vulnerable during regression periods—moments when their emotional investment exceeds the perceived returns. In these periods, the Psychological Mathematics of Mood Temperatures skew negative: the Chaser feels that they are giving more than they are receiving. This imbalance can lead to feelings of frustration, self-doubt, and despair.

Regression periods often occur when the Runner pulls back even further, either intentionally or unintentionally. This withdrawal intensifies the Chaser's longing and emotional turmoil, creating a cycle of pursuit and retreat that can be difficult to break.

Recalculating and Recalibrating the Dynamic

The key to balancing a Runner and Chaser dynamic is to appropriate the Psychological Mathematics of Mood Temperatures. When you are hot, chasing someone, and giving them 70%, or 80%, or 90% while they give the remaining fraction, the only thing you can do is go cold and give them the amount of effort they are giving you which in turn will cause them to make up the difference and give the amount of effort you were previously giving. Human beings are like shadows. Once you turn around and walk away, they will follow. However, if the dynamic is too lopsided and overwhelmed, and the excessive chasing has pushed them away too far, it is extremely difficult to readjust the Balance of Power.

The Influence of Dating Pools

The dynamics of Running and Chasing are also influenced by the broader context of Dating Pools. The availability and scarcity of potential partners significantly affect who assumes the role of Runner and Chaser.

Male-Benefitting Dating Pools

In Dating Pools where men are scarce and highly sought after, women are more likely to become Chasers. Men, knowing they are in high demand, often adopt the role of Runner, leveraging their scarcity to dictate the terms of relationships. This dynamic is common in environments where men's economic or social status gives them an advantage.

Female-Benefitting Dating Pools

Conversely, in Dating Pools where women are scarce and in high demand, men are more likely to become Chasers. Women, aware of their leverage, often assume the role of Runner. This dynamic is prevalent in settings where women's desirability is amplified by cultural or societal factors.

Dominated vs. Validated Relationships

The interplay of running and chasing shapes the type of relationship that emerges. Broadly speaking, relationships can be categorized as Dominated or Validated, as previously mentioned, based on who assumes the role of Runner, and who assumes the role of Chaser.

Dominated Relationships

In Dominated Relationships, the male is the Runner, and the female is the Chaser. These relationships are often characterized by the man's emotional distance and the woman's persistent pursuit of his love and approval. While these dynamics can create passion and intensity, they also risk perpetuating unhealthy Power Imbalances.

Validated Relationships

In Validated Relationships, the female is the Runner, and the male is the Chaser. These relationships often revolve around the man's pursuit of the woman's affection and the sense of achievement he gains from winning her over. But because of Mood Temperatures and men remaining hot when already hot, male Chasers are more likely to remain in this perpetual cycle of unhealthy Power Imbalances.

Alpha, Beta, and Omega Dynamics in Running and Chasing

The roles of Runner and Chaser are also influenced by individual priorities and behavioral modes.

Alpha Males and the Runner Role

Alpha Males, who often prioritize sex over love, are more likely to assume the role of the Runner. They lead with confidence, assertiveness, and emotional detachment, often withholding affection or commitment as they focus on physical connection. For Alpha Males, the pursuit of love may seem secondary or even unnecessary compared to their emphasis on conquest and dominance in romantic contexts.

Omega Males and the Chaser Role

Conversely, Omega Males, who prioritize love over sex, are more inclined to become Chasers. Their focus is often on emotional connection, partnership, and stability, which leads them to invest heavily in relationships. These men value reciprocity and mutual affection, which makes them more vulnerable to assuming the Chaser role in pursuit of genuine love.

Beta Males and Both the Runner and Chaser Role

Beta Males, however, being mid-tier and having more fluidity, can be either Runners or Chasers. A Beta Male who is dating an Alpha

Female is more likely to take on the Chaser role, and a Beta Male who is dating an Omega Female is more likely to take on the Runner role. It's also important to note that a Beta Male who prioritizes sex over romance is more likely to take on the Runner role, and a Beta Male who prioritizes romance over sex is more likely to take on the Chaser role.

Romantic Mode vs. Erotic Mode

A man's behavioral mode also determines his role:

- **Romantic Mode:** When a man is in Romantic Mode, prioritizing connection, emotional intimacy, and long-term bonding, he is more likely to take on the role of the Chaser. His actions reflect vulnerability, openness, and a deep desire for reciprocated affection.

- **Erotic Mode:** When a man is in Erotic Mode, focused on physical attraction and sexual fulfillment, he naturally gravitates toward the Runner role. This mode is characterized by emotional detachment, leading to the withholding of love and commitment.

Women and Shifts Between Roles

Women, too, can shift between Runner and Chaser roles depending on how they approach relationships:

- **Leading with Love:** If a woman leads with love, offering emotional connection first, and she's in a Female-Benefitted dating pool, she may initially take on the role of the Runner. But if this emotional connection results in a more sexual desire and erotic requirement, she may later transition to the Chaser role in a different dating pool, particularly if she feels she has achieved her emotional goal or has grown emotionally detached. However, if a woman leads with love, and she's in a Male-Benefitted dating pool, she may initially take on the role of a Chaser, but she might transition to a Runner role when it results in a more sexual desire and erotic requirement if the man she's chasing doesn't also transition into Erotic Mode along with her.

- **Leading with Sex:** Conversely, a woman who leads with sex, allowing physical connection to precede emotional intimacy, and she's in a Female-Benefitted dating pool, will often start as the Runner. But she will most likely remain a Runner because she has more options than the men who are pursuing her. However, a woman who leads with sex, and she's in a Male-Benefitting dating pool, may initially take on the Chaser role, but she will most likely remain in the Chaser role even if this sexual dynamic evolves into genuine emotional connection and she desires deeper affection and validation because she'll be competing with other women.

By understanding how individual priorities, modes, and behaviors influence the Runner and Chaser dynamic, individuals can better navigate the complexities of their roles in relationships. Recognizing these patterns allows for more conscious choices and healthier connections.

Relationships Are Never Perfectly 50/50

In any relationship, effort is rarely distributed equally at all times. It can fluctuate—60/40, 70/30, or even 80/20—and this is a natural part of human dynamics. However, a relationship remains healthy as long as these imbalances average out to approximately 50/50 over time. Both parties must contribute to the relationship's success, even if the effort levels shift occasionally.

A prolonged imbalance—70/30, 80/20, or worse—90/10—creates an unhealthy and unbalanced relationship. In such cases, one person holds exclusive Relational Power while the other consistently overextends, leading to resentment, burnout, and emotional dissatisfaction. It's essential to recognize when these prolonged disparities occur and address them openly to restore balance. Healthy relationships thrive on mutual effort and shared responsibility, not on one-sided exertion.

The Dating Game of Tag

It is impossible for two people to chase each other at the same time. Even in a childhood game of "tag," only one person can be "it" at a time. The same goes for intersexual dynamics. Usually, one person is running, and the other person is chasing.

The Balance of Power is Physics

Relationships, at their core, are systems of motion. People come together with histories, emotional velocities, and patterns of resistance or pull. Nowhere is this more visible than in the push-pull dynamic often described as the "runner and chaser" — a relationship loop where one partner seeks closeness while the other flees from it. On the surface, this may seem purely psychological, but at a deeper level, it mirrors the very principles that govern the physical universe.

Newton's Laws of Motion — foundational truths in classical physics — can serve as a compelling framework for understanding the emotional mechanics behind human connection, resistance, pursuit, and balance. These laws, which explain the behavior of physical objects, also illuminate the invisible forces at work in the dynamics of love, power, and pursuit. What happens when one person accelerates toward intimacy while another recoils in fear? What creates change in a dynamic locked in repetition? And how does power shift when one stops reacting altogether?

Now let's explore the parallels between Newton's Laws of Motion and the relationship dynamics of Runners and Chasers, uncovering how the Balance of Power is often governed by laws as constant as gravity itself.

Newton's First Law: Inertia and Emotional Momentum

"An object at rest stays at rest, and an object in motion stays in motion unless acted upon by an external force."

In relationships, inertia takes the form of emotional habits. A Runner, often emotionally withdrawn or avoidant, remains in a state of distance not always because of malice or disinterest, but because it is the natural continuation of their internal momentum. Their emotional state — shaped by past experiences, trauma, or attachment styles — keeps them at rest, resistant to change.

The Chaser, conversely, may be in constant motion, propelled by anxiety or a desire to resolve emotional distance. They initiate contact, pursue connection, and seek answers. But unless a new force enters the system — often an internal shift or a refusal to continue the same emotional pattern — the dynamic remains fixed. The Runner keeps running. The Chaser keeps chasing. The system remains stable in its dysfunction.

This law teaches us that nothing changes unless something shifts. Emotional Dynamics are subject to inertia; they resist change until a force — clarity, detachment, confrontation, or growth — is applied.

Newton's Second Law: Force, Resistance, and Emotional Weight

"Force equals mass times acceleration (F = ma)."

This law speaks to the relationship between effort and resistance. Imagine the Chaser pouring emotional energy — calls, messages, pleas, presence — into someone who is emotionally heavy with fear, doubt, or past wounds. The greater the "mass" (emotional resistance), the more effort it takes to move that person emotionally.

And yet, often, no amount of force seems to make a difference. The Runner doesn't respond proportionally. The emotional investment of the Chaser feels wasted, or worse — it backfires, pushing the Runner further away. This is because the acceleration is not just about the force applied but about how much resistance it's up against.

There is a painful imbalance here. When one person is doing all the emotional labor, trying to move the weight of another's fear or avoidance, they eventually exhaust their own capacity. The system becomes unsustainable. True movement in a relationship requires shared force — both parties applying effort. Otherwise, it's not a relationship; it's an emotional burden carried by one.

Newton's Third Law: Reaction and Emotional Equilibrium

"For every action, there is an equal and opposite reaction."

Perhaps the most striking law when applied to Emotional Dynamics. In the Runner-Chaser Relationship, the more one person leans in, the more the other leans out. This is not always conscious, but the response is reactive: closeness provokes withdrawal, pursuit provokes avoidance.

When the Chaser acts with intensity, the Runner often reacts with equal force in the opposite direction. This is not just about fear; it's about the system's equilibrium. The dynamic maintains balance through opposition — one runs, the other follows. But if one person stops acting, the reaction also ceases. When the Chaser stops chasing, the Runner may stop running — because the counterforce has been removed. This law reveals an important truth: reaction is not the same as response. Relationships thrive not when people react in opposition, but when they respond in cooperation.

The Physics of Intimacy

Newton's Laws remind us that relationships, like physical systems, obey certain principles. Effort without response leads to imbalance. Motion without disruption leads to repetition. And opposition begets opposition. In the Runner-Chaser Dynamic, the Balance of Power is often skewed by motion itself — by the constant pull and push that keeps both people locked in roles that feel fated but are not.

True intimacy requires both people to stop reacting and start responding. It requires the mutual application of force — vulnerability, effort, honesty — and the willingness to disrupt emotional inertia. Love is not just chemistry; it's physics too.

The 5 C's Mind States and Newton's Laws of Motion (Applied to Chasers)

The 5 C's Mind States — *Chase, Competition, Confusion, Curiosity,* and *Challenge* — represent the internal psychological forces that drive many people into unhealthy relationship patterns, especially the role of the chaser. When examined through the lens of Newton's Laws of Motion, these mind states reveal how emotional momentum, resistance, and reaction create and sustain the runner-chaser dynamic. Each law of motion — inertia, force, and equal reaction — can be mapped directly to the behaviors and thought patterns triggered by these five states, showing how our psychological impulses generate predictable emotional outcomes, just like physical laws govern the movement of objects.

Newton's First Law – Inertia: Why Chasers Can't Stop

"An object in motion stays in motion unless acted upon by an external force."

The dysfunctional Chaser is caught in emotional inertia — unable to stop moving toward someone, even in the absence of mutual effort. The *Chase* mind state drives compulsive pursuit: the belief that if they just say the right thing or prove themselves enough, love will finally settle. *Competition* adds pressure — needing to "win" someone who seems unavailable, especially if others are also interested. *Confusion* fuels the chase by interpreting mixed signals as signs of depth, instead of seeing them for what they are: avoidance or ambivalence. *Curiosity* leads to obsessive analysis — dissecting conversations, behaviors, or silences to find meaning or hidden affection. *Challenge* reinforces the false belief that the more emotionally difficult the person is, the more "worth it" they must be. This keeps the chaser in constant motion, convinced that effort equals love — when often, it's just repetition.

Newton's Second Law – Force and Resistance: When More Effort Makes Things Worse

"Force equals mass times acceleration (F = ma)."

This law explains the imbalance in emotional effort. In a *Chase* mind state, the more resistant or emotionally "heavy" the Runner is (due to fear, trauma, avoidance, or disinterest), the more force the Chaser applies. But rather than creating closeness, this force increases the pressure, making the other person retreat. A Chaser in a *Competitive* or *Challenge* mindset may even see that resistance as a signal to push harder — to "win" the person or overcome their defenses. *Confusion* makes it difficult to discern when effort is futile, and *Curiosity* creates a false belief that understanding the runner deeply will eventually unlock intimacy. The Chaser accelerates emotionally while the Runner remains still or moves backward — a setup for resentment and heartbreak. More effort does not always equal more connection. In this equation, force applied without reciprocation only leads to imbalance.

Newton's Third Law – Equal and Opposite Reaction: Why the Runner Always Pulls Away

"For every action, there is an equal and opposite reaction."

In emotional terms, chasing creates pressure — and pressure creates resistance. The more the Chaser pushes, the more the Runner pulls away. What the Chaser sees as affection or effort, the runner experiences as control or validation. The *Chase* mind state intensifies this, blurring the line between desire and desperation. *Competitive* energy turns intimacy into a power struggle, while *Challenge* creates a dynamic where love is earned, not shared. *Curiosity* and *Confusion* make the

Chaser reactive — constantly trying to interpret or outmaneuver the Runner's behavior. Every action becomes a trigger for its opposite. This is why the dynamic never resolves — both roles are locked in reaction rather than response. True change can only happen when one party stops reacting altogether.

The Runner – Why Running Feels Good but Costs Everything

While the Runner may appear emotionally distant, avoidant, or indifferent, there is often a psychological *reward* to the role. As previously mentioned, running can feed the ego: knowing someone is chasing you creates a sense of power. It provides *emotional leverage*, especially in uncertain or unstable relationships — the Runner controls the pace, the access, and the connection. There's a thrill to being pursued — a *sense of adventure* that feels exciting, validating, even romantic. And for many Runners, especially those wounded by past intimacy or afraid of emotional vulnerability, running feels like safety. It protects the self from engulfment, loss, or exposure.

But the emotional cost of running is far greater than the immediate reward. Running prevents connection. It avoids accountability. It relies on control, not vulnerability. Over time, the Runner becomes emotionally isolated — never seen, never truly known, never truly met. Intimacy requires presence. It requires stillness. And it requires the courage to let someone close enough to disappoint you, challenge you, or love you for who you are, not how well you can stay ahead of them. Runners who continue to flee from emotional engagement will never experience the richness of true love — not because they are unlovable, but because they are never *there long enough* to be loved. Running may feel like power. But it's really avoidance dressed in motion.

The Turning Point: How Emotional Force Triggers Role Reversal

Just as Newton's Laws of Motion helps explain the push-pull dynamic between Runners and Chasers, they also shed light on the sudden and often dramatic role reversals that can occur in relationships. When a powerful enough emotional force disrupts the system—such as betrayal, rejection, or the complete withdrawal of attention—the inertia shifts. The Runner, once confident in their control and distance, may find themselves chasing the very person they once took for granted. Meanwhile, the exhausted Chaser, finally detached and no longer applying force, becomes the one who pulls away. This reversal isn't random—it's a direct response to the emotional laws in motion, where imbalance eventually demands correction, often through drastic emotional consequences.

When the Roles Reverse: Runner Turns Chaser

In many relationships, the roles of the Runner and Chaser can suddenly reverse—especially when the Runner has done something major to damage the connection, such as cheating, lying, or committing some form of blatant disrespect. In these moments, the very person who once distanced themselves emotionally, neglected their partner's needs, or kept the relationship at arm's length suddenly becomes desperate to win their lover back.

But here's the catch: **it almost never comes from a truly genuine place.** It's rarely about real remorse or a newfound appreciation for the relationship. Instead, it's often about the emotional shock of potential loss—the sudden realization that the Chaser might actually be walking away for good.

The Psychology of Loss and Regret

This behavior is deeply rooted in human psychology. People tend to *only want what they have once it's gone*, or once they're faced with the looming possibility of losing it. We procrastinate. We delay effort until the last possible moment. A perfect metaphor is the day before a major performance or exam—panic sets in, energy spikes, and people throw themselves into preparation as if the event or exam suddenly snuck up on them.

Similarly, we often take people for granted when they're always around. We assume there's always time. But when a loved one falls ill or death feels imminent, we drop everything to be present. Not because we're better people all of a sudden—but because *reality has finally set in*. That's the same force that drives the Runner to chase when they sense the Chaser is finally done.

"Acting Right" Isn't the Same as "Being Right"

When the Chaser finally starts pulling away—emotionally detaching, healing, or even finding someone new—the Runner might begin to "act right." They might suddenly do all the things the Chaser begged them to do before: communicate better, show affection, express love. But it's important to understand that this is often *reactionary*, not *transformational*. They're not acting right because they've evolved; they're acting right because **they're losing**. It's a panic response. It's "fix it or lose it." And once the Chaser gives in again, thinking the Runner has truly changed, the dynamic often resets, and the Runner slowly slips back into their old behavior—because they were never changed by love, only shaken by fear.

Don't Reward Repeated Disrespect

A Chaser should never give a Runner too many chances. If someone continuously hurts you, betrays you, or disrespects the relationship—and only acts right when you're halfway out the door—it's not love. It's manipulation. At that point, they're playing a game. They're doing it **because they can**, and because **you've taught them that you'll always come back**. Real change comes from inner transformation, not desperation. And a relationship based on fear of loss is not sustainable love.

How to Stop Being a Chaser

To stop being a chaser, one must first stop mistaking effort for value. Love isn't proven by how much you fight for it — it's proven by how freely it flows between two people without force. The key is to shift from reaction to awareness. If you find yourself caught in the Chase, fueled by Competition, Confusion, Curiosity, or Challenge, pause and ask: *Is this connection mutual? Or am I running after a feeling that only I'm committed to sustaining?* Let go of the belief that love has to be earned through performance, problem-solving, or emotional pursuit. Instead, anchor yourself in self-worth. The healthiest relationships are not built on pursuit, but on presence. They begin when two people move toward each other — not when one person is doing all the moving.

How to Stop Being a Runner

To stop being a runner, one must recognize that distance is not safety — it's exile. Emotional avoidance may protect you from vulnerability, but it also locks you out of real love. The ego boost, the control, the thrill of being chased — none of it lasts, and none of it fills the deeper longing to be known and loved. If you're always running, ask yourself: *What am I avoiding?* Is it fear of rejection, fear of being responsible for someone else's emotions, fear of being truly seen? True connection requires stillness. It requires you to stop managing the relationship and start participating in it. The moment you stop hiding behind distance, you give yourself the chance to be met — not just desired but deeply understood. And that's when love becomes real. Not a game. Not a performance. But a home.

Highlighting the Roles and Dynamics

The Law of Running and Chasing highlights the intricate dance of dominance and desire that underpins all relationships. By understanding the roles of Runner and Chaser, individuals can navigate their relationships with greater awareness and intentionality. The key lies in recognizing the psychological and emotional dynamics at play and using this knowledge to create connections that are fulfilling, balanced, and authentic.

Chapter 8

The Law of Withholding and Activating

In the delicate dance of Relationship Dynamics, one of the most fundamental yet misunderstood principle is the ability to trigger a response from your partner. Relationships don't have to remain stagnant or one-directional, but in order to tilt the scales, and or create movement, one must activate desire. The Law of Withholding and Activating states that an emotional desire can be created and or stimulated from the absence and or deprivation of sexual energy and or sexual actions, and a sexual desire can be created and or stimulated from the absence and or deprivation of emotional energy and or emotional actions. At its core, the law suggests that power is not equally distributed between partners; it is gained or lost through the subtle management—or mismanagement—of emotional and sexual energy. When one partner withholds affection, attention, intimacy, or desire, they gain leverage, activating the other partner's emotional or sexual yearning. Conversely, when one partner gives too much too soon, they surrender that leverage, setting the stage for an imbalance that can shift Relational Power in the other direction.

No Spark Without a Trigger: Why Withholding Activates a Connection

For anything to **ignite**, **spark**, **generate**, or **charge**, there must be a **trigger**—a specific action or condition that sets the process in motion. This principle applies across all areas of life, from mechanical systems to relationship dynamics.

Take a **light switch** for example. The light doesn't turn on just because it exists. You have to **flip the switch** to complete the electrical circuit. That single action—**the trigger**—allows electricity to flow and power the bulb. Without it, the light remains off.

Similarly:

- A **car won't start** if the **battery is dead**. You can turn the key all you want, but without a charged battery, there's no ignition.

- A **cell phone won't turn on** if the **battery is drained**. No matter how high-tech it is, without power, it's useless.

The same principle applies to **romantic and sexual relationships**. If the relationship is **dead, dying, or dull**, something must **activate** it. Something must trigger a shift in emotional or sexual energy to generate momentum again. You can't just expect connection to magically appear—it must be sparked.

In many cases, especially where one partner has been **over-giving** or **over-available**, the necessary **trigger is withholding**. When one partner stops giving what was once freely offered—whether it's love or sex—it creates **a disruption**, a **void**. That absence forces the other person to notice, feel, and potentially **re-engage**.

- If love has been over given and taken for granted, withholding it can activate emotional curiosity and desire.

- If sex has been freely offered without appreciation, withholding it can activate physical intrigue and effort.

Withholding isn't about manipulation—it's about **restoring value**. Just like flipping a switch or charging a battery, it's the intentional disruption of the current pattern that gives new energy a chance to flow. And without that shift, the relationship remains in the dark—unlit, uncharged, and uninspired.

The Root of the Balance of Power

The Balance of Power in any romantic dynamic rests upon and is governed by the Law of Withholding and Activating. In essence, the dance between withholding and activating is a continual attempt by each partner to regain or maintain power within the relationship. In this framework, power manifests differently for men and women: a man's power is derived from *Control*, while a woman's power is rooted in *Attention*. When one partner withholds a particular form of energy—be it love or sex—it disrupts the balance, leading the other to become activated in an effort to restore their own sense of power.

Control as a Man's Form of Power

For men, (especially narcissistic and toxic men), power in a relationship is closely tied to control, specifically over the dynamics of affection, closeness, and interaction. When a man withholds love, he is not only keeping his emotions at a distance but also limiting the amount of attention he gives his partner. This act of withholding deprives the woman of power by denying her the attention she desires, leaving her activated erotically and wanting more from him. In this way, he maintains control over the pace and depth of the relationship, setting the boundaries of emotional intimacy and engagement.

Because men experience power as control, their emotional activation is a natural response to losing this control. When a man feels as though he is no longer in control of the relationship—perhaps because the woman is withholding sex, withdrawing, or establishing her independence—he is activated emotionally. This activation is essentially a bid to regain control and, thereby, his sense of power. The more he feels the need to chase, the more he is reacting to a loss of control and attempting to restore the Balance of Power.

Attention as a Woman's Form of Power

In contrast, women, (especially narcissistic and toxic women), experience power primarily through attention. A woman's influence within a relationship often hinges on the level of attention she receives from her partner. When a woman withholds sex, she is not only setting boundaries around physical intimacy but also limiting the amount of control the man can exert over her. By withholding, she deprives him of power, as he lacks access to the form of intimacy that substantiates his control within the relationship. This leaves him activated and seeking ways to engage her, which can include emotional or material investments in an attempt to restore balance.

A woman's erotic activation, then, is a response to a lack of attention. When she feels deprived of attention, whether through a man's emotional distance, disinterest, or focus elsewhere, she is naturally inclined to seek ways to regain that power. Her erotic activation is a reaction to the attention deficit, and by becoming more sexually available, she attempts to restore her influence over him, drawing him closer and rebalancing her power in the relationship.

Activation as the Quest for Balance

At its core, activation is the natural response to an Imbalance of Power. When one partner withholds love or sex, the other's reaction is driven by an instinctual attempt to bring the scales back into equilibrium. Each partner's form of power is rooted in their primary need—control for men and attention for women—and withholding or giving is a means of maintaining or shifting the balance. Let's further elaborate and break down this principle.

Withholding as Leverage: Rebalancing Power in Unequal Relationships

In many relationship dynamics, when one partner is being **treated poorly**, it's often not simply because the other is inherently toxic or cruel—it's because the **power dynamic is off**. One person has given too much, too soon, or too consistently without receiving the same in return. Whether it's **sexual control** or **emotional attention**, giving too much power without boundaries often invites imbalance, entitlement, and neglect. To **tilt the scales back**, the most effective tool isn't confrontation—it's **withholding**.

When Women Are Treated Poorly: Too Much Sexual Control Given Away

When a woman is consistently treated poorly in a relationship, it's often because she has **given her man too much power**—specifically, by surrendering too much **sexual control**. She may be **faithful and sexually exclusive**, even if he isn't. She may be **completely sexually available**, regardless of how emotionally absent, distant, or disrespectful he becomes.

By continuing to give sex freely while receiving little in terms of love, respect, or commitment, she **feeds his power**. He doesn't have to earn her intimacy—so he takes it, and her, for granted.

- **How to Tilt the Scales**:

    The only way to shift the power dynamic is to **withhold sex**. This isn't manipulation—it's a realignment. When she stops giving her body to someone who doesn't respect her, he immediately **loses sexual control**, which reduces his overall **Relational Power**.

- **Why It Works**:

    Sex is a man's most sought-after connection point in many relationships. Without access, he becomes **activated emotionally**. He feels **powerless**, like something valuable is slipping away, and will often make efforts—whether through apologies, gifts, or changed behavior—to **regain that access**.

- **Example in Real Life**:

    Women instinctively use this method when hurt or disappointed. A phrase like, *"You're sleeping on the couch tonight!"* is a default signal of sexual withholding. And men, knowing what that implies, often respond with pleading or attempts to regain favor because the **loss of sex = loss of control**.

When Men Are Treated Poorly: Too Much Emotional Attention Given Away

On the flip side, when a man is being disrespected or emotionally mistreated in a relationship, it's usually because he has **given the woman too much power**—specifically, by offering **too much emotional attention**. He may **listen to her problems, comfort her emotionally,** and **romantically pursue her** even when she isn't reciprocating.

He may show up for her over and over, despite emotional coldness, criticism, or lack of effort on her end. By continuing to provide love, attention, and validation without any balance, he gives her **emotional dominance**. She doesn't have to earn his attention—so she stops valuing it.

- **How to Tilt the Scales**:

    The only way to rebalance the dynamic is to **withhold love**. That means pulling back on Romantic Attention, becoming emotionally unavailable, and creating **emotional scarcity**.

- **Why It Works**:

    Romantic Attention is a woman's form of power and validation. When a man **goes quiet, pulls back,** or **stops chasing**, it interrupts the emotional rhythm. She suddenly feels **the absence of his energy**, which causes her to become emotionally **activated** and often desperate to re-engage.

- **Common Advice to Men**:

    Society reinforces this strategy all the time—phrases like *"Just ignore her, she'll come running back"* or *"Go cold, and she'll warm up"* stem from the understanding that a woman who's used to receiving romantic attention will panic when it's gone. The **silent treatment**, while controversial, works because it **disrupts her emotional power supply (loss of love = loss of attention).**

The Activation of Withholding Creates a Runner a Chaser

The Law of Withholding and Activating is also deeply rooted in the dynamic of running and chasing, which taps into deep psychological triggers. When someone withholds something—whether it's sex or love—it activates a strong emotional and or sexual response in the other party. This withholding creates a void that the Chaser feels compelled to fill.

In many cases, the Runner is not withholding out of malice but simply following their nature or prioritizing their own boundaries. However, this dynamic still activates a psychological response in the Chaser, who becomes emotionally and or erotically heightened and more invested in winning over the Runner.

The Gender Dynamics of Runners and Chasers

In Unbalanced Relationships, we often see the manifestation of "Runners" and "Chasers," as previously mentioned. The Runner, holding power, controls the emotional or sexual dynamic, whether consciously or unconsciously, by withholding love and or sex. The Chaser, on the other hand, is in pursuit, seeking approval, love, or sexual fulfillment from the Runner, which places them in a position of lower power.

Men and women alike can take on either role depending on the circumstances, but the pattern is clear: the one who withholds tends to maintain control and runs away, while the one who chases becomes emotionally committed and or sexually submissive because they are activated. This dynamic of withholding and activating often leads to frustration for the Chaser, who feels powerless in the face of the Runner's indifference or distance.

Gender Dynamics and Emotional Activation

The interplay of running and chasing often follows gendered patterns, shaped by societal norms and biological tendencies. Female

Runners typically withhold sex, activating male Chasers emotionally. Conversely, male Runners often withhold love, activating female Chasers erotically. This dynamic reveals a fundamental truth: the Runner's power lies in their ability to withhold what the Chaser craves most.

For the male Chaser, the pursuit of a female Runner evokes a heightened emotional response, often characterized by longing, admiration, and a deep sense of purpose. For the female Chaser, the pursuit of a male Runner triggers a powerful sexual activation, driven by a desire to bridge the gap and secure the Runner's affection.

Female Runners and Male Chasers

In relationships where the woman is the Runner and the man is the Chaser, and the dynamic is revolving around the withholding of sex, the woman, consciously or unconsciously, uses sexual availability as a lever to increase her perceived value. This dynamic activates the male Chaser emotionally, compelling him to prove his worthiness and pursue her more enthusiastically.

This scenario aligns with societal narratives that equate a woman's worth with her sexual exclusivity. The male Chaser's pursuit becomes a reflection of his desire to conquer and win over a woman who seems unattainable.

Male Runners and Female Chasers

Conversely, relationships where the man is the Runner and the woman is the Chaser, and the dynamic is centered on the withholding of love or emotional connection, the man's perceived emotional unavailability creates a sense of mystery and challenge for the woman. Her pursuit is driven by a desire to unlock his emotional depth and gain his commitment.

This dynamic taps into traditional narratives that emphasize men's emotional aloofness and women's nurturing instincts. The female

Chaser's vulnerability often makes her more sexually and emotionally invested, while the male Runner enjoys the benefits of her attention, care, and heightened sexual readiness.

Alpha Males, Omega Males, and Their Approach to Withholding Love

Alpha Males:

Alpha Males, who prioritize sex over romance, are naturally more inclined to withhold love. For them, emotions are secondary to physical attraction and sexual connection, making it easier for them to maintain emotional distance. This emotional withholding activates women erotically because women instinctively work harder to gain Romantic Attention from emotionally distant men. This dynamic positions Alpha Males as Runners in many relationships, as they hold the power by selectively offering emotional availability only when it suits them, ensuring women stay activated and invested.

- **Why They Withhold Love**: Emotions are not their primary focus, so withholding love comes naturally. They value control and use it strategically to maintain dominance in relationships.

- **Ease of Activation**: Alpha Males' emotional distance and confidence often intrigue women, making it relatively easy for them to activate women erotically and maintain Relational Power.

Omega Males:

Omega Males, on the other hand, prioritize romance over sex, making emotions their primary focus. Because of this, they are less likely to withhold love, as they often lead with emotional availability and vulnerability. While this makes them genuine and emotionally connected, it also reduces their ability to activate women erotically. Women may view Omega Males as too emotionally available or even needy, which can limit their ability to create or maintain interest or a Balanced Power Dynamic.

- **Why They Struggle to Withhold Love**: Their focus on romance makes it challenging for them to pull back emotionally, even when it might benefit the Relational Balance.
- **Difficulty in Activation**: Because they are more emotionally available, they often fail to create the mystery or challenge that activates women erotically.

Beta Males:

Beta Males exist between these two extremes and adapt their approach depending on their partner. They are more likely to withhold love from **Omega Females** and romance-prioritizing **Beta Females**, as these women are already emotionally focused and might be easier and or more logical to pursue. In contrast, Beta Males are less likely to withhold love from **Alpha Females** or sex-prioritizing **Beta Females**, as they feel they must actively pursue these women to keep their attention.

- **Why They Vary in Withholding Love**: Beta Males are adaptive and tend to withhold or give love based on the Relational Power Dynamic. They withhold when it gives them an advantage and release when they feel it's necessary to maintain a connection.
- **Effectiveness in Activation**: Beta Males can sometimes activate women, but they lack the dominance and confidence of Alpha Males, making their activation less consistent.

Romantic Mode and Erotic Mode: Their Impact on Withholding and Activation

In the dynamics of relationships, **Romantic Mode** and **Erotic Mode** also play crucial roles in determining whether withholding and activation are possible. Each mode serves a distinct purpose, making it difficult—or even impossible—for one party to withhold their form of Relational Power in that mode. This, in turn, prevents the activation of the other partner.

Romantic Mode: Why Men Struggle to Withhold Love

In Romantic Mode, the focus is on emotional connection, bonding, and intimacy. For both men and women, this mode is about creating and deepening an emotional relationship. Because love and emotional availability are the essence of Romantic Mode, men find it difficult to withhold love in this state.

- **Why Men Can't Withhold Love:**
  - The purpose of Romantic Mode is to offer love, emotional intimacy, and vulnerability. Withholding love in this mode contradicts its purpose and disrupts the emotional flow.
  - As a result, women are not erotically activated because the emotional bond is already being fulfilled, leaving no challenge or withholding to stimulate sexual intrigue.
- **Effect on Women:**
  - Women in this mode are often comfortable and secure emotionally, but they are not erotically activated because there is no scarcity or mystery surrounding the man's Romantic Attention.

Women, however, don't need to withhold love in Romantic Mode because a woman withholding love does not activate a man neither emotionally nor erotically. A man in Romantic Mode will typically remain in Romantic Mode whether or not the woman is also in Romantic Mode.

Erotic Mode: Why Women Struggle to Withhold Sex

In Erotic Mode, the focus shifts to physical intimacy, exploration, and sexual satisfaction. For women, this mode is centered on giving and receiving sexual energy. Because sexual connection is the essence of Erotic Mode, women struggle to withhold sex in this state.

- Why Women Can't Withhold Sex:
  - The purpose of Erotic Mode is to embrace and engage in sexual intimacy. Withholding sex in this mode would undermine the very essence of what it represents.
  - As a result, men are not emotionally activated because their primary need in this mode—sexual fulfillment—is already being met.
- Effect on Men:
  - Men in this mode are satisfied physically but are not emotionally activated because there is no withholding of sexual energy to create a sense of longing or desire for deeper connection.

Men, however, don't need to withhold sex in Erotic Mode because withholding sex does not activate a woman neither erotically nor emotionally. A man in Erotic Mode will typically remain in Erotic Mode whether or not the woman is also in Erotic Mode.

Dynamics of Dominated and Validated Relationships

Dominated Relationships:

In a Dominated Relationship, the man typically withholds love, activating the woman erotically. His emotional distance forces the woman to seek his approval and affection through sexual availability. This dynamic keeps the man in a position of power, as he continually benefits from her efforts to satisfy him sexually.

- **How Withholding Love Works**: The man maintains control by keeping his emotions guarded, leaving the woman activated and striving for his love and attention.

- **Cycle of Activation**: The woman remains erotically activated because her efforts to gain his love often go unrewarded, causing her to keep trying. This creates a cycle where her sexual investment reinforces his dominant position.

Validated Relationships:

In a Validated Relationship, the woman typically withholds sex, activating the man emotionally. By controlling access to physical intimacy, she positions herself in a validating role, where the man is constantly trying to earn her affection through romantic gestures and emotional investment.

- **How Withholding Sex Works**: The woman maintains power by controlling when and how intimacy occurs, leaving the man emotionally activated and striving to meet her needs.
- **Cycle of Activation**: The man remains emotionally activated because his efforts to gain sexual intimacy often go unrewarded until she decides to reward him, ensuring he continues to pursue her romantically, giving her attention and validating her position.

Calculated Relationships: A Balanced Alternative

Calculated Relationships are different from Dominated and Validated Relationships because they focus less on withholding and more on intentional activation. Partners in a Calculated Relationship understand the value of their own emotional and sexual energy and choose to direct it where they will benefit from it. These relationships are based on sexual satisfaction and or emotional gratification and strategic investment, rather than control, attention, or power imbalances.

- **Use of Activation**: In a Calculated Relationship, activation is not about chasing or withholding but about leveraging the energy created by activation to increase the overall benefit.

- **Avoidance of Withholding**: While withholding might still occur, it is not used to maintain power. Instead, partners focus on finding ways to avoid losing the sexual and or emotional benefit of the relationship or relationships.

The Dynamics of Withholding and Activation Within Dating Pools

The Relational Power Dynamics in Dating Pools are significantly influenced by whether the Dating Pool benefits men or women. In these environments, the abundance of options available to the favored gender makes it easier for them to withhold their respective form of power—love for men and sex for women—while simultaneously activating multiple partners who compete for their attention, exclusivity, and commitment.

Male-Benefitting Dating Pools: Men Withhold Love

In Male-Benefitting Dating Pools, men have an abundance of options, giving them a significant advantage in Relational Power. Because they don't need to try hard to win anyone over, withholding love becomes second nature. This emotional unavailability, combined with their scarcity as desirable partners, allows them to keep multiple women erotically activated at the same time.

- **Why Men Withhold Love**:
  - They don't need to overextend emotionally because they have numerous options.
  - Their emotional distance increases their value, making women work harder to gain their Romantic Attention, exclusivity, and commitment.

- **Erotic Activation of Women:**
  - Men in Male-Benefitting Dating Pools create a dynamic where women are erotically activated by the challenge of securing their attention.
  - Women compete with one another to gain his exclusivity, often through sexual and nurturing competition, such as offering physical intimacy, caretaking, or emotional support.
- **Multiple Women Activated:**
  - These men can juggle the attention of several women at once, keeping all of them activated through emotional unavailability and selective attention.
  - The competition among women reinforces the man's power, as each woman strives to outdo the others in hopes of winning his affection or commitment.

Female-Benefitting Dating Pools: Women Withhold Sex

In Female-Benefitting Dating Pools, women have an abundance of options, giving them the upper hand in Relational Power. Because they don't need to try hard to attract suitors, withholding sex becomes their natural advantage. This sexual unavailability, combined with their scarcity as willing partners, allows them to keep multiple men emotionally activated simultaneously.

- **Why Women Withhold Sex:**
  - They don't need to be sexually available to gain attention because the abundance of suitors guarantees their desirability.
  - By withholding sex, they increase their value, compelling men to invest more effort in the hope of gaining physical intimacy.

- **Emotional Activation of Men:**
  - Women in Female-Benefitting Dating Pools create a dynamic where men are emotionally activated by the challenge of securing their Sexual Attention, exclusivity, and commitment.
  - Men compete for her exclusivity and intimacy through romantic gestures, financial investment, and emotional effort.
- **Multiple Men Activated:**
  - These women can entertain the attention of several men simultaneously, keeping all of them emotionally activated through selective engagement.
  - The competition among men reinforces the woman's power, as each man strives to stand out by offering greater romantic or financial commitment.

The Law of Leading and Resulting: The Mechanism of Runner and Chaser Roles

The Law of Leading and Resulting directly impacts the dynamics of the Law of Withholding and Activating. This principle reveals how the Runner or Chaser roles are often determined by whether an individual leads with sex or love, which sets the initial tone and trajectory of the relationship. Leading with sex or love determines whether one withholds or gives away, influencing whether they start as a Runner or Chaser and, in some cases, whether they remain in that role.

1. **Women Leading with Love:**
   a. If a woman leads with love—prioritizing emotional connection and withholding sex—she enters Romantic Mode. If she's in a Male-Benefitting Dating Pool, by withholding sex, she initially assumes the role of the Runner, activating the man emotionally. However, if her withholding results in the need for physical

intimacy and erotic exploration, she may find herself shifting from Runner to Chaser. As soon as she enters Erotic Mode and begins giving away sexual energy, the man's interest may begin to shift, and she may start to pursue his affection and emotional availability, effectively becoming the Chaser.

b. On the contrary, if a woman leads with love, enters in Romantic Mode, and is in a Female-Benefitting dating pool, she will also initially assume the role of the Runner by withholding sex. However, her withholding is less likely to result in the need for physical intimacy and erotic exploration because her scarcity, refusal of sexual energy, and men's deprivation of Sexual Attention will cause them to continually and consistently pursue her in a romantic manner.

2. **Women Leading with Sex:**

a. Conversely, if a woman leads with sex, enters Erotic Mode, focusing on physical attraction, and is in a Male-Benefitting Dating Pool, she begins the relationship as a Chaser, because she is not withholding sex, thus is not activating men emotionally. However, if her physical openness results in the need for emotional connection or leads to Romantic Mode, she will remain a Chaser because the scarcity of men caused a refusal of romantic energy from the men, which then causes her to have a deprivation of Romantic Attention. This then will cause her to continually and consistently pursue him in a sexual manner and or with a nurturing competitive mindset.

b. On the contrary, if a woman leads with sex, enters Erotic Mode, and is in a Female-Benefitting Dating Pool, even if she's not withholding sex and not activating men emotionally, she will begin the relationship as a Runner because of her scarcity. However, her physical openness will less likely result in the need for emotional connection and she will remain in Erotic Mode because her scarcity causes her to remain sought after, but men's pursuit of her remains in a sexual manner because there is no refusal of sexual energy or deprivation of Sexual Attention causing them to become emotional.

3. **Men Leading with Sex**: When a man leads with sex, he enters Erotic Mode and simultaneously withholds love. By holding back emotional availability, he maintains control and begins the relationship as the Runner. His focus on sex over romance enables him to avoid falling into the Chaser role, as he maintains a position of control by keeping emotional distance. This approach generally means that he will remain a Runner, as he can keep activating the woman sexually and does not risk the loss of his dominant position.

4. **Men Leading with Love**: If a man leads with love, he enters Romantic Mode and, by giving away emotional availability, foregoes withholding love. In doing so, he places himself in the Chaser role, seeking a woman's approval or affection. Because he has not created sexual energy through withholding, he is likely to remain in the Chaser role throughout the relationship. His lack of withholding from the start makes it difficult for him to gain control or establish the dynamic necessary to become the Runner.

Regression Periods and Progression Periods

As previously mentioned, relationships naturally fluctuate between **Progression Periods** (growth and connection) and **Regression Periods** (stagnation or imbalance). The ability to shift a relationship from Regression back into Progression often hinges on how Relational Power is managed, and one's ability to withhold Relational Power.

Regression Periods: Using Withholding to Reverse the Mood Temperature

When a relationship is in a Regression Period, one partner typically holds more Relational Power due to the other continually relinquishing their power—whether through over-giving love or sex. The way to shift the relationship back into a Progression Period is for the partner with less Relational Power to withhold their form of power—either love or sex—depending on the dynamic.

- **How Withholding Reverses the Mood Temperature**:
  - The partner with less power must stop giving away their primary resource.
    - If the partner with less power has been over-giving love, they should withhold Romantic Attention, creating scarcity and activating the other partner erotically.
    - If the partner with less power has been over-giving sex, they should withhold Sexual Attention, creating scarcity and activating the other partner emotionally.
  - This reversal disrupts the stagnant dynamic or downward trajectory, forcing the other partner to re-engage and rebalance the Relational Energy.
- **Why It Works**:
  - Withholding shifts the Balance of Power by creating a sense of value and scarcity around what the other partner had previously taken for granted.

Progression Periods: Avoiding Regression

A relationship in a Progression Period can easily fall into a Regression Period if one or both partners fail to manage their Relational Power effectively. Specifically, a **constant and continual release of Relational Power**—either love or sex—without activating the other partner emotionally or erotically, leads to an imbalance that causes stagnation or downward trajectory.

- **How Relationships Regress:**
  - Over-giving love: When one partner gives too much Romantic Attention without any reciprocation, the other partner becomes complacent, leading to a sexual disengagement.
  - Over-giving sex: When one partner gives too much Sexual Attention without any reciprocation, the other partner takes the physical connection for granted, leading to a lack of emotional engagement.
- **The Risk of Failing to Activate:**
  - A relationship requires a balance of emotional and erotic activation to maintain growth and connection. If one partner consistently fails to activate the other, the relationship loses its spark and falls into a Regression Period.

Power Dynamics and the Cycles of Withholding and Activating

The cycles of withholding and activating serve as mechanisms to maintain or restore power within relationships. Each time one partner withholds a form of energy—whether it's love or sex—the other partner's activation is an attempt to achieve a new balance. The Balance of Power, therefore, is not static; it fluctuates based on how each partner manages their withholding and activating behaviors.

When a relationship reaches a stable balance, both partners have found an equilibrium between their needs for control and attention. However, when one partner consistently withholds without allowing the other to regain balance through activation, the relationship may tip into a prolonged imbalance, often resulting in one partner continually holding power over the other. This is when the dynamic of Runners and Chasers becomes entrenched, and the relationship loses its potential for a genuine, balanced connection.

The Emotional Trap: When Withholding Follows Intensity

In many Relationship Dynamics, one of the most powerful and manipulative techniques involves first overwhelming someone with attention, praise, and affection—then suddenly pulling it away. This creates an emotional rollercoaster where the highs feel euphoric and the lows feel unbearable. At first, the connection feels magical, even fated. The affection is intense, constant, and consuming. You feel seen, valued, and chosen.

But then, without warning, the energy shifts. The calls slow down. The compliments fade. The attention that once came freely is now inconsistent or withheld altogether. This sudden absence doesn't make you lose interest—it makes you *want them more*. Emotionally, you become activated. You long for the return of those early moments. You replay the good times. You chase the high that once felt effortless. Your brain is now wired to crave them, not because of who they are, but because of how the dynamic was constructed: through cycles of emotional flooding followed by emotional deprivation.

This pattern is a textbook example of the Law of Withholding and Activating in action—flood someone with emotional intensity, then withhold it to trigger longing, dependency, and pursuit. When done intentionally to control or manipulate, this isn't love—it's **love bombing**.

What is Love Bombing?

Love bombing is a psychological manipulation tactic where someone overwhelms you with excessive affection, attention, praise, and gifts early in a relationship to create emotional dependency and fast-track attachment. It often feels like a fantasy—like you've finally met "the one." But in reality, it's a **strategic overinvestment** designed to pull you in quickly and gain control over your emotions. You're showered with compliments: *"I've never felt this way before."* You receive constant texts and calls: *"I just can't stop thinking about you."* They make grand promises early: *"I can see myself marrying you."* They escalate physical or emotional intimacy fast: *"I've never connected with anyone like this.* At first, it feels magical. But behind the charm is often a desire for **control**, **validation**, or **manipulation**—not genuine love.

Why Love Bombing is Addictive

Love bombing is so powerful because it **hijacks the brain's reward system**, flooding you with feel-good chemicals that are normally released gradually in healthy relationships. But in this case, the neurochemical surge happens **all at once**, creating a high that mimics romantic euphoria—and eventually, **dependency**.

1. Dopamine Overload

Love bombers create **constant stimulation**—texts, compliments, intense eye contact, touch, future-planning. Your brain releases **dopamine**, the same neurotransmitter released during gambling or drug use. You feel euphoric, addicted to their presence, and begin to **crave the high** they give you.

2. Oxytocin Bonding

Physical touch, sexual intimacy, and emotional vulnerability trigger **oxytocin**, the bonding hormone. Even if the relationship is new, the oxytocin makes you feel **deeply connected**, creating a premature sense of trust and attachment. You begin to believe the intensity must mean it's *real love*, when in fact it's often engineered.

3. Fast-Tracked Emotional Dependency

Because everything escalates so quickly, your brain doesn't have time to assess the relationship logically. You become emotionally dependent on their affection and approval, and any pullback or silence triggers anxiety, panic, and a desperate need to reconnect. The **fear of losing the connection** keeps you hooked, even if red flags appear.

The Withdrawal: The Most Addictive Part

Once you're fully emotionally invested, the love bomber often **pulls away**—either suddenly or gradually. This withdrawal creates a psychological crash: Dopamine levels plummet, oxytocin is no longer being released, cortisol (stress hormone) spikes. You go from feeling loved and euphoric to anxious and confused. This sudden emotional vacuum feels devastating—and that's exactly what makes it **addictive**. You start chasing the high, trying to get back to that early "honeymoon phase."

This is how the **cycle of trauma bonding** begins:

- Intense affection → sudden withdrawal → emotional confusion → desperate reattachment → repeat.

Each time they pull away and then give you a little more attention again, your brain gets another dopamine hit. Like a slot machine, you start chasing the **unpredictable reward**, which is one of the most addictive behavioral patterns in human psychology.

Why It Works

Love bombing works because it **mimics the natural arc of emotional intimacy**, but in **fast-forward**: What should take months of trust-building happens in days or weeks. Your brain registers it as "real love" because of the hormonal surges. Your emotional logic is bypassed by chemical dependency. Even when you *know* something feels off, your body is already **addicted to the feeling**.

Key Signs You're Being Love Bombed

They move **too fast**: talking about the future, commitment, or soulmates within days. They **overwhelm you** with compliments and gifts. They **make you feel guilty** for needing space or questioning the pace. They **become irritable or cold** when you don't reciprocate their intensity. The relationship feels more like a **rollercoaster** than a steady climb.

Love Bombing Isn't Love—It's Emotional Abuse

True love is built slowly, with **consistency, respect,** and **emotional balance.** Love bombing is about creating a **chemical and psychological dependency** that keeps you chasing validation from someone who never planned to offer it consistently. Once you understand the **addictive nature** of love bombing, you can start to detach from the fantasy and see the pattern clearly. Healing from it requires not just emotional distance but also **neurological detox**—retraining your brain to stop craving emotional intensity and start recognizing **emotional stability** as real love.

The Reciprocal Influence of Withholding and Activating on Power

The interplay between withholding and activating reveals that power in relationships is less about dominance, validation, or calculation, but more about balance. Both partners influence each other reciprocally, and the natural desire to maintain or regain power motivates them to adjust their behaviors. This dynamic creates a flow in which control and attention are continually negotiated, either fostering growth and mutual respect or reinforcing imbalanced roles.

Understanding the Balance of Power in relationships is essential for recognizing how the Law of Withholding and Activating functions. Through this lens, partners can see how their behaviors—whether withholding or releasing—affect the overall equilibrium. By recognizing the root motivations behind each partner's power needs, individuals can navigate their relationships with greater awareness, aiming for a connection that respects each partner's need for both (positive) control and (positive) attention, ultimately leading to a more harmonious and Balanced Dynamic.

Why Withholding Works

Whether it's a man being taken for granted emotionally, or a woman being used sexually, the solution lies in understanding **Relational Power** and the balancing it out: If you are **constantly giving**, you are **not activating** the other person. If you are **never withholding**, you are **never challenging** them. If you are **always available**, you are **not valuable** in their eyes. **Withholding** love or sex—whichever form of power you've been giving away too freely—is often the only way to: create distance, restore respect, ignite activation, and trigger a power rebalancing.

Withholding Isn't Manipulation—It's Protection

Withholding, when done with **self-awareness and respect**, is not about playing games. It's about protecting your value and **forcing a recalibration** in a relationship that has gone lopsided. If you continue to give while receiving nothing in return, you're not being loving—you're being exploited. If your partner only values you when you're withholding, then you've discovered the truth of the Relationship Dynamic. And if the power never balances—even after you reclaim yours—**the most powerful thing you can do is walk away.**

SECTION 3
THE ESSENTIALS

Chapter 9

The Law of Relational Respect

In the complex dance of dating, respect serves as the foundation upon which all meaningful connections are built. This chapter explores the crucial role of Relational Respect in creating a dynamic where both individuals feel valued, heard, and appreciated. The Law of Relational Respect states that the longevity and loyalty of all relationships, casual or serious, are highly dependent upon respect being established and or earned by both parties since the inception of the relationship, and failure to establish and or earn respect will likely cause a disruption and or discrepancy in the dynamics of the relationship. Whether it's honoring boundaries, showing genuine consideration, or embracing each other's individuality, respect is the silent force that fosters trust and intimacy. Without it, even the strongest attraction or chemistry can falter. In this chapter, we'll uncover how cultivating mutual respect can transform dating from a fleeting encounter into a pathway towards a lasting connection.

Respect Is the Foundation of All Human Interaction

In every aspect of life, **respect is not optional—it's essential.** Whether you're a politician commanding the attention of a nation, a businessman or businesswoman negotiating high stakes deals, a professional athlete leading a team, an entertainer influencing millions, or a religious leader guiding a community, **respect is what gives your words and actions weight.** Without it, people will not listen, they will not follow, and they certainly won't take you seriously.

People instinctively **test boundaries and look for leverage**—and if they sense that you lack self-respect or the respect of others, they will try to exploit that weakness. In any career or social environment, **you**

cannot rise, influence, or lead if you're not respected. You may be liked, you may be noticed, but without respect, you won't be valued.

The exact same principle applies in **intersexual dynamics and romantic relationships**, whether they're **casual or committed**. You cannot build healthy attraction, maintain desire, or create emotional safety without respect. At its core, **respect is not just necessary—it's mandatory**. It's what determines whether someone will value your presence or take you for granted, whether they will pursue you or push you away.

Respect sets the tone and trajectory of every relationship you enter. It dictates whether your connection will evolve into something meaningful or fade into disinterest. In every environment, every friendship, every romance—**respect is the currency that buys influence, intimacy, and loyalty.** Without it, you're just noise. With it, you become a force.

The Importance of Respect

Respect and love are inseparably intertwined; without respect, love cannot truly take root. It is impossible for someone to fall in love with a person they do not genuinely respect. Respect forms the framework for admiration, trust, and emotional safety—all essential ingredients for love to flourish. When someone respects you, they see your worth, value your opinions, and honor your individuality. This recognition lays the groundwork for deeper feelings of connection and affection. On the other hand, if respect is absent, the relationship becomes imbalanced, undermined by dismissiveness or disregard. Love requires a foundation of respect because it elevates both partners, creating an environment where vulnerability and closeness can thrive. Simply put, without respect, love is an illusion; with it, love becomes limitless.

The Modern Labels: "Simp" and "Pick Me"

In modern society, two terms have emerged to describe men and women who **favor the opposite sex while disregarding their own**:

- **"Simp"** – A term used to describe a man who is overly generous, overly accommodating, or excessively chivalrous toward women, often at the expense of his own self-respect and dignity.

- **"Pick Me"** – A term used to describe a woman who is overly understanding, nurturing, or defensive of men's issues, often to the point of distancing herself from other women in an attempt to be more appealing to men.

Both terms are **usually used as insults**, implying that the individual is behaving in a way that **lacks self-respect** and is **motivated by a desire for approval from the opposite sex** rather than genuine character.

Respect vs. Seeking Validation

It is important to recognize that **treating the opposite sex with respect is not wrong**—in fact, it is essential for healthy intersexual relationships. The problem arises when **respect is given in hopes of securing attraction, admiration, or validation** rather than as a natural extension of one's own values.

- A man who is **kind and respectful** toward women is not a "simp"—unless he is **doing so to seek approval, admiration, or attraction** rather than as an expression of his authentic self.

- A woman who **acknowledges male struggles and treats men with fairness** is not a "pick me"—unless she is **doing so with the intention of distancing herself from other women to be more desirable to men** rather than standing in her truth.

Securing Relational Respect Before Displaying Partnership Qualities

In intersexual relationships, the key to **long-term attraction and respect is securing Relational Respect first before showcasing one's ability to be a good partner.**

- **For Men:** Before displaying romantic generosity, emotional availability, or deep devotion, a man must **establish Romantic Respect** by **demonstrating value, self-respect, and boundaries.** If he starts with excessive giving, he risks being seen as weak or desperate rather than desirable.

- **For Women:** Before showcasing nurturing qualities, deep emotional investment, sexual availability and expertise, or unwavering understanding, a woman must **establish Sexual Respect** by **ensuring that her value is recognized before fully investing.** If she starts by over-caring too soon, she risks being taken for granted rather than deeply appreciated.

How Respect Determines Relationship Power

- **Romantic Respect is created by withholding Romantic Attention.**

  o When a person gives **too much Romantic Attention too soon or without Romantic Respect being earned**, they reduce their perceived value in the eyes of their partner.

  o By **withholding** Romantic Attention, it forces the other person to work for and appreciate the connection. This creates **mystery, challenge, and admiration,** leading to Romantic Respect.

- **Sexual Respect is created by withholding Sexual Attention.**
  - When sex is given too freely without emotional depth, it often reduces perceived value and makes it harder to generate long-term investment.
  - By **withholding** Sexual Attention, it sets a standard that sexual access is exclusive and meaningful. This forces the other person to demonstrate higher levels of commitment and investment, leading to Sexual Respect.

The Biological Difficulty of Relational Respect

However, the catch is, the more attracted to and interested a man is in a woman, the harder it will be for him to establish and or earn Romantic Respect. And the more attracted to and interested a woman is in a man, the harder it will be for her to establish and or earn Sexual Respect. This is because when a man falls in love, his testosterone levels decrease, making him more agreeable and passive. And when a woman falls in love, her testosterone levels increase, making her more competitive and raising her sex drive. Simply put, it's harder to establish and or earn Relational Respect from someone you like and easier to do so from someone you don't like.

The Activation Mechanism: Withholding Love and Sex

One of the most critical aspects of The Law of Relational Respect is how it directly correlates with The Law of Withholding and Activating. The withholding of love or sex triggers an activating response in the other person. For instance, when a man withholds love—by not giving too much Romantic Attention too early or by not acting needy—he activates a woman's sexual desire. Women are often more turned on by men who are challenging, mysterious, or emotionally distant. The activation happens because she feels that she must work for his affection, and this challenge creates intrigue and desire. She begins to chase him emotionally and sexually because his withholding has made her "weak" for him.

Similarly, when a woman withholds sex—by not giving in to physical lust too soon or by not being overly sexual—she activates a man emotionally. Men are wired to pursue, and when a woman is not immediately accessible, they become more intrigued by her as a person, not just as a sexual partner. The act of withholding Sexual Attention forces the man to engage emotionally, creating a deeper attachment. He starts to chase her, not just for sex, but for her Emotional Attention as well. She has gained Relational Power by withholding what he desires most.

Romantic Respect and The Friend Zone

In heterosexual relationships, a common occurrence is women "friend-zoning" men. This often happens when a woman does not have Romantic Respect for the man pursuing her. Romantic Respect is critical in maintaining a Balanced Dynamic. When a woman feels that a man is giving her too much Romantic Attention—by showering her with affection, compliments, or constantly being available—without first establishing Romantic Respect, she gains Relational Power. The imbalance begins to tip in her favor.

When a woman places a man in the Friend Zone, it is often because she does not see him as a viable romantic partner. She might appreciate his emotional support and attention, but without Romantic Respect, she will not be sexually or romantically attracted to him. The imbalance becomes evident as the man continues to give without receiving the same level of emotional or romantic reciprocation. His excessive giving places him in the Chaser role, where he is continually seeking approval or a shift in her feelings. But that shift rarely happens because the more he gives, the more she withholds.

The Power of Withholding Romantic Attention

The paradox is that Alpha Males who prioritize sex over romance tend to gain more Romantic Respect from women. This is because these men are better at withholding excessive Romantic Attention, which prevents women from gaining an upper hand in the Relational Power Dynamic. When a man focuses more on physical attraction and refrains from over-investing emotionally, a woman must work harder to gain his affection, causing her to be more intrigued by him. The activation here is subtle—his withholding of love makes her desire it more, turning the tables on the usual dynamic. This gives the man a higher level of control, as he avoids falling into the Chaser role.

Alpha Males are more difficult for women to categorize into the Friend Zone because they do not make themselves emotionally available in the way that other men, eager to please do. In a typical scenario, the woman begins to chase, wanting to unlock that part of him that remains hidden behind his restraint. Her sexual and emotional curiosity is stimulated because of his ability to withhold, making him more attractive.

Sexual Respect and The Sex Zone

Just as men are friend-zoned when they fail to acquire Romantic Respect, women are "sex-zoned" when they do not earn a man's Sexual Respect. Sexual Respect is essential for a woman to avoid becoming just a sexual conquest in a man's eyes. When a woman gives away too much Sexual Attention—either by being overly eager to please sexually, by being too sexually available, or by being extremely sexually explicit—she loses leverage in the relationship. The man gains Relational Power because he no longer has to chase or earn her sexual interest.

This creates a dynamic where the woman is pursuing emotional fulfillment while the man remains disengaged, having already secured what he was looking for sexually. The woman, having given away too much too soon, finds herself in the Chaser role, seeking more than just a physical connection, but often to no avail.

The Power of Withholding Sexual Attention

Beta and Omega Females who prioritize romance over sex, on the other hand, tend to gain more Sexual Respect. Their ability to withhold sexual attention makes men more intrigued and activated. Men, wired to pursue, become more emotionally engaged when sex is not immediately accessible. The chase becomes about more than just physical satisfaction; it turns into an emotional pursuit as well. A woman who can refrain from giving away too much sexual energy too soon is better able to maintain Relational Power, keeping the man invested in her both emotionally and physically.

The Dynamic Between Erotic Mode and Romantic Respect for Men

For men, being in **Erotic Mode**—where he is primarily operating from a place of sexual energy, desire, and physical attraction—makes it easier for him to **establish or earn Romantic Respect** from a woman. This is because, in Erotic Mode, he naturally exudes confidence, assertiveness, and mystery—qualities that women often find attractive and respect-inducing. When a man prioritizes his own desires and maintains a sense of independence, he creates a dynamic where a woman has to **earn his Romantic Attention**, which in turn makes her value and respect it more when it is given.

On the other hand, when a man is in **Romantic Mode**—where he is prioritizing emotional connection, affection, and devotion—it can be harder for him to establish Romantic Respect. This is because over-giving Romantic Attention too early, especially without Romantic Respect being earned, can cause a woman to take it for granted. If a man is **too available, too emotionally invested too soon, or overly**

eager to please, it may lower the sense of challenge or excitement for the woman, reducing her Romantic Respect for him.

The Dynamic Between Romantic Mode and Sexual Respect for Women

For women, the dynamic works in reverse. When a woman is in **Romantic Mode**—where she leads with love, nurturing energy, and emotional connection—it makes it easier for her to **establish or earn Sexual Respect** from a man. This is because men tend to place higher value on sex when it is tied to sexual exclusivity and a deep connection. If a woman presents herself as sexually unavailable first, a man is more likely to see her as worthy of commitment and admiration in addition to physical attraction.

However, when a woman is in **Erotic Mode**—where she leads with sex and physical desire—it becomes harder for her to establish Sexual Respect. If a man is given physical access too quickly without emotional depth, he may subconsciously **devalue the connection**, making it more difficult for her to later shift the relationship toward something deeper. If respect wasn't built on the foundation of the connection, it will be harder to introduce it later.

The Experience Paradox: Love for Sex, Sex for Love

Experience and self-esteem play a crucial role in how these dynamics unfold. Men with less experience and or low self-esteem often find themselves giving love in order to receive sex. They believe that by being overly romantic or attentive, they can secure a woman's physical affection. However, this strategy backfires more often than not, as it places them firmly in the Friend-Zone and Chaser role, where they are giving away their Romantic Attention too early without securing Romantic Respect first. Once they are perceived as overly eager or needy, their chances of shifting the Power Dynamic becomes slim.

Women with less experience and or low self-esteem, on the other hand, tend to give sex to get love. They believe that by being sexually available, they can gain emotional closeness or affection from a man. But just as with men, this dynamic places them at a disadvantage. By giving away Sexual Attention too early, they often lose the opportunity to gain Sexual Respect from the man. He gets what he wants, and she is left chasing emotional fulfillment that may never come. Needless to say, this places them firmly in the Sex-Zone and Chaser role.

Learning From Your Mistakes

With experience comes knowledge, so a man who gives love to get sex or a woman who gives sex to get love at an early age should learn from these mistakes as they get older. Giving love or giving sex to your partner is not wrong, but it's important to only do so because they are interested in you, not as an attempt to get them to be interested in you. It's important to establish Romantic or Sexual Respect before you give out Romantic or Sexual Attention.

The Catch-22 of Relational Power

One of the most complex aspects of The Law of Relational Respect is the inherent catch-22 that exists, particularly for men. Women, with their ability to shift between Erotic Mode and Romantic Mode, are naturally more adept at managing Relational Power. They can also transition from being distant to being available and vice versa. This flexibility allows women to regain or shift power in a relationship more easily.

Men, on the other hand, do not possess the same capacity for emotional and sexual fluidity. Once a man has given away too much Romantic Attention and failed to secure Romantic Respect, it becomes nearly impossible for him to regain that power. He becomes stuck in the Chaser role, constantly seeking the approval or affection that was never fully earned. His inability to withhold love after giving away too much too soon places him in a position of potentially permanent disadvantage.

However, men who have mastered the art of withholding love from the outset, gaining Romantic Respect early in the relationship, have a much better chance of maintaining the upper hand. These men understand the art of navigating a woman's mood shifts, knowing when to withhold and when to engage. By balancing their emotional and sexual energy, they avoid falling into the trap of over-giving, ensuring that the relationship remains balanced—or in their favor.

The art of obtaining and maintaining Relational Respect is a subtle, powerful mechanism that activates desire in relationships, but the catch lies in understanding when and how to employ it. Those who master this law maintain control, while those who falter find themselves chasing what may never be returned.

The Validated vs. Dominated Relationship

The imbalance created by giving too much too soon leads to two specific types of relational disadvantages. For men, giving too much Romantic Attention without first gaining Romantic Respect pushes them into the disadvantaged side of a "Validated Relationship." This means that they are constantly seeking approval from the woman, hoping that their emotional efforts will eventually be rewarded with affection and or sexual attraction. This hope is rarely fulfilled, as the woman holds the upper hand and can continue to withhold the emotional or physical attention the man craves.

For women, giving too much Sexual Attention without gaining Sexual Respect places them in a "Dominated Relationship." Here, the woman seeks emotional closeness from the man, but he holds the power by controlling access to his emotional world. She becomes the Chaser, emotionally chasing a man who is primarily interested in maintaining a physical relationship. In both cases, the partner giving too much too soon loses their ability to influence the Relationship Dynamics.

The Role of Convenience in a Dominated Relationship

In a Dominated Relationship, the Runner holds Sexual Power and allows the Chaser to continue pursuing them, capitalizing on the convenience this dynamic provides. The Chaser, usually having given away too much Sexual Attention too soon and failed to acquire Sexual Respect, finds themselves striving to earn something more meaningful in return. Yet the Runner has little incentive to change the situation; the Runner's withholding of love ensures the Chaser stays activated, invested in the hope of a deeper connection or intimacy. This leads to a convenient setup for the Runner, who can enjoy the benefits of consistent sex, support, and affection without having to reciprocate on the same level.

In many cases, the convenience for the Runner manifests as a sort of "guaranteed access" to the Chaser's resources and commitment. This can include easy access to what might be called "partner privileges" that resemble traditional wife and husband roles—being nurtured, cared for, or catered to. The Chaser often provides these things with the hope that the Runner will eventually reciprocate emotionally or romantically. But as long as the Runner withholds love, the Chaser will remain activated sexually and will continue to give away power. This convenient setup for the Runner can prolong the relationship indefinitely, as they are in a position where they receive without having to truly give.

If a woman fails to secure Sexual Respect early on and finds herself in the Sex-Zone, a man seeking a Dominated Relationship will logically form an Artificial Relationship with her as long as she provides convenience. A lack of Sexual Respect combined with a lack of convenience will result in a purely casual relationship.

The Role of Comfort in a Validated Relationship

In a Validated Relationship, the dynamic is the opposite and also unbalanced. Here, the Runner withholds sex, creating a setup where the Chaser is primarily activated on an emotional level. The Chaser, seeking a deep emotional bond, becomes committed to proving their worth and stability to the Runner, often through acts of financial support, gifts, or fulfilling traditional husband and wife roles—taking care of household responsibilities, covering expenses, and spoiling the Runner with attention.

For the Runner in this situation, the comfort of this dynamic is highly appealing. They receive steady emotional support, as well as tangible benefits like financial security and acts of devotion, without having to fully commit physically or emotionally. This comfort incentivizes the Runner to maintain the dynamic as long as the Chaser remains emotionally invested and willing to chase. In this sense, the withholding of sex by the Runner creates a dynamic where the Chaser continues to seek approval, prolonging the relationship through a cycle of unfulfilled emotional needs.

If a man fails to secure Romantic Respect early on and finds himself in the Friend-Zone, a woman seeking a Validated Relationship will logically form an Artificial Relationship with him as long as he provides comfort. A lack of Romantic Respect combined with a lack of comfort will result in a purely platonic relationship.

Male-Benefitting Dating Pools: Men as Runners, Women as Chasers

In a Male-Benefitting Dating Pool, where men have more options, men naturally assume the role of the Runner, as previously mentioned. The abundance of choices available to them means that men can secure Romantic Respect relatively easily. They don't have to work as hard to prove their value, and they don't have to be emotionally available to women. Because they are not compelled to give excessive Romantic Attention, they avoid coming across as needy or overly available.

The ease with which these men can establish Romantic Respect allows them to withhold love, thus activating women erotically. Women, aware of the competition and scarcity of emotionally invested partners, are driven to chase, hoping to secure a man's affection or attention. This dynamic reinforces the position of men as Runners; their willingness to withhold love maintains their control, while women, chasing after emotional validation, often fall into the role of Chasers. The men are in Erotic Mode, leading with sexual energy and activating women erotically without having to sacrifice their position of power or risk appearing overly invested.

Female-Benefitting Dating Pools: Women as Runners, Men as Chasers

In Female-Benefitting Dating Pools, where women have a multitude of options, the dynamic flips. Women assume the role of the Runner while men become the Chasers, again, as previously mentioned. With a wide range of choices, women can secure Sexual Respect easily, meaning they don't have to prove themselves physically or come across as overly sexually available. The abundance of options enables them to withhold sex, which, in turn, activates men emotionally.

Because men perceive the scarcity of sexual availability and understand the competitive nature of such an environment, they become invested in chasing. In these cases, women lead with love rather than physical intimacy, which maintains their control over the dynamic and incentivizes men to pursue emotional connections rather than merely physical ones. By withholding sex, women can stay in Romantic Mode, activating men's emotional investment and prolonging the Relationship Dynamic with themselves in the dominant position.

The Consequence of Leading with Love vs. Leading with Sex

- **When a woman leads with love without requiring emotional unavailability, it may result in the need for erotic stimulation later on.**
  - If a man is unable to **refrain from over-giving Romantic Attention**, she may lose Romantic Respect for him.
  - This happens because **she didn't have to earn his romantic energy**, so it lacks the necessary weight to maintain attraction and respect.
  - If he continuously **prioritizes emotional availability over maintaining a sense of mystery and desire**, he may become too predictable or unchallenging, reducing the sense of passion.
- **When a woman leads with sex, but it results in the need for an emotional connection, she will struggle to generate Sexual Respect.**
  - Since the relationship started on **a foundation of physical desire**, emotional depth wasn't part of the original dynamic.
  - If a man initially sees a woman as a source of physical pleasure without deeper connection, **his level of investment will remain surface-level**.
  - She may later crave emotional connection, but because she **didn't establish sexual exclusivity or depth first**, the man may resist shifting the dynamic.

Again, as mentioned before, the back-end result can happen early on in the relationship, or years down the line. This is why you sometimes see long-term relationships or marriages that are happy and committed, but then something switches, and the woman says she's not happy (but actually just not satisfied) and loses interest in the relationship. The second scenario is when a man and a woman are in a casual relationship, but she now wants it to be a more serious and committed relationship, but the man refuses to take it in that direction because Sexual Respect was not established or earned upfront, thus he only sees her as a sexual conquest.

The Relationship Cycle: Progression to Regression

A relationship naturally follows a **Progression** when Relational Respect is maintained, allowing attraction, connection, and intimacy to deepen over time. However, when **Relational Respect begins to diminish**, the relationship will shift into **Regression**, where the emotional and physical dynamics weaken, and disinterest or frustration begins to take hold.

Once in **Regression**, the relationship can turn cold, leading to emotional or physical withdrawal. At this stage, the **only way to reignite passion and move the relationship back into Progression is by reestablishing respect**. Without respect, the relationship cannot sustain itself in a meaningful way, as attraction without respect leads to indifference, and love without respect leads to resentment.

However, the **key** to successfully reestablishing respect is that **it must have been there in the first place**. If a relationship was built without true respect—whether Romantic Respect or Sexual Respect—then attempting to restore it will likely be impossible. Respect must be rooted in the foundation of the relationship; if it was absent from the beginning, then there is nothing to restore.

The Runner & Chaser Dynamic: A Game of Respect

When a relationship enters Regression, the person who **loses respect first** often becomes the **Runner**—the one pulling away, losing interest, and emotionally detaching. The person who feels the loss and tries to **reignite the connection** becomes the **Chaser**—the one seeking approval, over-giving attention, and trying to restore what was lost.

- **A person becomes a Runner because they failed to establish or earn Respect.**
  - This means that either Romantic Respect or Sexual Respect was never solidified, making the Runner lose attraction and feel the need to withdraw.
- **A Chaser can only reverse roles and become a Runner by demanding Relational Respect.**
  - If a person who was initially undervalued suddenly **demands respect**—whether Romantic or Sexual—they can **shift the dynamic** and make the former Runner work to gain their respect.
  - This role reversal only works if the person making the demand **genuinely upholds their own standards** and does not revert back to over-giving attention.

Ultimately, **the person who controls respect controls the direction of the relationship**—whether it remains passionate and exciting or fades into disinterest and detachment.

Understanding Commitment and Submission

Before diving into the deeper dynamics of attraction and power in relationships, it's important to clarify two often misunderstood terms: **commitment** and **submission**.

- **Commitment** is a conscious decision to invest in and remain loyal to one person. It's when a man (or woman) chooses to prioritize one relationship above all others, offering time, energy, emotional presence, and long-term intention. True commitment goes beyond convenience or obligation—it's a choice rooted in value and respect.

- **Submission** in the context of a healthy relationship is not about dominance or control—it's about **trust** and **influence**. When a woman submits to a man, it means she is willingly allowing him to lead certain aspects of the relationship, not because she's weak, but because she respects his strength, stability, and emotional leadership. It's not about losing power—it's about **trusting someone else with it.**

Generally speaking, in long term relationships, women value commitment from a man, and men value submission from a woman.

The Deep, Dark Secret Behind Commitment and Submission

There is an unspoken truth about what really drives these two forces in intersexual dynamics—one that many don't say out loud, but it plays out in relationships every day:

Men only commit to women they can't control sexually. Women only submit to men they can't control emotionally.

Let's break this down.

Why Men Commit: The Power of Sexual Respect

A man will not truly commit to a woman he can **easily control sexually.** If he feels that sex is too readily available, given without effort, or used as a tool to gain his affection, he will lose a sense of value for it—and ultimately, for the woman.

But when a woman **commands Sexual Respect**—by withholding sexual access until it's earned, by valuing herself, and by maintaining high standards—he realizes **he doesn't have control.** This lack of control breeds desire, focus, and respect.

And when a man **respects a woman sexually,** he **values her beyond the physical,** and that's when **commitment becomes possible.** He doesn't commit out of convenience—he commits because he knows she's rare, not easily obtained, and worthy of exclusivity.

Why Women Submit: The Power of Romantic Respect

On the flip side, a woman will not truly submit—emotionally, sexually, or relationally to a man she can **easily control emotionally**. If he is too available, overly expressive, gives all his romantic energy upfront, or constantly seeks her approval, she senses that she holds all the power—and she begins to lose Romantic Respect.

But when a man maintains **emotional composure**, respects himself, and does not overextend Romantic Attention without it being earned, he becomes **less predictable, more grounded, and more emotionally centered**. She cannot control him emotionally, and that very stability draws her in.

When a woman **respects a man romantically**, she naturally lets go of the need to lead emotionally and instead chooses to **submit to his leadership, his energy, and his influence**—not because she has to, but because she **wants to**.

The Core of Respect in Commitment and Submission

- The only way a man loses **sexual control** over a woman is if he has **Sexual Respect** for her.

- The only way a woman loses **emotional control** over a man is if she has **Romantic Respect** for him.

Without these two forms of respect:

- Commitment from a man feels like obligation or manipulation.

- Submission from a woman feels like force or desperation.

But **when respect is real**, everything shifts. The man commits not because he has to—but because **he can't walk away from someone he deeply respects**. The woman submits not because she's told to—

but because **she trusts a man who is emotionally unshakable and worthy of leading.**

Respect Is Key

At the deepest level, the **Balance of Power and desire in relationships** is maintained through **respect**, not control.

- A man gives commitment **only when he can't own a woman sexually.**
- A woman gives submission **only when she can't dominate a man emotionally.**

This is why **respect isn't just the key to love—it's the key to power, desire, and deep connection.**

Toxic Dynamics: How Misused Relational Power Distorts Relationships

As we explore the deeper mechanics of commitment, submission, and respect, it's important to also understand **how Relational Power can be misused**, especially in **toxic dynamics**. Men and women generally wield a different form of Relational Power, and when that power is driven by **extreme ideologies or distorted beliefs**, it can lead to manipulation, imbalance, and emotional harm.

A Man's Relational Power Is Control

As previously mentioned, in relationships, **a man's form of Relational Power is typically control**—the ability to dominate or influence a situation or a partner's behavior. A **toxic man**, especially one influenced by **extreme masculine ideologies** ("Men rule the world. The world is owned by men"), will exploit this power if it feeds his ego or sense of dominance.

- He may **keep a woman around whom he has no intention of committing to,** and whom he does **not respect sexually,** as long as he can **easily control her sexually.**

- She becomes a vessel for his **desire for sex and power,** not someone he genuinely values.

- Because **he does not see her as emotionally equal or sexually worthy,** he feels no internal pressure to commit—but will continue the relationship to maintain dominance, physical gratification, and control.

This is a critical warning: **just because a man stays doesn't mean he respects you.** If he can control you sexually and doesn't view you as someone of value, **he will stay only to use you,** not to grow with you.

A Woman's Relational Power Is Attention

Also as previously mentioned, on the other hand, **a woman's form of Relational Power is attention**—the ability to attract, receive, and hold emotional focus from others. A **toxic woman,** especially one influenced by **extreme feminine ideologies** ("Women run the world. The world is owed to women"), is less likely to keep a man around **whom she doesn't respect romantically or want to submit to,** even if she can control him emotionally.

- Why? Because she has **no desire for control**—her need is for **constant attention, validation, and admiration.**

- If a man becomes **too emotionally available,** too predictable, or needy, she quickly loses Romantic Respect for him.

- Once she realizes she **can easily manipulate his emotions,** she **kicks him to the curb**—because he does not satisfy her craving for emotional challenge and the desire to be led.

This is why **overly emotional, needy, and approval-seeking men** often find themselves **discarded or ghosted quickly**—not because they loved too much, but because they **gave too much too soon**, without establishing any Romantic Respect.

Respect and Power: The Real Relationship Currency

Here's what this all boils down to:

- A **toxic man** will exploit **sexual control** if there's no respect.
- A **toxic woman** will discard a man if **emotional attention** becomes too easy and unearned.

In both cases, **the absence of respect turns power into manipulation**. This is why it's crucial to:

- **Withhold Romantic Attention** until Romantic Respect is earned.
- **Withhold Sexual Attention** until Sexual Respect is earned.

Because if you lead with your Relational Power **without the foundation of respect**, you don't attract love—you attract users, manipulators, or people who only value what you give them, not who you are.

The Bottom Line

- **Men must guard against giving emotional energy before earning Romantic Respect**—or risk being used for attention, then discarded.
- **Women must guard against giving sexual access before earning Sexual Respect**—or risk being kept for control, but never truly valued.

In toxic dynamics, people don't want **you**—they want what they can get **from you**.

Respect is what makes them want *you* — your presence, your essence, your partnership. That's the difference between being **kept** and being **chosen**.

Romantic Respect and Sexual Respect: Understanding the Historical Double Standard

Historically, societal narratives around love, sex, and relationships have been shaped by the underlying dynamics of **Romantic Respect** and **Sexual Respect**—often without explicitly naming them. These unspoken principles have governed much of how men and women are told to behave, especially when it comes to attraction and relationship strategy.

- **Romantic Respect is why men have been told to avoid "catching feelings."**

    Society has long encouraged men to pursue **casual relationships** and avoid appearing emotionally invested too early. Why? Because a man who is actively seeking commitment is more likely to be **emotionally available, give too much Romantic Attention**, and **fail to establish Romantic Respect**. When a man leads with emotional generosity before a woman has had the chance to earn it, it often results in a loss of attraction and respect.

- **Sexual Respect is why women have been told to avoid being "fast" or "easy."**

    Women have historically been encouraged to pursue **committed relationships** rather than casual ones. Why? Because a woman who leads with sexual availability is more likely to **give too much Sexual Attention** before a man has had the chance to earn or value it. This often leads to a lack of Sexual Respect, causing men to detach emotionally and lose long-term interest.

These dynamics have fueled outdated gender expectations—but **it's important to evolve our thinking**.

Respecting Individual Choice Without Judgment

As a modern society, we must move beyond rigid stereotypes and understand that **there is nothing wrong with a man preferring a committed relationship**. That doesn't make him "soft," "needy," or "less masculine." He's simply being true to himself and pursuing what feels fulfilling and meaningful to him.

Likewise, **there is nothing wrong with a woman preferring a casual relationship**. That doesn't make her "less than," "promiscuous," or "unworthy of love." She is exercising autonomy over her life and her body, and expressing her sexuality in a way that aligns with her personal freedom.

What matters most is not *what* kind of relationship someone wants—but *how* they navigate it.

Incorporating Respect into Your Chosen Path

- **Men who are "suckers for love" must learn to incorporate Romantic Respect.**
  - This means not rushing to emotionally overinvest before a woman has shown the same level of interest and value.
  - It means **withholding Romantic Attention** until there's mutual effort and respect, allowing attraction to build on solid ground.
  - It's not about playing games—it's about **being intentional with your emotional energy**.
- **Women who are sexually liberated must remember to incorporate Sexual Respect.**

- This means not giving sexual access to those who haven't shown emotional presence, effort, or sincere interest beyond the physical.

- It's about **withholding Sexual Attention** not to manipulate, but to ensure it's **valued and respected** in the way it deserves.

- Casual doesn't mean careless—**empowerment still requires boundaries**.

The Core Truth

Whether you desire love, sex, or both—**respect must come first**. Romantic Respect and Sexual Respect are not tools of control—they are **standards of self-worth**. They protect you from being undervalued and help you build connections where your energy, love, and presence are truly appreciated.

So, no matter your gender or relationship goals:

- Lead with **authenticity**,
- Operate with **clarity**,
- And always hold yourself and others to a standard of **Relational Respect**.

Because the kind of love or connection you desire can only thrive where respect lives.

Respect Is Never Given—It Must Be Earned

One of the most fundamental truths about respect is this: **it is never given freely—it must be earned**. No title, status, or intention automatically guarantees you the respect of others. You can't demand it, beg for it, or assume it based on who you think you are. Whether you're trying to influence a boardroom, lead a team, win a crowd, or build a romantic relationship, **respect is something that others grant you only when you consistently show that you deserve it**.

In politics, business, sports, entertainment, and religion, it doesn't matter how talented, smart, or charismatic you are—**if people don't respect you, they won't follow you, support you, or stand by you.** You become vulnerable to manipulation, criticism, and being overlooked. The same is true in your personal life. In relationships—casual or serious, short-term or long-term—**you must earn Relational Respect through your actions, your self-worth, and your boundaries.**

You earn **Romantic Respect** by being selective with your emotional investment and refusing to over-give where it isn't reciprocated. You earn **Sexual Respect** by valuing yourself enough to not offer physical access without emotional presence, commitment, or mutual effort. **When you don't require respect before giving yourself to someone, you teach them that they don't need to value you.**

Ultimately, **respect is the gatekeeper to all meaningful relationships and success**—professional or personal. It's what gives your presence power. It's what turns attention into admiration, and admiration into loyalty. And because it's earned—not given—it's also what makes people fight to keep you once they have you.

CHAPTER 10

The Law of Dating Connections

In the intricate world of dating, relationships take many forms, shaped by varying levels of connections. Whether we're conscious of it or not, the dynamics of these connections govern the course of every relationship we engage in, defining its intensity, duration, and ultimately, its success or failure. The Law of Dating Connections states to ensure a higher probability of success, relationships require varying forms of connections that must be mutual, however if any necessary form of connection is not mutual, the relationship will have a lower probability of success, nonetheless, if any necessary form of connection is not present, the relationship will also have a lower probability of success. Understanding the Law of Dating Connections requires us to break down these dynamics into three core categories: sexual, emotional, and social. Each one on its own can lead to a very different type of relationship, but their combinations—whether strong or lacking—determine the nature of the bond formed.

The Three Types of Connections

At its most fundamental level, human connection is about creating links between two people, but not all links are equal. In the context of dating, the connections we form can be categorized as sexual, emotional, and social. Let's take a closer look at each of these types.

1. **Sexual Connection:** This is often the first type of connection that people think of when they think about dating. It's the spark, the chemistry, the attraction that drives physical intimacy. A sexual connection is fueled by desire and often a strong, physical draw between two people. In many cases, it is what people crave when they talk about "chemistry" in a

relationship. However, while a sexual connection is often intense, it can also be fleeting.

2. **Emotional Connection:** This type of connection goes beyond the physical. It's about feeling understood, valued, and emotionally safe with another person. Emotional connections develop over time through deep conversations, shared vulnerabilities, and mutual care. It's the bond that makes people feel like they can truly rely on each other, confide in one another, and have each other's back.

3. **Social Connection:** The social connection is more about the companionship and shared activities that create the fun and structure in a relationship. It's enjoying each other's company, doing things together, and fitting into each other's lives in terms of friends, family, and daily routines. A strong social connection can make you feel like you are part of a team, building a life together.

You Need All Three for a Lasting Relationship

- **A Sexual Connection (Chemistry)** lights the fire.
- **An Emotional Connection (Commitment)** keeps it warm.
- **A Social Connection (Compatibility)** keeps it alive.

True love thrives when all three align. However, these three types of connections tend to exist separately or combine in different ways to form the fabric of any relationship. When two people meet, the relationship is shaped by which connections are present and which ones are lacking. The combinations that arise from these connections can create very different dating experiences.

The Possible Combinations

Understanding the combinations of these connections is key to making sense of the variety of relationships that people engage in.

When you break them down, you begin to see that each combination has its own dynamics, intensity, and potential outcomes.

1. Sexual and Emotional Connection: Passionate Romance

When sexual attraction and emotional intimacy are combined, the result is often a fiery and passionate romance. This is the type of relationship that people describe as "soul-shaking" or "intense." The emotional bond fuels a sense of closeness and vulnerability, while the sexual connection keeps the passion alive. Couples in this type of relationship often feel deeply connected on multiple levels, leading to a relationship that can be both fulfilling and tumultuous.

However, the intensity of such a connection can sometimes lead to instability if other aspects of the relationship, like social compatibility, are not as strong. Without a social connection to ground the relationship, these romances can burn bright and fast, sometimes fizzling out just as quickly as they started.

2. Social and Sexual Connection: The Fling or Friends with Benefits

When a sexual and social connection are present without emotional depth, the relationship often takes the form of a casual fling or a friends-with-benefits arrangement. In these cases, there's physical attraction and the enjoyment of spending time together, but there's no deep emotional investment. The relationship tends to be lighthearted, focused on fun and physical satisfaction without the commitment or complications of deeper emotional involvement.

For many people, this type of relationship works well for a time. It's low-maintenance and free of emotional entanglement, but it rarely lasts long-term. Without emotional intimacy, these relationships often run their course once the novelty or excitement wears off, leaving both parties to move on to other experiences.

3. Emotional and Social Connection: Close Friendship

A relationship built on emotional and social connections, but lacking sexual attraction, often leads to a close friendship. These relationships are characterized by mutual support, trust, and companionship. They're the kind of relationships where two people can spend hours talking, confiding in each other, and feeling safe in the knowledge that they have each other's best interests at heart.

While these relationships are deeply fulfilling in terms of emotional and social support, they don't typically evolve into romantic or sexual relationships unless a new dimension of sexual attraction is introduced later on. In some cases, one person may desire more, but if the other doesn't share that same sexual interest, the relationship remains a close friendship.

4. Sexual, Emotional, and Social Connection: The Complete Relationship

The holy grail of relationships is the combination of all three types of connections—sexual, emotional, and social. When all three elements are present, the relationship has the potential for long-term success and deep fulfillment. Couples with this kind of connection not only enjoy physical intimacy and emotional support but also thrive in each other's company in a variety of social settings.

This type of relationship is often described as the complete package because it satisfies on every level. The sexual (connection) chemistry fuels passion, the emotional connection (commitment) fosters trust and intimacy, and the social connection (compatibility) ensures that the couple enjoys spending time together outside of the bedroom. In other words, a relationship without chemistry can feel like friendship, a relationship without commitment can feel empty, and a relationship without compatibility can feel chaotic. While achieving this balance is rare, it is often the goal for those seeking lasting, meaningful partnerships.

The Importance of Social Connection in Dating

When people think about strong relationships, they often focus on **emotional connection** (commitment) or **sexual connection** (chemistry). But what truly holds those two together is the often-overlooked **social connection** (compatibility). This is the axis point of a relationship—the central force that keeps everything balanced and functional.

A **social connection** is how well two people get along in day-to-day life. It's about:

- Enjoying each other's company
- Sharing values, humor, and routines
- Feeling comfortable in silence
- Being able to coexist without pressure

It's not driven by passion or emotional intensity—it's driven by **natural ease**.

Without this axis point:

- **Sexual attraction** begins to fade without shared enjoyment or companionship.
- **Emotional intimacy** starts to feel heavy or unstable without a sense of social comfort.

Even the deepest emotional bond and the strongest sexual attraction can fall apart if the two people aren't compatible in how they live, think, and move through the world together.

In short, **social connection is the glue** that keeps emotional connection and sexual connection from pulling apart. It creates the rhythm and the everyday joy that make love sustainable—not just intense.

Social Connection Is the Axis—But Not the Whole Wheel

Although a **social connection** is extremely important and should never be overlooked, it's only part of the equation. A relationship also needs a **sexual connection** (chemistry) and an **emotional connection** (commitment) to truly thrive.

After all, an **axis point has no purpose if there's nothing to connect**, and **glue serves no purpose if it has nothing to hold together**. Social compatibility keeps the relationship balanced—but it must be anchoring something meaningful on both sides: physical desire and emotional depth. Without all three, the relationship lacks direction, passion, or heart.

The Pitfalls of Unbalanced Connections

The complexity of dating relationships comes from the fact that all three connections (sexual, emotional, and social) don't always align perfectly. In fact, many modern relationships are defined by an imbalance of connections, which can lead to dissatisfaction, confusion, or even heartbreak.

1. Sexual and Social for Men

One of the common patterns in today's dating landscape is that men often prioritize a sexual and social connection, while women often prioritize a sexual and emotional connection. For men, this might mean they're looking for fun, physical intimacy, and casual companionship without necessarily seeking deep emotional involvement. They may enjoy the sexual connection and the social aspect of hanging out but lack the emotional depth needed for a long-term bond.

2. Sexual and Emotional for Women

On the other hand, women, in many cases, look for a combination of sexual attraction and emotional intimacy. They may value the connection that comes from physical intimacy and also crave the emotional depth that makes them feel safe and loved. However, a strong social connection is often seen as platonic and not necessary for a romantic relationship. This difference in priorities can lead to mismatched expectations and misunderstandings, particularly when one person is looking for something more serious than the other.

The Friend Zone and the Sex Zone

When connections are unbalanced, it can also lead to the dreaded "friend zone" or "sex zone" situations. Men who prioritize emotional and social connections but fail to establish a sexual connection often find themselves in the friend zone. They may develop a close friendship with a woman, sharing deep conversations and spending a lot of time together, but without that sexual spark, the relationship never progresses to romance. This can be frustrating for men who feel emotionally close but fail to transition to a romantic relationship.

Conversely, women who prioritize sexual and social connections, but neglect an emotional connection can find themselves in the "sex zone." They may enjoy the physical aspect of the relationship and the social compatibility, but without the emotional depth, the connection remains shallow. The result is often a fling or friends-with-benefits situation, where the relationship is primarily physical and lacks the emotional investment necessary for long-term commitment.

Shared Priorities: The Foundation of Mutual Connection

One of the most important aspects of dating is ensuring that both people prioritize the same things. Whether you prioritize sex over romance or romance over sex, the key is to find someone who shares that focus.

- **If You Prioritize Sex Over Romance**: Look for partners who value sexual chemistry as much as you do. When both people lead with passion and physical connection, there's a better chance of mutual fulfillment in the relationship.

- **If You Prioritize Romance Over Sex**: Look for partners who are focused on building emotional intimacy and love first. This alignment ensures that both individuals are on the same wavelength, fostering a connection that feels balanced and secure.

Why this matters: When both people share the same Relational Priorities, it's easier to build trust, avoid miscommunication, and maintain a connection over time. Misaligned priorities often lead to frustration, with one person feeling undervalued or misunderstood.

Aligning Relational Modes: Romantic Mode vs. Erotic Mode

Every person enters the Dating Pool with a Relational Mode—**Romantic Mode** or **Erotic Mode**—that reflects their priorities and approach to relationships. These modes influence how connections form and whether they can be sustained.

- **Romantic Mode**: This mode prioritizes emotional connection and love. Individuals in Romantic Mode often seek deeper intimacy, trust, and shared life goals before focusing on physical aspects.

- **Erotic Mode**: This mode prioritizes sexual chemistry and physical connection. Individuals in Erotic Mode may value passion and attraction over emotional depth initially.

For a genuine connection to form, both individuals must be in the same mode. When one person is in Romantic Mode and the other in Erotic Mode, their priorities are misaligned, creating frustration and emotional imbalance. You will never truly connect with someone unless you both share the same Relational Mode. Misaligned modes lead to misunderstandings, unreciprocated efforts, and one-sided attachments.

The Law of Leading and Resulting Meets the Law of Dating Connections

In the strategic chess game of modern dating, two foundational principles and essentials—**The Law of Leading and Resulting** and **The Law of Dating Connections**—intersect in powerful and often misunderstood ways. While many relationships are built on either emotional or sexual connections, how they **begin** (leading) versus how they **evolve** (resulting) is often shaped by **biological shifts, psychological needs**, and **unconscious mating strategies**—especially on the part of women.

Understanding how these laws work together explains why seemingly strong relationships break down and why casual ones unexpectedly escalate. It also reveals why **men and women often interpret the same connection in very different ways**, especially as the biological and emotional landscape of a relationship shifts over time.

Emotional Connection First: Romantic Leading, Erotic Resulting

Sometimes, a man and a woman begin their relationship in **Romantic Mode**—leading with emotional connection. The focus is on shared vulnerability, communication, and bonding. They don't initially see the lack of strong sexual chemistry as a problem because the emotional depth feels fulfilling enough.

This works—*until it doesn't*.

What Happens When Emotional Turns Erotic?

Over time, **the woman biologically shifts from emotional to erotic**. This is part of her **Dual Mating Strategy**—a biological tendency to seek emotional safety in one phase, and erotic stimulation in another. When this shift occurs, the deep emotional connection that once held the relationship together suddenly **feels incomplete**. She begins craving **passion, desire, and satisfaction**—things that emotional intimacy alone can't provide. This is when the **emotional-only relationship collapses**. The man is often blindsided, confused, and heartbroken.

"But we had such a deep emotional bond. I don't understand why she left."

Why She Left (and Isn't Pushing for More):

- She was **happy but** not **satisfied**.

- There was emotional connection, but **no sexual chemistry** to sustain her biologically.

- She felt emotionally safe but **biologically unfulfilled**—so she left to seek passion.

This reflects the painful truth of the **Dual Mating Strategy: Women tend to leave when they are happy (emotionally connected) but not satisfied (sexually unfulfilled).**

Sexual Connection First: Erotic Leading, Romantic Resulting

In other cases, a man and a woman begin in **Erotic Mode**, leading with sexual attraction, chemistry, and physical compatibility. They both treat it casually. Neither party demands emotional vulnerability or labels. The relationship works because it's light, fun, and physically satisfying.

Until—again—it *doesn't*.

What Happens When Erotic Turns Emotional?

Over time, **the woman biologically "catches feelings"** due to oxytocin surges from consistent sexual intimacy. She begins to crave more than just sex—she seeks **love, commitment, and emotional**

depth. Her Erotic Mode starts shifting into Romantic Mode. She tries to **add an emotional connection to an already existing sexual one.**

This is where you start hearing:

"What are we?"

"I need to know where this is going."

"It feels like I'm giving more than I'm getting."

Meanwhile, the man—still operating in Erotic Mode—feels confused or pressured. To him, nothing changed. But **for her, everything changed.**

Why She Stays (or Starts Pushing for More):

- She is **satisfied but** now wants to be **happy**.
- She's emotionally activated, often through oxytocin, and now wants to deepen the bond.
- Her biological state demands a more emotionally secure environment, not just physical pleasure.

But the man may not be ready to transition from Erotic Mode to Romantic Mode. To him, the connection was sexual, casual, and convenient. Now he's faced with a dilemma—**commit or disconnect.**

This often results in the woman **feeling misled**, even though the man's intentions haven't changed. This is a classic disconnect between **leading and resulting modes**, where **expectations diverge** because of **biological shifts.**

The Collision of Connection and Evolution

When **The Law of Leading and Resulting** is paired with **The Law of Dating Connections,** it becomes clear that **how a relationship starts** is rarely how it ends—unless both people **adapt their connection to match evolving needs.**

- A relationship that starts with **emotional depth** needs sexual chemistry to **survive biological shifts.**

- A relationship that starts with **sexual chemistry** needs emotional bonding to **satisfy relational evolution.**

If the connection doesn't **grow**, it will **break**. And if the man or woman doesn't shift modes when the other does, the bond becomes one-sided, imbalanced, and ultimately unsustainable.

To build something lasting, you must not only ask:

"Do we connect?"

You must also ask:

"Are we aligned not just in this moment, but in where we're headed?"

That's the difference between a passing flame and a real relationship. And that's the power of understanding connection through the lens of evolution, emotion, and timing.

The changes in connections can shift over time, but they can also shift from time to time. Let's take a closer look at short-term fluctuations of connections.

The Fluctuation of Dating and Relationship Connections

In the ever-changing dynamics of relationships, the connections between two individuals are rarely static. They tend to fluctuate over time, influenced by emotional intensity, sexual attraction, and external factors. These fluctuations, governed by the **Psychological Mathematics of Mood Temperatures**, highlight the delicate balance required to maintain a strong and lasting connection. When one party in a relationship becomes emotionally or sexually "cold" while the other remains "hot," the resulting imbalance can cause significant strain on the connection and lead to attachments, fixations, or pursuits that are often unreciprocated.

The Hot and Cold Dynamic

At the heart of every dating or relationship connection is the concept of emotional and sexual intensity—whether one or both parties are "hot" (intensely engaged) or "cold" (detached). In the **Psychological Mathematics of Mood Temperatures**, maintaining equilibrium is essential for sustaining a relationship.

1. **When Both Parties Are Hot:**

   a. A connection is strongest when both individuals are fully engaged, either emotionally, sexually, or both. For example, when two people are equally attracted to each other physically and emotionally, they build a deep bond that feels passionate and fulfilling.

   b. However, this equilibrium is fragile. If one party begins to "cool off," losing either emotional or sexual interest, the connection becomes unbalanced. The other person, still "hot," may struggle with feelings of rejection, confusion, or desperation, which can lead to overcompensation or obsessive behavior.

2. **The Danger of One-Sided Heat:**

   a. When only one party remains "hot" while the other goes "cold," the relationship risks disconnection. The person who is still emotionally or sexually engaged may find it difficult to "cool off," leading to significant emotional damage. This can manifest as unreciprocated efforts, over-pursuit, or deep attachment to a connection that no longer exists on both sides.

   b. If the hot party is unable to recalibrate their emotional or sexual intensity, the dissonance often results in frustration, hurt, and an eventual severing of ties.

Fluctuations in Sexual Connections

When a relationship begins with a **sexual spark**, the trajectory of that connection is heavily influenced by what each person seeks beyond the physical intimacy.

1. **When a Woman Seeks Emotional Connection:**

   a. A sexual spark that leads to a sexual connection often results in the woman seeking an emotional bond to complement the physical one. However, if the man remains focused on the sexual aspect without investing emotionally, the connection becomes lopsided.

   b. **For the Woman:** She develops a **sexual attachment**, driven by her desire to deepen the relationship emotionally. Again, this attachment is fueled by the release of oxytocin during physical intimacy, which intensifies her feelings of attachment, even if those feelings are not reciprocated.

   c. **For the Man:** Because of the constant release of dopamine, he develops a **sexual fixation**, remaining tied to the physical aspects of the relationship without progressing toward emotional intimacy. The fixation keeps him engaged sexually and superficially, but his lack of emotional involvement leaves the woman feeling unfulfilled and trapped in a one-sided attachment.

2. **The Resulting Imbalance:**

   a. The woman's attachment leads her to continue offering physical intimacy in hopes of achieving emotional closeness. Meanwhile, the man's fixation keeps the relationship stuck in an erotic loop, often leaving both parties dissatisfied and frustrated. This dynamic underscores the fragility of relationships that prioritize sexual connections without addressing emotional needs.

Fluctuations in Emotional Connections

Conversely, when a relationship begins with **romantic energy** and a strong emotional connection, the trajectory changes if one party seeks to incorporate physical intimacy into the bond.

1. **When a Woman Seeks Sexual Connection**:

   a. A relationship that begins with emotional openness and mutual understanding often leads to the woman seeking a sexual connection to solidify the bond. However, if the man remains emotionally focused and fails to build physical chemistry, the dynamic shifts.

   b. **For the Man**: He develops an **emotional attachment**, becoming deeply invested in the emotional bond without successfully transitioning to a physical connection. This attachment makes him cling to the emotional aspects of the relationship, often misinterpreting the woman's actions as validation of their emotional closeness.

   c. **For the Woman**: She engages in a **sexual pursuit**, sometimes elsewhere, hoping that introducing physical intimacy will strengthen the connection, or she will look for a new connection with someone else. Her desire to merge emotional and physical aspects of the relationship can create pressure, as she perceives the lack of physical engagement as a missing piece.

2. **The Resulting Imbalance**:

   a. The man's emotional attachment and the woman's sexual pursuit create a mismatch of relational energy. The woman may feel unfulfilled by the lack of physical connection, while the man feels overwhelmed by the expectation of transitioning the relationship into something he may not be prepared for. This disconnect can lead to frustration on both sides, with the man feeling emotionally drained and the woman feeling physically and emotionally unsatisfied.

Alignment is Necessary for Balance

These scenarios illustrate the **Psychological Mathematics of Mood Temperatures**, where emotional and sexual connections must align to maintain balance. When one party remains "hot" in a specific area—whether emotionally or sexually—while the other "cools off" or fails to match the intensity, the resulting imbalance causes strain.

Key patterns to understand include:

1. **Unbalanced Emotional and Sexual Energy**: When emotional and sexual energies do not align, one party often compensates with attachment (emotional or sexual) while the other withdraws or fixates.

2. **Attachments vs. Connections**: Attachments form when one party remains "hot" while the other disengages. These attachments are often one-sided and lead to prolonged emotional or sexual suffering for the invested party.

3. **Transition Failures**: When a sexual connection doesn't transition to an emotional one, or vice versa, the relationship remains in a state of imbalance, creating frustration, pursuit, and eventual collapse.

Oxytocin and the Power of Attachment Over Connection

A significant element in the dynamic of connections is the role of oxytocin, often called the "bonding hormone." Oxytocin is released during physical touch, especially during sexual activity, and creates feelings of attachment and closeness. However, it's crucial to understand that while oxytocin can make you feel attached, it doesn't necessarily create a true connection.

Connections and attachments are not the same thing. A connection is a mutual bond formed between two people, while an attachment is only one-sided. Oxytocin can foster attachment even in relationships that lack emotional or social depth. This is why people can feel intensely attached to someone with whom they share only a sexual relationship, even if the other person doesn't feel the same emotional connection. This often leads to one-sided relationships, where one person becomes deeply attached while the other remains distant.

Attachments without connections are the root of many of the heartaches that come from modern dating. When one person forms an attachment, but the connection isn't reciprocated, the relationship becomes unbalanced, leading to feelings of rejection or confusion. Understanding the difference between connection and attachment is essential to navigating the complex world of relationships.

The Illusion of Connection in Dominated and Validated Relationships

Many relationships appear to be built on strong sexual or emotional connections, but upon closer examination, they are often **imbalanced dynamics fueled by hormonal and psychological responses** rather than genuine mutual connection. Two of the most deceptive relationship structures—**Dominated Relationships** and **Validated Relationships**—create intense attachments and fixations that mimic true connection but lack **genuine emotional or sexual reciprocity**.

Dominated Relationships: Sexual Attachment vs. Sexual Fixation

A **Dominated Relationship** is not defined by a genuine sexual connection but rather by a one-sided sexual attachment from the woman and a sexual fixation from the man. **This is not the same as a true mutual sexual bond.** Instead, the relationship is driven by

hormonal responses that create different psychological experiences for each party.

Why is there no true sexual connection?

A **sexual connection** is when both individuals experience **mutual attraction, chemistry, and fulfillment** through physical intimacy. However, in a **Dominated Relationship**, the woman is not experiencing a real **connection**—she is experiencing an **attachment** due to oxytocin surges, while the man is experiencing a **fixation** due to dopamine and testosterone boosts.

The Woman: Sexual Attachment

- Frequent sexual intercourse triggers **oxytocin surges**, making her feel bonded to the man.

- She mistakes her **attachment** for an actual connection, believing that sex will eventually lead to deeper emotional involvement.

- Since the man provides **no emotional investment**, her body compensates by deepening her **attachment** in hopes of stabilizing the relationship.

- She becomes the Chaser and **chases validation through sex**, and giving sex to get love, even when it becomes emotionally draining.

The Man: Sexual Fixation

- Frequent sexual intercourse **releases dopamine**, creating a cycle of **pleasure and reward** that reinforces his **fixation**.

- His **testosterone levels spike**, intensifying his **desire for dominance, power, and control** rather than emotional closeness.

- The act of frequent sex **boosts his ego**, making him feel powerful and in control of the relationship dynamic.
- Instead of bonding emotionally, he **fixates on maintaining access to sex**, often withholding emotional connection to ensure the woman stays attached.

The Psychological Trap

- The **woman mistakes her attachment for love**, leading her to **overinvest emotionally** in a relationship that lacks depth.
- The **man mistakes his fixation for desire**, reinforcing his **avoidance of emotional connection** and maintaining control over the woman.
- This cycle repeats until one person **breaks the attachment or fixation**, usually resulting in the woman being emotionally drained while the man moves on unscathed.

Validated Relationships: Emotional Attachment vs. Emotional Fixation

A **Validated Relationship** is **not based on a true emotional connection** but rather on an **emotional attachment from the man** and an **emotional fixation from the woman**. This dynamic creates an **illusion of closeness**, but in reality, the two individuals are engaging with the relationship **for different reasons**.

Why is there no true emotional connection?

A **true emotional connection** is built on **shared values, vulnerability, and mutual emotional fulfillment**. In a **Validated Relationship**, however, the **man experiences an attachment** while the **woman experiences a fixation** due to dopamine boosts.

The Man: Emotional Attachment

- Spending time with the woman and **investing in emotional interactions** leads to an **increase in oxytocin,** making him feel bonded.

- His **testosterone levels decrease,** making him **more emotionally vulnerable** and causing him to feel deeply attached.

- Since he is "catching feelings," he starts **overinvesting emotionally,** often **prioritizing the woman's needs over his own** in an attempt to solidify the relationship.

- He becomes the **Chaser**, seeking deeper intimacy and **offering love in exchange for sex.**

The Woman: Emotional Fixation

- The **constant attention and validation** she receives from the man **triggers dopamine surges,** making her feel **a sense of pleasure and reward.**

- She becomes fixated on the **power and comfort of receiving emotional investment**, rather than the actual relationship itself.

- She enjoys being the **center of his emotional world,** but she does **not reciprocate his depth of feelings**—instead, she remains in control of the relationship dynamic.

- She keeps the connection **at an emotional distance,** giving just enough **to keep his attachment intact while maintaining her position of power.**

The Psychological Trap

- The **man mistakes his emotional attachment for love,** leading him to **overcommit to someone who does not share his depth of feelings.**

- The **woman mistakes her fixation for genuine emotional engagement,** when in reality, she is **chasing the dopamine rush that comes from being desired and validated.**

- This cycle **reinforces emotional imbalance,** leaving the man emotionally drained while the woman remains emotionally and or sexually indifferent.

Prioritize True Connections: Aligning Intentions in the Dating Pool

Navigating the Dating Pool can be challenging, but one of the most essential truths to remember is this: **date people you truly connect with**. A genuine connection cannot be forced or fabricated and confusing an attachment for a connection can lead to heartache and frustration. Successful relationships stem from mutual understanding, shared priorities, and the alignment of Relational Modes—whether **Romantic Mode** or **Erotic Mode**.

Connection vs. Attachment: Know the Difference

As previously mentioned, a **connection** is a mutual bond where two people are equally engaged and invested. It is built on shared emotional, sexual, and social energy. Conversely, an **attachment** is often one-sided, formed when one person remains "hot" while the other becomes "cold" or disengaged. Attachments can create a sense of longing, but they are not the foundation of a Balanced Relationship.

When dating, it's vital to ask yourself:

- Are we both investing in this relationship equally?

- Do we both share the same Relational Priorities?
- Am I pursuing this because I feel truly connected, or because I am attached to the idea of what this relationship could be?

By distinguishing between connection and attachment, you can avoid chasing Unbalanced Relationships that leave you unfulfilled.

The Impact of Unequal Options in the Dating Pool

Another factor to consider is the imbalance of options within the Dating Pool. It's harder to make a genuine connection with someone who has significantly more options than you. This imbalance often occurs in **Male-Benefiting** and **Female-Benefiting** Dating Pools.

- **If You're a Woman in a Male-Benefiting Dating Pool**: Men with an abundance of options are less likely to invest deeply, often leading with sexual attraction and maintaining minimal emotional connection. Women in this scenario may find themselves chasing love through physical intimacy, creating an unbalanced dynamic.

- **If You're a Man in a Female-Benefiting Dating Pool**: Women with more options may maintain control by prioritizing their own needs while withholding deeper emotional and or physical commitment. Men in this scenario often find themselves emotionally overinvesting in the hope of building a stronger bond, and or establish a sexual relationship.

When there is an imbalance in options, one party often has less incentive to prioritize or nurture the connection. This dynamic makes it challenging to create and sustain a meaningful relationship. **The solution?** Date within pools where the playing field is more balanced and mutual investment is possible.

How the Runner and Chaser Dynamic Affects Dating Connections

The **Runner and Chaser dynamic** is one of the most common and damaging patterns in modern dating, and it has a profound impact on how dating connections—sexual, emotional, and social—form, function, and fall apart. In this dynamic, one person (the Chaser) becomes emotionally or sexually activated and begins to pursue the other, while the other person (the Runner) avoids depth, commitment, or vulnerability and maintains control by pulling away. This imbalance distorts the natural development of mutual connection and often leads to confusion, frustration, and emotional burnout.

From a **sexual connection** standpoint, the Chaser may offer physical intimacy in hopes of building closeness, while the Runner accepts the sex but avoids giving emotional reciprocity. This leads to a **sexual attachment** for the Chaser and a **sexual fixation** or convenience dynamic for the Runner. In **emotional connections**, the Chaser may overextend—offering love, reassurance, and constant communication—while the Runner remains distant or inconsistent, keeping emotional engagement just out of reach. Over time, this creates a one-sided bond where the Chaser becomes more invested, and the Runner becomes more detached.

The **social connection** in Runner and Chaser dynamics is often superficial or performative. The Runner might participate in social interactions just enough to keep the Chaser hopeful but avoids spending quality, meaningful time that builds true companionship. This leads to a relationship that may appear functional on the outside but is emotionally hollow on the inside.

Ultimately, the Runner and Chaser dynamic prevents genuine connections from developing. A real bond—whether sexual, emotional, or social—requires **mutual pursuit and shared investment**. When one person is constantly reaching and the other is constantly retreating, the result is not a relationship—it's a **cycle of**

longing, control, and imbalance disguised as chemistry. The longer this dynamic lasts, the harder it becomes for the Chaser to discern between real connection and one-sided emotional addiction.

How Withholding and Activating Affects Dating Connections

In the context of **Runner and Chaser dynamics**, the **Law of Withholding and Activating** plays a central role in shaping how dating connections evolve. The Runner maintains power and distance by **withholding** emotional, sexual, or social energy, while the Chaser becomes increasingly activated—offering more love, sex, or attention in an attempt to bridge the gap. This imbalance distorts the natural development of mutual connection and often leads to dysfunctional patterns of pursuit and retreat.

When it comes to **sexual connection**, a Runner may activate the Chaser's desire by showing just enough interest or engaging in physical intimacy, then withdraw shortly after. This inconsistency keeps the Chaser emotionally hooked and sexually activated, leading to **sexual attachment** without stability. The Chaser may then offer more sex or physical closeness in hopes of reactivating the Runner's interest, but because the sexual energy is being used as leverage—not mutual expression—the connection becomes transactional and emotionally draining.

In **emotional connections**, the same pattern occurs. The Runner may withhold affection, vulnerability, or words of affirmation, while the Chaser doubles down on emotional availability—offering more reassurance, love, and openness. But without reciprocity, the emotional connection becomes unbalanced. The Chaser feels emotionally depleted, while the Runner remains disengaged, yet still benefits from the attention. This creates an illusion of closeness without true emotional safety.

Even the **social connection** is affected. A Runner may withdraw socially—stop texting, cancel plans, or become distant—knowing that the absence will activate the Chaser's anxiety or desire for reconnection. The Chaser, in turn, initiates more, reaches out more, and tries to fill the gap. But when one person is always showing up while the other disappears and reappears on their terms, the social bond becomes inconsistent and fragile.

Ultimately, the Law of Withholding and Activating explains how **emotional and sexual power is exchanged** in the Runner and Chaser cycle. The Runner stays in control by withholding, while the Chaser becomes more desperate by over-activating. This imbalance prevents real connection from forming, because **healthy connections require mutual timing, shared energy, and reciprocal effort**—not power plays disguised as interest.

How the Law of Relational Respect Affects Dating Connections

In every romantic relationship, people tend to focus on building emotional bonds, maintaining sexual chemistry, and enjoying social compatibility. But there's a deeper force at play that determines whether those connections truly *last*—and that's **Relational Respect**. The **Law of Relational Respect** teaches us that no matter how strong a connection may feel, it can't thrive or sustain itself without mutual respect for each other's *relational value*. Respect in this context goes beyond general kindness—it's about how much one person *values* the other within the framework of a sexual, emotional, or social connection. When relational respect is present, each partner sees the other as someone worth investing in, honoring their presence, boundaries, and intentions. When it's missing, even the most intense connections become imbalanced, one-sided, or exploitative.

In dating, a lack of **Sexual Respect** turns physical intimacy into a tool for control or convenience. A lack of **Emotional Respect** turns affection into a tool for attention and comfort. And without **social**

respect, time and companionship are taken for granted, often used out of boredom or self-interest rather than genuine connection. That's why some people feel deeply connected but still end up heartbroken—because the **respect needed to sustain the connection was never mutual**. Respect is the silent force that solidifies the emotional energy, sexual chemistry, and social effort each person brings. Without it, a connection is reduced to a **transaction**, not a relationship.

Ultimately, Relational Respect is what gives *meaning* to a connection. It's what transforms attention into intention, sex into significance, and time into presence. You can't have a real relationship without it—because respect is what keeps all forms of connection **mutual, healthy, and sustainable**.

Build Connections That Last

In the ever-shifting landscape of modern dating, one principle remains constant: **Genuine connections thrive on mutuality**. To create, build, and maintain a meaningful connection, both parties must be equally invested, aligned in their priorities, and operating in the same Relational Mode.

Remember:

- **Never force a connection.** If it's not mutual, it's not real.

- **Know the difference between connection and attachment.** Attachments are one-sided; connections are shared.

- **Align your Relational Mode.** Ensure that you and your partner are both in Romantic Mode or both in Erotic Mode for a harmonious relationship.

- **Balance the playing field.** Avoid chasing people with significantly more options than you, as this often leads to Unbalanced Dynamics.

- **Share the same priorities.** Whether it's sex or romance, mutual focus lays the groundwork for a strong and lasting bond.

By being intentional and mindful of these essentials, you'll not only navigate the dating pool with greater confidence but also increase your chances of finding a partner who truly complements you.

Balancing Dating Connections and Combinations

The Law of Dating Connections shows that no two relationships are the same, but they all operate within the framework of sexual, emotional, and social dynamics. While certain combinations can lead to fleeting flings, close friendships, or passionate romances, the most fulfilling relationships tend to be those that balance all three connections.

However, the reality is that many people find themselves stuck in relationships where one or more connections are missing. The imbalance of these dynamics is further complicated by the hormonal effects of attachment, which can make a relationship feel more significant than it truly is. In the end, understanding the Law of Dating Connections provides valuable insight into why certain relationships thrive while others falter. By recognizing the importance of balancing sexual, emotional, and social connections, individuals can better navigate their relationships and avoid the traps of one-sided attachments or unbalanced expectations.

Chapter 11

The Law of Intentional Interest

Relationships are built on the foundation of interest and intentions. At the core of every relationship lies the questions: *How much does this person like me? What does this person want from me, and why?* The Law of Intentional Interest states that for a relationship to thrive, both parties must have a sufficient level of romantic interest in one another from the very beginning, and both parties must intend on establishing and maintaining a genuine relationship with one another from the very beginning. In the event that one or both components, intention and or interest, are nonexistent, the relationship will most likely languish. Interest alone is not enough—without good intentions, interest can quickly turn into manipulation, exploitation, or indifference. Good intentions alone aren't enough either because without interest, good intentions can quickly turn into boredom, resignation, or pity. Understanding the interplay between someone's interest level and their relational intentions is crucial because it sets the tone for how the relationship will unfold. Whether they chose to be with you or felt obligated to be with you, and whether they see you as a partner to invest in or a resource to take from will determine the Balance of Power, the flow of energy, and ultimately, the success or failure of the relationship.

The Power of Mutual Interest

One of the most important yet overlooked essentials in dating is the simple truth: **date someone who is genuinely interested in you.** When someone has a high level of interest, everything flows more naturally—they're more patient with your flaws, more considerate of your feelings, and more willing to cooperate in building something meaningful. Real interest creates effort, attentiveness, and emotional availability. You won't have to chase clarity or beg for consistency, because genuine interest reveals itself through action.

However, it's just as important to **avoid one-sided interest**. Being too invested in someone who isn't equally invested in you can quickly lead to frustration, emotional imbalance, or even obsession. Interest should be mutual, not lopsided. You deserve to be with someone who is just as curious about you, excited to know you, and eager to grow with you as you are with them. When both people are truly interested, the connection deepens with ease—and both individuals are empowered to show up as their best selves.

Why Interest and Intentions Can Change—and Why It Matters

Nonetheless, in the world of dating, one of the most confusing experiences is watching someone "switch up"—going from deeply invested to suddenly distant, from passionately attentive to emotionally unavailable. To make sense of this, we have to separate two key concepts: **interest** and **intentions**. They may feel similar on the surface, but they are driven by very different forces.

Interest is emotional. Intentions are strategic. Interest is fueled by hormones, mood, and chemistry—it's unpredictable, reactive, and constantly in flux. Intentions, on the other hand, are based on mindset and long-term goals. They're more stable and deliberate, but they can be hidden or misunderstood. Understanding the distinction between these two can prevent a lot of confusion—and a lot of heartache.

Why Women Can Lose Interest Suddenly

Interest is biologically wired, especially for women, to respond to their **hormonal environment**. Chemicals like **dopamine (pleasure), oxytocin (bonding), estrogen (emotional sensitivity), cortisol (stress), and serotonin (mood regulation)** all influence how much emotional energy a woman is willing to give to a relationship.

Because of this, **a woman can genuinely feel in love with a man one week and emotionally disconnected the next**—not always because something went wrong, but because her internal emotional chemistry shifted. Maybe she's stressed, overthinking, or no longer feels the emotional safety or excitement she once did. Her **emotional interest is sensitive and responsive**, which makes it less predictable and more vulnerable to sudden decline.

This is why **many men feel blindsided** when a woman who was once warm and invested suddenly becomes cold or disinterested. She may not have lied about her feelings—**her feelings simply changed.** And unless a man understands how female interest works, it can feel like betrayal when in reality, it's biology and emotional rhythm at play.

The good news is that **with experience**, a man can **learn the skill of maintaining a woman's interest.** By understanding her emotional cycles, creating consistent excitement and security, and avoiding behavior that triggers withdrawal (like neediness and over-validation), he can build a stronger emotional foundation. **Interest may be fragile—but it can be sustained.**

Why Men's Intentions Are More Consistent

Unlike interest, **intentions—especially in men—are often stable and clear from the beginning,** whether they're communicated or not. If a man starts a relationship looking only for something casual or sexual, that intention is unlikely to change over time. He may show affection, spend time, and even act emotionally connected—but those actions don't always reflect his true goal.

Likewise, if a man is serious from the start—if he sees a future with a woman, respects her, and wants to build something—his intentions are usually consistent, even through rough patches. **Men tend to know what they want early on**, and if their behavior changes later, it's often not because they changed their mind. It's because **they were wearing a mask, and the mask finally came off.**

However, it's important to note that **not all men who disappoint women are being deceptive**. Sometimes, **women see the red flags early**—his lack of effort, his inconsistent communication, his avoidance of commitment—and **choose to overlook them**, hoping that his intentions will change. They fall in love with his potential, not his patterns. And when the relationship inevitably falls apart, it's not always because he changed. Sometimes, it's because he **was never serious to begin with—and she hoped he would become serious over time**.

To Give or To Take Is the Question

In the world of dating, just as there are Runners and Chasers, there are also Givers and Takers. These archetypes are not merely roles people assume for strategic advantage; they often stem from deeply ingrained patterns shaped by personality, upbringing, and self-esteem. It's important to note that Givers tend to also be Chasers and Takers tend to also be Runners. Understanding the dynamics of Givers and Takers is crucial for navigating relationships with clarity, purpose, and self-awareness. This chapter explores how someone's interest level and intentions can be deciphered through the lens of giving and taking, and how these intentions and interest level ultimately determine the trajectory of a relationship.

The Giver and the Taker Dynamic

At its core, the relationship between Givers and Takers reflects a balance—or imbalance—of energy.

- **Givers** are those who, because of their nurturing tendencies, derive fulfillment from contributing to others. They find joy in providing emotional support, acts of kindness, and solutions to problems. Often, their sense of worth is tied to how much they can offer, especially in relationships.

- **Takers** seek relationships that maximize what they can receive. This is not always malicious; it can stem from a sense of entitlement, unmet emotional needs, or even a subconscious habit of seeking comfort without reciprocation.

The interplay between these two archetypes creates a Balance of Power, which frequently tilts in favor of the Taker. Why? Because Givers, particularly those with low self-esteem or a strong desire to feel needed, may unconsciously overextend themselves. Takers, meanwhile, often have an intuitive ability to identify and attract Givers, perpetuating the dynamic.

Interest and Perception in Giving and Taking

Interest and intentions in dating are sometimes heavily influenced by the interplay of how much of a Taker someone is and how much of a Giver they perceive you to be—and vice versa.

1. **The Taker's Interest in the Giver:**

   A Taker's interest often increases when they perceive you as a Giver. They may view your willingness to give as an opportunity to fulfill their needs, whether emotional, physical, or material. While this dynamic can sometimes appear to work initially, it often results in imbalance and eventual resentment if the Taker's interest is purely self-serving.

2. **The Giver's Interest in the Taker:**

   Givers, especially those with nurturing tendencies or low self-esteem, may feel drawn to Takers because they see an opportunity to "fix," help, or nurture them. This attraction can feel rewarding at first but can also lead to burnout if the Giver's needs are not reciprocated.

3. **Two Givers Together:**

   When two Givers come together, the relationship tends to flow harmoniously. Mutual giving fosters trust, security, and emotional intimacy. However, it requires conscious effort to avoid over-giving to the point of losing individual boundaries.

4. **Two Takers Together**:

   Two Takers in a relationship often clash, as both may feel entitled to more than they are willing to offer. This dynamic typically results in a short-lived connection, marked by power struggles and unmet expectations.

The Role of Intentions

Someone's intentions—whether they are conscious or subconscious—will ultimately determine the trajectory of the relationship.

- **Good Intentions**: When someone approaches a relationship with good intentions, they prioritize mutual respect, honesty, and collaboration. Even if one partner leans more toward giving or taking, the dynamic has a chance to balance itself out because the intention is to build something sustainable and equitable.

- **Bad Intentions**: If someone enters a relationship with selfish or exploitative intentions, the relationship will likely become strained. Takers with bad intentions often manipulate Givers, taking advantage of their nurturing nature while offering little in return. Similarly, Givers with bad intentions may over-give in hopes of gaining control or validation, or in hopes of finding self-worth or a sense of accomplishment, creating resentment over time.

Tilting The Balance of Power

As previously mentioned, in many relationships, the Balance of Power tilts in favor of the Taker. This is because Givers are often willing to sacrifice their own needs to maintain harmony, while Takers are more inclined to assert their desires unapologetically. Over time, this imbalance can create a dynamic where the Giver feels drained, and the Taker feels entitled.

However, this imbalance is not inevitable. When a Giver becomes aware of their own worth and sets healthy boundaries, they shift the Balance of Power. Likewise, when a Taker develops self-awareness and chooses to give rather than take, the relationship dynamic transforms.

How to Determine Intentions

To discern someone's intentions, pay attention to their actions over time. Words can be deceptive, but consistent behavior reveals truth. Here are some questions to ask yourself:

- Do they reciprocate your efforts, even in small ways?
- Are they genuinely interested in your well-being, or do they primarily focus on what you can provide for them?
- Do you feel energized and supported in their presence, or drained and taken for granted?

By answering these questions honestly, you can identify whether someone's intentions align with a healthy relationship or an exploitative dynamic of artificial connections and artificial interest.

The Danger of Artificial Connections and Artificial Interest

In the dating world, not every connection is genuine, and discerning between genuine connections and genuine interest as opposed to artificial connections and artificial interest and are essential for emotional well-being. This brings us to a crucial point within the Law of Intentional Interest: the presence of artificial connections and artificial interest. Artificial connections and artificial interest often lead to imbalanced, manipulative dynamics that serve the needs of one party while leaving the other feeling emotionally drained or misled. In some cases, individuals fabricate certain connections as a means to gain power, control, attention, comfort, or convenience.

Identifying and Guarding Against Artificial Connections

Understanding and recognizing the signs of artificial connections can protect you from falling into these unbalanced dynamics. Here are some indicators of a potential artificial connection:

- **One-Sided Effort**: If one person is always initiating, planning, or compromising, this can signal an imbalance where only one side is genuinely invested.

- **Lack of Genuine Sharing**: In artificial connections, the person fabricating interest may share less of themselves emotionally, keeping things at surface-level or evading deep conversations.

- **Withholding Certain Types of Connection**: If you find that someone is expressive in one area (e.g., sexually) but cold or distant in another (e.g., emotionally), it may indicate that they are not interested in a full and genuine connection.

- **Feeling Insecure or Unsure**: Artificial connections often leave you feeling off-balance, unsure of where you stand or constantly searching for answers. Genuine connections, by contrast, tend to feel secure and mutual.

In the world of dating, where signals are often mixed and motivations vary, the power lies in understanding these dynamics and choosing connections that are based on authenticity, respect, and shared values. By being vigilant and discerning in your connections, you can avoid falling into the "Chaser" role, where you're giving more than you receive. The Law of Intentional Interest is not just about understanding how relationships form; it's about learning to identify genuine connections and genuine interest to protect yourself from Unbalanced Dynamics that lead to one-sided attachment.

Real, balanced connections require mutual interest, effort, and sincerity. Artificial connections, on the other hand, are often a means to gain power, manipulate, or use another person for one's own benefit, leaving the other to chase a relationship that doesn't truly exist. Let's examine how these deceptive dynamics play out for both men and women.

The Manipulation of Sexual Attraction Without Emotional Connection

Consider a man who feels a strong sexual attraction to a woman but lacks genuine emotional interest in her. Rather than being upfront, he may pretend to share a romantic connection, perhaps displaying just enough emotional involvement to make her believe there is more to the relationship. His true intention is to gain control and receive benefits from the situation, whether for convenience or personal gratification.

This dynamic creates a powerful, often confusing situation for the woman. When a man expresses sexual interest without genuine emotional intention, it often triggers a Chase response in the woman. Her Sexual Activation, fueled by the attraction, compels her to seek more closeness and intimacy, believing that she can eventually build a full emotional connection with him. Yet because he withholds emotional energy and refrains from developing a real emotional connection, she finds herself in an endless cycle of pursuit.

Since the emotional connection remains incomplete, a sexual attachment forms instead. The result is that she becomes the "Chaser," constantly seeking validation and a deeper connection. In her quest for love, she offers sex, hoping that it will eventually lead to the emotional fulfillment she craves. This creates an unbalanced dynamic where she is effectively "giving sex to get love," while he maintains power without reciprocating genuine emotional investment. The root of this dynamic is because the Chaser failed to obtain Sexual Respect from the beginning.

The Manipulation of Emotional Attraction Without Sexual Connection

On the other side of the spectrum, a woman might have a strong emotional attraction to a man but lack genuine sexual interest. Rather than addressing this difference, she may pretend to have sexual interest to keep him invested, using seduction as a means of obtaining power and or comfort. By giving the impression of a potential sexual connection, she keeps his interest alive, leading him to believe that a more sexually charged relationship could be on the horizon.

When a woman expresses emotional interest without any sexual intentions, it often activates a Chase response in the man. His emotional activation, motivated by her attractiveness, draws him closer, creating the illusion that they could build something more intimate and passionate. However, because she withholds sexual energy and refrains from building a real physical connection, he too becomes trapped in an unbalanced pursuit.

Since the sexual connection remains incomplete, an emotional attachment forms instead, leaving him in the role of the "Chaser." In this dynamic, he offers his love, hoping that it will eventually lead to the physical intimacy he desires. Caught in this cycle, he finds himself "giving love to get sex," while she maintains power by keeping physical intimacy just out of reach. The root of this dynamic is because the Chaser failed to obtain Emotional Respect from the beginning.

The Exchange of Love and Sex: The Power Play in Dating Dynamics

Love and sex are often seen as the two main currencies in dating, but how they are exchanged depends largely on self-esteem and intent. When someone operates from a place of low self-worth, they tend to give what they value least in hopes of receiving what they crave most. Conversely, those with exploitative intentions and ulterior motives tend to offer what the other person desires most, in order to extract what benefits them. This strategic exchange creates a Power Dynamic that plays out differently for men and women.

Women Who Give Sex to Get Love vs. Women Who Give Love to Get Favors

For women, love is often a verification of importance, an acquisition of attention, and a celebration of femininity. How a woman pursues this validation is determined by whether she operates from low self-esteem or manipulative intent.

1. Women With Low Self-Esteem: Giving Sex to Get Love

A woman with low self-esteem often believes that her worth is tied to her desirability. Because of this, she may use sex as a means to secure love, thinking that if she is sexually available, the man will develop emotional attachment and commitment.

- She associates sex with approval and validation.
- She fears that without sexual access; the man will lose interest.
- She equates a man's post-sex affection with genuine love, even if it's temporary.

This dynamic leaves her vulnerable to men who take advantage of her need for love, offering just enough emotional breadcrumbs to keep her invested without ever truly committing.

2. Women With Exploitative Intentions: Giving Love to Get Favors

On the other hand, a woman with exploitative intentions understands that love is a powerful tool in maintaining power. She doesn't necessarily seek deep emotional connection—rather, she uses the illusion of love to gain tangible benefits.

- She strategically nurtures a man's emotions to make him invest in her.

- She gives just enough affection and emotional closeness to keep him romantically hooked.

- Once he is emotionally invested, she leverages his commitment for financial support, favors, or lifestyle upgrades.

For this type of woman, love is less about emotional fulfillment and more about securing resources and influence. She understands that men, especially those seeking long-term commitment, value love and emotional security, so she dangles the possibility of it in order to extract what she wants.

Men Who Give Love to Get Sex vs. Men Who Give Sex to Get Favors

For men, sex is an extension of dominance, an assertion of control, and a reaffirmation of masculinity. How a man navigates this depends on whether he operates from low self-esteem or exploitative intent.

1. Men With Low Self-Esteem: Giving Love to Get Sex

A man with low self-esteem often believes that his worth is tied to his ability to secure sexual validation. However, if he lacks the confidence, looks, or social status to attract women sexually, he may attempt to "earn" sex through emotional investment.

- He showers women with love, attention, and commitment in hopes that it will lead to physical intimacy.

- He sees an emotional connection as the price he must pay to receive sex.

- He may overextend himself, over-romanticize the relationship, and even ignore red flags just to secure sexual access.

This approach often results in him being "friend-zoned" or being used for his emotional availability without receiving the sexual validation he truly seeks.

2. Men With Exploitative Intentions: Giving Sex to Get Favors

In contrast, a man with exploitative intentions views sex as a means to gain power and extract benefits. Instead of offering love in exchange for sex, he offers sex in exchange for what he wants.

- He uses his sexual appeal to make a woman emotionally and physically hooked.
- Once she is attached, he leverages the connection for financial favors, emotional labor, or lifestyle benefits.
- He keeps the relationship undefined, ensuring that she remains available to him while he extracts maximum value.

For this type of man, sex is less about pleasure and more about strategic positioning. He understands that women who develop emotional connections through intimacy are more likely to invest in him beyond just sex—whether that means financial support, emotional support, social status, being nurturing, or other advantages.

The Power Shift in Relationships

At its core, this exchange of love and sex creates a **Power Imbalance**, where the person who values one more than the other is at a disadvantage.

- **Women who seek love and give sex freely often end up with men who value sex over love.** These men receive what they want without having to reciprocate emotionally.
- **Men who seek sex and give love freely often end up with women who value love over sex.** These women enjoy the emotional investment but may not reciprocate sexually in the way he desires.
- **Women who give sex strategically gain control over men who are emotionally invested.** These women often dictate

the terms of the relationship, deciding when and how physical or emotional intimacy occurs.

- **Men who give love strategically gain control over women who are physically hooked.** These men use emotional detachment as a form of dominance, keeping the relationship on their terms.

This highlights why many relationships feel like a power struggle—each person is trying to secure what they value most while giving up what they value least.

The Connection Between Priorities, Intentions, and Interest

A person's approach to relationships—whether they prioritize **sex over romance** or **romance over sex**—is a strong indicator of their **intentions** and the **authenticity of their interest**. The fundamental difference lies in what they seek from a relationship:

- **Someone who prioritizes sex over romance** is more likely to seek **casual relationships**, which are often self-serving and transactional. As a result, they are more prone to displaying **artificial interest** and **artificial intentions** to maintain access to sex without true emotional commitment.

- **Someone who prioritizes romance over sex** is more likely to seek **serious relationships**, which require emotional depth and investment. Because of this, they tend to exhibit **genuine interest** and **genuine intentions**, as their goal is to build something meaningful rather than extract temporary gratification.

This distinction is critical in understanding Dating Dynamics—someone's **end goal** determines the **authenticity of their actions** and how much they are truly invested in a relationship.

How Prioritizing Sex Leads to Artificial Interest and Intentions

A person who **prioritizes sex over romance** most likely operates with a **short-term mindset**, where **pleasure takes precedence over emotional connection.** Because of this, their approach to dating is often filled with **artificial interest and intentions,** meaning they:

- **Pretend to care more than they do** to maintain sexual access.

- **Act emotionally invested** when it benefits them but withdraw when deeper connection is required.

- **Mimic romantic behavior** (such as sweet talk, affectionate gestures, or future-faking) to create the illusion of genuine connection—only to disappear or lose interest once sex is obtained.

- **Remain non-committal,** avoiding serious relationships because their true goal is physical rather than emotional.

Because they are **more interested in what they can get** rather than **who they are with,** their approach to relationships lacks true emotional depth. They may say all the right things and act interested, but if their **core motivation is sex,** their **intentions remain surface-level and self-serving.**

How Prioritizing Romance Leads to Genuine Interest and Intentions

On the other hand, a person who **prioritizes romance over sex** is **naturally inclined toward genuine connection.** Their goal is not just **what they can receive,** but **who they can build with,** which leads to a very different type of interest and intention:

- **They genuinely invest in getting to know the other person**—their values, emotions, and long-term compatibility.

- **Their affection is not conditional on physical intimacy**, meaning their attraction remains strong regardless of whether sex is on the table.
- **They prioritize emotional bonding**, leading to a desire for deeper commitment, trust, and partnership.
- **Their consistency reveals their authenticity**—because they are not just looking for a temporary high, they remain engaged even when the relationship faces challenges.

Because their goal is to build something lasting, they approach relationships with real emotional investment, making them more likely to be sincere, committed, and emotionally available.

Casual Relationships vs. Serious Relationships: The Intention Gap

The type of relationship someone seeks directly reflects how real or fake their interest is:

- **Casual relationships** place a greater emphasis on personal gratification, which **requires less emotional investment** and more **surface-level interest** to keep the arrangement going.
- **Serious relationships** require genuine commitment and deep emotional engagement, which means **interest and intentions must be real for the relationship to work**.

This is why **people who prioritize sex over romance tend to avoid serious relationships**—because genuine emotional connection is not their focus. Instead, they rely on **artificial displays of affection and false promises** to sustain casual arrangements without forming real bonds.

Scarcity and the Role It Plays in Intentions and Interest

In the realm of Dating Dynamics, the concept of scarcity and abundance significantly influences someone's intentions, interest, and the authenticity of their connections. When someone occupies the "benefitting side" of the Dating Pool—whether male or female—they are often in a position of relative scarcity, which grants them more options and advantage in the Dating Market. This abundance can lead to a reduced need to act with good intentions, express genuine interest, or foster real connections, simply because they don't face the same pressures or constraints as those on the other side of the equation.

Men on the Male-Benefitting Side of the Dating Pool

For men, the Male-Benefitting side of the Dating Pool typically includes those who possess traits or circumstances that make them highly desirable, such as wealth, status, physical attractiveness, or social influence. These men often have a larger pool of potential partners vying for their attention, which can create a sense of abundance.

This abundance, while advantageous, can sometimes lead to:

- **Bad Intentions**: They may approach relationships with a mindset of personal gain rather than mutual respect and connection.

- **Artificial Interest**: To maintain their abundance of options, they might express interest insincerely, using charm or flattery to create the illusion of emotional investment.

- **Artificial Connections**: Because they are not in a disadvantageous position and don't have a short supply of options, they may lack the urgency or motivation to build genuine connections, instead prioritizing surface-level connections that fulfill their immediate desires.

The scarcity of desirable men in this category gives them the power to be selective, often with little accountability for how their actions impact others. Without a "dire need" for authentic connections, they may adopt a mindset of convenience over an authentic connection.

Women on the Female-Benefitting Side of the Dating Pool

Similarly, women on the Female-Benefitting side of the Dating Pool—those perceived as particularly attractive, socially desirable, or in high demand—experience a similar dynamic. Their scarcity within the Dating Pool gives them access to more options and a greater ability to choose partners on their terms.

This abundance can lead to:

- **Bad Intentions**: Some women in this position may approach dating with an entitlement mentality, focusing on what they can gain (e.g., attention, gifts, validation) rather than seeking a meaningful connection.

- **Artificial Interest**: They might fabricate interest to maintain control or manipulate outcomes, especially if they are not emotionally invested.

- **Artificial Connections**: With a surplus of options, they may prioritize the thrill of attention or temporary excitement over deeper, more genuine connections.

Because they are scarce within the Dating Pool, they, too, lack the pressure and urgency to act with good intentions or invest deeply in relationships. Like their male counterparts, their abundance can create an environment where comfort often outweighs an authentic connection.

The Common Thread: Scarcity Creates Imbalance

The key factor driving this behavior in both men and women on the benefitting side of the Dating Pool is scarcity. When someone is scarce in the Dating Market, they naturally have more of an advantage, less urgency, and fewer incentives to approach relationships with genuine intentions. This imbalance creates a dynamic where those with abundance often develop patterns of taking rather than giving, and they may exploit the interest of others without feeling the need to reciprocate authentically.

The Dominated Relationship: Sexual Attraction Without Emotional Connection

A man seeking a **Dominated Relationship** often prioritizes sexual attraction over emotional intimacy. While he may exhibit artificial interest to gain the trust or attention of his partner, the underlying intention isn't love, connection, or mutual growth—it's **power, control, and convenience**. He also only has intentions of Taking and not Giving and will target a woman or women with nurturing tendencies and or low-elf-esteem to fulfill his sexual and emotional needs.

Key Traits of a Dominated Relationship:

- **Artificial Interest**: He may fake emotional engagement, showing just enough romantic gestures or care to keep the woman invested. However, these actions are surface-level and lack depth.

- **Sexual Attraction Without Emotional Connection**: The relationship is primarily driven by physical desire. He seeks the benefits of sexual intimacy without investing emotionally or building a genuine bond.

- **Motivations of Power and Control**: His primary aim is to maintain dominance in the relationship. By controlling the pace and depth of the connection, he ensures that his needs are met while avoiding emotional vulnerability.

- **Convenience**: The relationship operates on his terms, requiring minimal effort or commitment. He may pull back emotionally when it's inconvenient for him, leaving the woman in a state of longing and pursuit.

Women involved in this dynamic often develop **sexual attachments**, mistaking his artificial romantic interest for affection and genuine intentions. This imbalance can leave them chasing a deeper connection that the man has no intention of providing.

The Validated Relationship: Emotional Attraction Without Sexual Connection

On the other side of the spectrum, a woman seeking a **Validated Relationship** may exhibit artificial interest by pretending to have a sexual connection with a man. Her true motivation lies not in physical attraction but in securing **power, attention, and comfort** through the man's emotional investment. She also only has intentions of Taking and not Giving and will target a man or men who is generous and has low self-esteem to fulfill her emotional and material needs.

Key Traits of a Validated Relationship:

- **Artificial Interest**: She may fake sexual desire or flirtation, using suggestive behavior to keep the man engaged. However, her primary focus is on eliciting emotional validation and financial benefits rather than building a genuine sexual connection.

- **Emotional Attraction Without Sexual Connection**: The woman prioritizes the man's emotional attention, care, and support but does not reciprocate physical interest.

- **Motivations of Power and Attention**: She seeks to maintain power by keeping the man emotionally invested. His longing for intimacy and connection allows her to dictate the pace and nature of the relationship.

- **Comfort**: The relationship fulfills her emotional needs without requiring her to invest sexually. She may offer emotional rewards, such as praise or acknowledgment, to keep him seeking her approval.

Men involved in this dynamic often develop **emotional attachments**, mistaking her artificial sexual interest for affection and genuine intentions. This imbalance leaves them chasing physical intimacy that she has no intention of reciprocating.

The Calculated Relationship: Multiple Connections, Flexible Engagement

A person seeking a **Calculated Relationship** operates with a different approach entirely. Rather than focusing on one individual, they may simultaneously develop multiple connections with multiple people, strategically managing these relationships to suit their needs at any given time.

Key Traits of a Calculated Relationship:

- **Multiple Connections**: They build relationships across various individuals, creating a network of emotional, sexual, and social connections that provide them with different forms of support and satisfaction.

- **Avoidance of Strong Connections**: To maintain power and flexibility, they often avoid developing deep or strong connections with anyone. This prevents emotional entanglement and allows them to disengage easily.

- **Turning Connections On or Off**: They may demonstrate interest or withdraw it as needed. For instance, they might intensify a connection when they want something (e.g., support, intimacy, or validation) and then go cold once their needs are met.

- **Adaptability**: Their ability to shift between Romantic Mode and Erotic Mode allows them to navigate different dynamics depending on the individual and the situation.

The motivations behind Calculated Relationships are often rooted in a desire for **freedom, variety, and self-preservation**. By keeping their options open and controlling the depth of their connections, they ensure that they remain in a position of power while minimizing emotional vulnerability.

The Fluidity of Intention and Interest

Although Relationship Formats tend to be set in stone (Dominated Relationship, Validated Relationship, Calculated Relationship), intention and interest are not static—they can evolve over time, influenced by the dynamic interplay of emotions, desires, and external factors. One significant determinant of how intentions and interest shift lies in whether someone leads with love or sex in a relationship. These starting points often set the tone for how someone engages with their partner, but they are not absolute, as emotions and circumstances can lead to unexpected changes in behavior.

When a Female Taker Leads with Sex

A Female Taker who leads with sex and initially exhibits bad intentions and artificial interest may do so because her primary goals are validation, financial gain, or romantic benefits. However, emotions are unpredictable, and even someone with artificial interest can experience a shift.

- **The Transition to Romantic Mode**: If this person unexpectedly "catches feelings," her interest may transform. What started as a casual dynamic may evolve into genuine interest and emotional investment. In Romantic Mode, she becomes more focused on connection, vulnerability, and mutual growth. Her initial artificial interest is replaced by a desire for something deeper and more meaningful.

This shift is not guaranteed, and highly unlikely, but it highlights the fluid nature of interest and how emotions can override initial motivations.

When a Female Taker Leads with Love

On the flip side, a Female Taker who leads with love and initially exhibits good intentions and genuine interest may undergo a different transformation.

- **The Shift to Erotic Mode**: If the relationship progresses into a desire for a more physical phase or Erotic Mode, her interest level may change. What began as a pursuit of emotional connection can shift toward seeking personal gratification, validation, or attention. This switch may leave her partner feeling as though the dynamic and connection has become less authentic, especially if the relationship becomes imbalanced.

Why Men Tend to Stay Consistent

In contrast, men generally remain consistent in their approach.

- **Men Who Lead with Sex**: Men who lead with sex often maintain that focus throughout the relationship. Their interest and intentions are aligned with physical connection, and while emotional attachment can develop, it is less likely to completely override their original motivations.

- **Men Who Lead with Love**: Men who lead with love tend to stay in that mode, prioritizing emotional connection, partnership, and long-term compatibility. Their intentions and interest level are more likely to remain stable, even as the relationship evolves.

While there are exceptions, these patterns underscore how gendered approaches to love and sex often differ in their trajectory.

The Role of Progression and Regression

As previously discussed, relationships are rarely linear; they go through periods of **Progression** and **Regression**, during which intentions and interest can fluctuate.

- **Progression**: When things are going well, emotions are high, and the relationship feels positive, both partners tend to show increased interest and stronger intentions. This is a period of growth, intimacy, and connection.

- **Regression**: During colder periods—whether due to conflict, disinterest, or external stressors—interest and intentions may weaken. One partner might pull away, creating an imbalance where one person appears distant and the other overcompensates with increased effort and interest.

Interest and Intentions Regarding the Psychological Mathematics of Mood Temperature

As per the Psychological Mathematics of Mood Temperatures, mood temperature significantly affects how interest and intention are expressed.

- **Mood Temperature Shifts**: When the mood shifts in favor of one person (e.g., they feel more confident, desired, or in control), their interest and intent tend to decrease. This creates a Power Imbalance where the other person, sensing the distance, shows increased interest and intent to close the gap.

This fluctuation creates a dynamic where the "hot" person becomes less invested, while the "cold" person becomes more eager to reconnect.

- **Authenticity Matters**: If the connection is genuine, these mood-driven fluctuations are temporary and often resolve with communication and effort. However, if the connection is artificial, the shifts in mood temperature can expose the lack of authenticity. Once interest and intent weaken due to emotional distance or external changes, the relationship often crumbles.

The Key to Combining Intentions and Interest

Interest can fluctuate, especially for women, because it's tied to hormones, mood, and emotional connection. Intentions, especially in men, tend to stay the same—whether those intentions are good or bad. But neither interest nor intentions exist in a vacuum. **With maturity and experience**, you can learn how to **sustain interest, recognize true intentions**, and avoid getting attached to potential instead of reality.

In the end, the key is not just to find someone who *likes* you, but someone who is **genuinely interested in you and intends to treat you with purpose**—from the very beginning.

Bringing Interest and Intentions Together: The Law of Intentional Interest

Although **interest and intentions need to combine, they are two separate forces**, and the key to understanding real connection lies in knowing **how and when they align**. Interest is emotional—it can rise, fall, and fluctuate with mood, hormones, and life circumstances. Intentions, on the other hand, are directional—they reflect what someone *wants* from you, what they *plan* to do with the relationship, and what role they *expect* you to play in their life.

According to the **Law of Intentional Interest**, true connection and lasting love only happen **when intention and interest are aligned from the beginning**. That means someone—especially men—must already *intend* to build something real with you *before* the emotions kick in or deepen over time. A man doesn't just "accidentally" fall in love. He may not say it outright, but he has to make that internal decision early on: *"If this goes well, I could see something real with her."* That foundational intention determines how far his interest will go.

Why Love Requires Intentional Interest

A person with **selfish, manipulative, or exploitative intentions** is not likely to suddenly wake up one day and see you in a new light. If they entered the relationship looking to take, use, or control—no matter how passionate it seems—it's tied to what *they* can gain, not what *you* both can build. Even if the chemistry feels intense, it's not rooted in mutuality—it's rooted in personal benefit.

This is why it's **extremely rare** for someone who started with **bad intentions** to develop good ones later. Emotional highs might come and go, but unless their *original goal* was authentic and relationship-focused, they are unlikely to sustain real romantic interest or grow into something long-term. More often, when their selfish needs are no longer being met, their interest fades—not because you did something wrong, but because **their original intent was never about building with you, only benefitting from you.**

When Interest Can Be Rekindled

On the other hand, **someone who had good intentions from the start**—someone who truly wanted something meaningful with you—*can* lose interest temporarily. Life happens. Emotions shift. The connection may dull. But because their **intentions were rooted in building, not using**, that person is far more likely to **regain interest**, reconnect emotionally, and be willing to work through the rough patches. Their commitment isn't just based on how they feel in the moment—**it's based on the decision they made from the beginning to value the relationship.**

So, while **interest can waver, intentions are the anchor.** And when someone's intentions are good, **even faded interest has the chance to be revived.** But if someone's intentions were selfish all along, **lost interest isn't just emotional—it's transactional.** They've stopped getting what they wanted, and therefore, they stop showing up.

Know When to Walk Away

Healthy relationships are built on a balance between **Givers and Takers**—not in the sense that one always gives and the other always takes, but in the sense that both people are willing to do **both**. A Balanced Relationship requires mutual exchange: giving love, support, effort, and presence—while also receiving those things in return. When that balance is present, the relationship feels natural, fulfilling, and secure. But when the dynamic shifts too far in one direction, where **one partner is always giving and the other is always taking**, the relationship becomes emotionally lopsided and unsustainable.

If you find yourself constantly in the role of the Giver, pouring into someone who only shows up to take, it's time to pause and reflect. That imbalance is rarely accidental—it usually points to a deeper issue: **either your partner has low interest, bad intentions, or both**. A Taker with low interest won't make the effort because they simply don't care enough to, and a Taker with bad intentions will continue extracting from you because they see you as a means to an end. Either way, it's not love—it's usage. And no matter how much you care; you can't force someone to value what they don't genuinely want or intend to build with. And you can't build a healthy, fulfilling relationship on one-sided effort.

If your giving is met with entitlement instead of appreciation, or silence instead of effort, it's not a relationship—it's a drain. Don't stay in a situation hoping they'll change. **Know your worth, recognize the signs, and be willing to walk away**. Because the right person won't just take from you—they'll give just as much in return. And staying in a relationship where your love is not matched with effort is not loyalty—it's self-neglect. You deserve a connection that's real, reciprocal, and rooted in both genuine interest and good intentions.

Chapter 12

The Law of Market Leveraging

The Dating Market, like any marketplace, is governed by the concept of leverage. Leverage in a marketplace refers to the **ability to influence outcomes or negotiate from a position of strength** due to having a desirable asset, resource, or advantage. In the Dating Market, leverage means the person with more options, desirability, or perceived value has **greater power to set terms, make choices, and dictate the pace of the relationship**. The Law of Market Leveraging states that the individual who holds more perceived or actual value in the Dating Market by default also obtains more Relational Advantage, therefore, said individual will inevitably also obtain more leverage in the dynamics of relationship. In other words, the person with more leverage will more likely have the ability and luxury to choose more and or better options, will be more likely to end the relationship, and be more likely to get away with things such as disrespect and infidelity. This Relational Advantage often determines who holds power in a relationship, and understanding this concept is key to maintaining balance and avoiding one-sided relationships.

In modern discussions, particularly those found on podcasts or in online debates, the question often arises: "Who is the prize in a relationship—men or women?" The answer, while culturally charged, is less about gender and more about leverage. The "prize" in any Relational Exchange is the individual with more options, desirability, or bargaining power. This leverage can come from various factors such as physical attractiveness, social status, or financial stability.

The Perception of the "Prize"

In cultural narratives, the debate over whether "women are the prize" or "men are the prize" misses the core truth: the "prize" is not determined by gender but by leverage. In any relationship, the "prize" is the person whose value in the broader Dating Market is higher relative to their partner. This value is influenced by societal norms, individual preferences, and the current dating landscape. Ultimately, the perception of who holds leverage can shift over time as circumstances, preferences, and external factors evolve. Nonetheless, the prize is usually the individual with more Sexual Capital.

What Is Sexual Market Value (Sexual Capital)?

Sexual Capital, also known as Sexual Market Value (SMV), is a term in Social Science used to describe a person's **perceived desirability and value in the dating and sexual marketplace.** It reflects how attractive someone is to potential partners based on a combination of physical, social, emotional, and psychological traits. Just like financial capital determines your worth in an economic system, **Sexual Capital determines your leverage in the romantic and sexual economy.**

Key components that contribute to SMV include:

- **Physical Attractiveness**: Facial symmetry, body composition, health, grooming, and overall appearance.

- **Age and Fertility (for women)**: Youth is often linked to higher SMV due to biological fertility cues.

- **Status and Resources (for men)**: Wealth, career success, confidence, and leadership raise male SMV.

- **Personality and Social Skills**: Charisma, humor, emotional intelligence, and confidence influence desirability.

- **Emotional Stability and Loyalty**: Trustworthiness and ability to form healthy connections are attractive long-term traits.

Importantly, **SMV is not the same as a person's moral or spiritual worth**—it's a measure of **how the dating market responds to someone** based on evolutionary cues, cultural trends, and individual preferences. It's also **fluid**, meaning it can change over time depending on self-development, aging, or shifts in social context. Again, Sexual Market Value is not the same as Personal Value. Every human being has inherent worth simply by being alive—life is precious, and no one's humanity is up for debate. However, **Sexual Market Value** operates on a different merit system, much like a credit score. It's a way of measuring perceived desirability in the Dating Market based on traits like appearance, status, charisma, or compatibility. Just as a low credit score doesn't mean someone is worthless—it just affects what loans they qualify for—having lower Sexual Market Value doesn't make someone less deserving of love, dignity, or happiness. It simply reflects how the dating market responds to certain traits, not the worth of a person's soul.

Hypergamy and Hypogamy: The Dynamics of "Dating Up" and "Dating Down"

To further understand the nuances of Market Leveraging, we must turn to two foundational concepts in social science: **hypergamy** and **hypogamy**.

- **Hypergamy** is the tendency to seek a partner of higher social status, higher social class, or perceived Sexual Capital (Sexual Market Value). In other words, it's the practice of "dating up" or "marrying up." This concept is often associated with women, who historically and biologically have sought partners that provide security, resources, or status. Hypergamy is not inherently a negative or manipulative practice; it is rooted in evolutionary psychology, where partnering with a higher-status individual could increase survival and reproductive success.

- **Hypogamy** is the opposite tendency, describing the act of "dating down" or "marrying down." Men are typically associated with hypogamy, as their mate selection often prioritizes physical attractiveness or youth over socioeconomic parity. Again, this is rooted in evolutionary strategies, where men may prioritize indicators of fertility over resource acquisition in a partner.

These tendencies are not rigid, but they help explain many patterns in Dating Dynamics. They also illuminate why the person with the higher perceived value in any given relationship may hold more leverage.

Leverage and Its Many Forms

Market Leverage doesn't come from a single trait; it's a combination of factors that contribute to someone's overall desirability and options in the Dating Market. These include:

1. **Physical Attractiveness**: This is often the most immediate form of leverage, as it is universally acknowledged and easily assessed. People who are conventionally attractive tend to have more options, increasing their leverage.

2. **Social Status**: This includes wealth, career achievements, reputation, and influence. High social status can make someone more desirable, particularly for those seeking stability or prestige.

3. **Personality and Emotional Intelligence**: Charm, humor, and emotional availability can be significant forms of leverage, especially in long-term relationship contexts.

4. **Scarcity of Alternatives**: The person with more viable alternatives or options will naturally hold more power in the Relationship Dynamic. If one partner feels the other is harder to replace, the latter gains leverage.

How Market Leveraging Shapes Relationships

Understanding leverage helps clarify why some relationships feel balanced and harmonious while others feel skewed or exploitative. When one partner holds significantly more leverage than the other, power imbalances can arise, potentially leading to resentment, manipulation, or dependency. For instance:

- A man with high social status and wealth may dominate the dynamic with a partner who relies on him financially.

- Conversely, a woman who is significantly more attractive than her partner may hold power due to his perceived inability to "trade up."

This leveraging effect often manifests in subtle but critical ways—how conflicts are resolved, who invests more in the relationship, or whose needs are prioritized.

Leveraging Experience in the Dating Market

An often-overlooked dimension of Relational Leverage is **experience**. The person with more dating experience typically holds an upper hand because they possess a greater understanding of Relationship Dynamics, emotional boundaries, and social cues. This allows them to navigate interactions with greater confidence and strategic awareness. Conversely, a person with less experience may feel unsure, reliant, or even intimidated, creating a natural imbalance in Relational Power.

This is why some individuals deliberately pursue partners with less dating experience. By doing so, they position themselves as the "expert" or more seasoned partner, which grants them a significant advantage. This can manifest in various ways:

- **Influence over decision-making**: The experienced partner often dictates the pace and direction of the relationship.

- **Control over relational dynamics**: The less experienced partner may be more forgiving of imbalances, unaware of healthier alternatives, or more likely to tolerate problematic behavior.

This dynamic highlights how leveraging experience can tip the Balance of Power, and it serves as a reminder of the importance of mutual respect and fairness, regardless of the disparity in relational knowledge.

Society's Perception of Relational Advantage

Because women tend to practice hypergamy—seeking partners with higher social status, experience, or resources—and men often practice hypogamy—preferring younger, less experienced partners—the dynamics of dating often result in women forming relationships with men who hold more **Relational Power**. This power imbalance can create a societal perception that women are more vulnerable in Romantic Relationships, as they are seen as more likely to be hurt or taken advantage of. When a couple breaks up, this perception often leads to the assumption that the man cheated or broke the woman's heart, rather than considering the possibility of the roles being reversed. This bias underscores how deeply ingrained these relational patterns are in societal narratives.

However, since women tend to practice hypergamy and date men with more experience than them, giving women a disadvantage, the reason why the Market Leverage can become balanced out is because of the fact that it's easier for women to accumulate options than it is for men, giving women an advantage. On the contrary, since men tend to have a harder time accumulating options than women do, giving men a disadvantage, another reason why the Market Leverage can become balanced out is because of the fact that men tend to practice hypogamy and date women with less experience than them, giving men an advantage.

The Asymmetry of Effort: Getting vs. Keeping in Modern Dating

In today's Dating Market, **women generally find it easier to get a man,** as previously mentioned. Due to biological factors, social conditioning, and the dynamics of attention in the sexual marketplace, women—especially in their youth—tend to attract a much higher volume of male attention than men attract from women. A woman can receive validation, interest, and offers with minimal effort, simply by existing in the space. However, while **getting a man is easy**, **keeping a man is often the harder challenge**. Many men pursue women for short-term reasons—sex, conquest, or curiosity—without long-term intentions. Because of this, women often struggle to secure lasting commitment from high-value men, especially if those men have options and aren't emotionally invested.

Conversely, **it's harder for men to get a woman**, particularly in the early stages of dating. Men are expected to initiate, impress, and pursue. The majority of men—especially average or Lower-Market Men—struggle to get noticed in a world where a handful of top-tier men dominate women's attention. However, once a man successfully earns a woman's interest—especially if she respects and admires him—it becomes **much easier for him to keep her**. Women, by nature and social conditioning, are generally more loyal and emotionally committed once they've formed a bond. If a man provides emotional safety, leadership, and consistency, most women will stick around, sometimes even long after they should.

This asymmetry in effort creates frustration on both sides: women ask, *"Why can't I keep the men I attract?"* while men ask, *"Why can't I attract the women I'd treat right?"* Understanding this paradox is crucial for navigating modern relationships. It shows that attraction and commitment require **two different skill sets**, and that success in love comes from mastering both—not just one.

The Gendered Dynamics of Dating and Marriage

The saying "women date who they want, and men date who they can; but men marry who they want, and women marry who they can" reflects a fundamental shift in leverage between the Dating and Marriage Markets. This dynamic underscores how the Balance of Power can shift based on what each person is seeking—and how effectively they leverage their strengths.

Women Date Who They Want

In the Dating Market, women often have the advantage because they typically receive more attention and have more options of potential partners. This advantage allows women to be selective, particularly in short-term or casual dating. However, this leverage diminishes when the goal shifts from dating to marriage, where men may have a greater ability to be selective.

Men Marry Who They Want

Marriage represents a long-term commitment, and men often gain leverage here because they tend to have more control over when and with whom they settle down. While women may be selective in dating, the pressure to secure a long-term partner as they age or prioritize family goals can shift the balance. Men, on the other hand, may delay marriage, increasing their ability to marry who they want when the time feels right for them.

Front End Leverage vs Back End Leverage

Although women tend to have more leverage on the front end (dating), and less leverage on the back end (marriage), and men tend to have less leverage on the front end (dating), and more leverage on the back end (marriage), both men and women can overcome the lack of front end or back end leverage if they position themself in the Dating Market based on their Sexual Market Classification.

Understanding Sexual Market Classification and Its Role in The Law of Market Leveraging

To fully grasp **The Law of Market Leveraging**, one must explore the concept of **Sexual Capital** (often referred to as Sexual Market Value) and how it interacts with **The Law of Natural Priority**. These two principles combine to create what I call **Sexual Market Classification**, a framework for understanding Relational Dynamics based on desire, sexuality, and emotional orientation.

Sexual Market Classification segments individuals into four categories, defined by their levels of **Sexual Capital** (how desired they are in the Dating Market) and **Natural Priority** (whether their orientation is primarily sexual or emotional). These classifications explain why some individuals hold significant leverage in the Dating Market while others may struggle.

The Four Sexual Market Classifications

1. **Highly Desired (High Sexual Capital) and Highly Sexual (Sexual Priority)**

    a. Individuals in this category are considered the **Alphas** of the Dating Market. They possess the most leverage due to their combination of desirability and sexual focus.

    b. **Advantages**: Alphas dominate the Dating Market because they are both physically or socially attractive (high sexual capital) and prioritize sexual fulfillment (sexual priority). Their ability to meet societal standards of attractiveness and exude confidence makes them highly sought after.

    c. **Unique Leverage**: Alpha Males, in particular, often gain additional power by **withholding love**, using their sexual focus to maintain control over Romantic Dynamics. This detachment can lead to gaining **Emotional Respect**, as their partners often feel they must "earn" emotional validation.

2. **Not Highly Desired (Low Sexual Capital) and Highly Sexual (Sexual Priority)**

   a. These individuals are **Betas** and prioritize sexual fulfillment but lack the desirability to command leverage in the Dating Market.

   b. **Challenges**: Although they may be willing to engage in relationships with a strong sexual focus, their low Sexual Capital makes them less influential in the Dating Market. They may struggle to form meaningful connections or gain respect from their partners.

3. **Highly Desired (High Sexual Capital) and Highly Emotional (Romantic Priority)**

   a. These individuals are also **Betas** and possess high desirability but prioritize emotional connection over sexual fulfillment.

   b. **Advantages**: Their desirability allows them to attract partners easily, but their romantic focus can make them more vulnerable to Power Imbalances if they encounter partners who are less emotionally invested.

   c. **Balanced Leverage**: This group can maintain leverage if they manage their emotional investments wisely, ensuring they're not overly dependent on the validation of their partners.

4. **Not Highly Desired (Low Sexual Capital) and Highly Emotional (Romantic Priority)**

   a. These individuals are considered the **Omegas** of the Dating Market. They possess the least leverage due to their low desirability and focus on emotional connection.

   b. **Disadvantages**: Omega Males, in particular, face significant challenges because their Romantic Priority makes them appear overly available, and their lack of Sexual Capital reduces their appeal. They often fail to command **Emotional Respect** due to their inability to withhold love or maintain emotional boundaries.

Implications of Sexual Market Classification

Understanding these classifications helps explain the disparities in Relational Power across different individuals. It also highlights why some people are able to dominate the Dating Market, while others may feel overlooked or undervalued. Key takeaways include:

1. **Leverage Is Multifaceted**: It's not just about being attractive or desirable; how one prioritizes sexuality, or emotional connection significantly impacts leverage in relationships.

2. **Romantic Respect Is Earned, Not Given**: Individuals who can balance their priorities and maintain emotional boundaries often command more respect and power in relationships.

3. **Awareness Creates Opportunity**: By recognizing their own classification and understanding where they fall short, individuals can work to increase their Sexual Capital or adjust their priorities to improve Relational Dynamics.

The Four Quadrants of the Dating Pool: Power Dynamics and Relationship Strategies

Because of Sexual Market Classification, the Dating Pool can be divided into four distinct quadrants based on who benefits more from the Relationship Dynamics—either men or women—and on the primary mode of engagement in each quadrant, whether Erotic or Romantic. These quadrants each reflect unique dynamics, with variations in emotional attachment, sexual attraction, and relational strategy. Let's break down each quadrant to understand these dynamics.

1. Male-Benefitting Side - Erotic Section

In the Erotic section of the Male-Benefitting side of the Dating Pool, the primary Relational Mode is Erotic Mode, the typical Male Role is Sexual Alpha Male Runner, and the typical Female Role is Female Chaser. Also, the primary dynamics revolve around sexual attraction with little emotional investment. Here, Alpha Males, who prioritize their own needs and maintain a dominant stance, set the pace and tone of the relationship. They are often focused on physical intimacy, with minimal effort put into emotional connection or long-term commitment. Nonetheless, women in this quadrant also prioritize sex over romance. Men withhold love and activate women sexually, and women give sex to get love.

Key Characteristics:

- **Men Begin and End in Erotic Mode**: These men view relationships through the lens of physical gratification and remain emotionally detached, prioritizing sex over romance.

- **Dominated Relationships**: Men maintain control, often providing minimal emotional or social input to keep themselves distanced from attachment.

- **Alpha Males:** Men in this quadrant are usually the most sought after because they have the most sexual charisma.

- **Male Runners, Female Chasers**: Women in this quadrant are typically the "Chasers," driven by an initial physical attraction that they hope will evolve into emotional connection. They lead with sex in the hope that it will turn into love, while men, in turn, give nothing to gain sex.

- **Overwhelming Psychological Mathematics of Mood Temperatures**: Women become emotionally invested due to the psychological impact of intimacy, creating emotional attachments that are not reciprocated by the men. This leads to an imbalance where women are fighting for love through sexual means, which ultimately reinforces their position as the "Chaser." A negative number multiplied by a positive number equals a negative number.

- **Emotional and Sexual Respect:** Men can secure Emotional Respect easily since they withhold emotions. Women on the other hand fail to secure Sexual Respect since they are activated sexually.

- **Sexual Connection and Emotional Attachment:** Both men and women have a sexual attraction, thus a sexual connection, however men don't have an emotional attraction leaving women with an emotional attachment.

- **Bad Intentions and Artificial Interest:** Men only intend on dating women for their own personal gain and sexual gratification and use artificial emotional interest to string women along.

- **Men are the Prize:** Men have high Sexual Market Value (Sexual Capital) because of physical attractiveness, social status, or financial success. They have more Market Leverage, because of their abundance of experience, thus tend to be the "prize." Because they are Highly Sexual and can easily Balance the Power, these men tend to date who they want, therefore can marry who they want, but prefer to hold off and enjoy a multitude of options and sexual benefits.

This quadrant tends to result in relationships that are often fleeting and imbalanced, driven by a purely sexual attraction from the man's side and emotional attachment from the woman's side. Although men are emotionally unattached, they may have a sexual motive because of the convenience the women in this quadrant provide.

2. Male-Benefitting Side – Romantic Section

In the Romantic section of the Male-Benefitting side of the Dating Pool, the primary Relational Mode is Romantic Mode, the typical Male

Role is Emotional Beta Male Runner, and the typical Female Role is Female Chaser. Also, the Relationship Dynamics shift towards an emotional connection. Women in this quadrant tend to prioritize romance over sex. However, in this quadrant, men are Beta Males who also prioritize romance over sex and are initially open to romance and even prioritize emotional intimacy over sexual conquest. This group of men approach relationships with a gentler, warmer demeanor and lead with affection. However, they are often able to calculate and switch between Romantic and Erotic Modes as needed. Men do not withhold love; therefore, women are not activated sexually. Instead, a woman's natural sexual desire must take its own course. Nonetheless, women give love to get love.

Key Characteristics:

- **Men Start Hot in Romantic Mode**: They lead with affection and emotional openness, which creates an initial bond with their partner.

- **Calculated Relationships**: These men understand the "Psychological Mathematics of Mood Temperatures" and navigate relationships with a sense of control that allows them to avoid becoming overwhelming.

- **Emotional Beta Males:** Men in this quadrant are usually balanced between giving sexual energy and giving emotional energy.

- **Male Runners, Female Chasers**: Women here lead with love in hopes of creating a relationship that combines emotional and physical intimacy. They give love to get love, while men withhold their full commitment (no love at all or give just enough love).

- **Shifts to Erotic Mode When Convenient**: Beta Males can switch to Erotic Mode when they perceive an opportunity to fulfill physical desires. The relationship often begins with romance but can easily turn into a physical connection without progressing toward long-term commitment. If a man fails to switch to Erotic Mode when the woman does, she will not try to convince him to do so. Instead, she will look elsewhere because the Psychological Mathematics of Mood Temperatures are not overwhelmed.

- **Emotional and Sexual Respect:** Men are able to secure Emotional Respect but can have a tough time maintaining it. Women are able to secure Sexual Respect easily because they prioritize romance over sex.

- **Emotional Connection and Slight Sexual Connection:** Both men and women have an emotional attraction, creating an emotional connection. However, sexual connections are hard to maintain because neither party is overly sexual.

- **Good Intentions and Artificial Interest:** Men tend to have good intentions because they are relationship seekers, however, a multitude of options can create the need for artificial interest in order to juggle options.

- **Men are the Prize:** Men have high Sexual Market Value (Sexual Capital) and have Market Leverage. However, they have a difficult time dating who they want because they are Highly Emotional and are unable to Balance the Power at times. Although they have a tough time dating who they want, they don't have a tough time dating (who they don't want).

In this quadrant, relationships may blend both emotional and sexual connections but remain imbalanced, with men having Market Leverage. Women invest emotionally while men remain more strategic, creating relationships that are "hot" but seldom evolve into lasting partnerships.

3. Female-Benefitting Side – Erotic Section

In the Erotic section of the Female-Benefitting side of the Dating Pool, the primary Relational Mode is Erotic Mode, the typical Male Role is Sexual Beta Male Chaser, and the typical Female Role is Female Runner. Also, both men and women prioritize sex over romance. However, women lead relationships on their own terms. Here, women engage in casual connections without emotional investment, practicing Calculated Relationships to avoid losing Relational Power. These women seek physical connections without the complications of attachment, often leaving men in the "Chaser" role. Women do not withhold sex; therefore, men are not activated emotionally. Instead, men remain erotically hot. Nonetheless, men give sex (sexual energy) to get sex.

Key Characteristics:

- **Women Lead with Sex for Sex's Sake**: These women engage sexually without emotional attachment, leading to relationships that begin and end in the Erotic Mode.

- **Female Runners, Male Chasers**: Men are often sexually activated by initial intimacy and become "Chasers," and sexually eager, while women remain detached.

- **Sexual Beta Males**: The men in this quadrant are often eager to connect sexually and may refrain from creating deeper emotional ties. However, they tend to struggle with creating strong sexual attraction since they aren't Alphas but instead Betas, which positions them as the "Chasers" in these dynamics.

- **Calculated Relationships and Controlled Emotions**: Women here are adept at maintaining emotional distance, focusing on the physical connection while avoiding attachment. The Psychological Mathematics of Mood Temperatures is manageable since they do not become emotionally overwhelmed. And since they don't get overwhelmed, women stay in Erotic Mode.

- **Men Give Sex to Get Sex**: Men in this quadrant exude sexual energy but never obtain Relational Power because women keep the relationship in their terms by giving little in return. The Psychological Mathematics of Mood Temperatures is not usually overwhelmed because both parties are giving of the same sexual energy and a positive number multiplied by a positive number equals a positive number.

- **Sexual and Emotional Respect:** Women fail to secure Sexual Respect; however Sexual Respect is not sought after by men in this quadrant. Men on the other hand secure Emotional Respect because they aren't overly emotional.

- **Sexual Connections and Little to No Emotional Connection:** Because sexual gratification is a priority and emotional investment is secondary for both parties, only a sexual connection is made, and an emotional connection is disregarded.

- **Bad Intentions and Artificial Interest:** Women tend to base relationships on superficial foundations. Interest is also used for superficial purposes.

- **Women are the Prize:** Women have High Sexual Market Value (Sexual Capital) and are Highly Sexual. However, because men in this quadrant are also Highly Sexual, and women in this quadrant are sexually available, women are the prize because they provide the sexual fulfillment that the men are seeking. Also, the women are scarce, hence men compete for sexual achievement. Nonetheless, women date who they want but have a tough time marrying who they want, but not a tough time marrying who they don't want.

Relationships in this quadrant are physically driven and ultimately fleeting, with both men and women having only sexual connections but little to no emotional connections or attachments. However, social connections may be present.

4. Female-Benefited Side – Romantic Section

In the Romantic section of the Female-Benefitting side of the Dating Pool, the primary Relational Mode is Romantic Mode, the typical Male Role is Emotional Omega Male Chaser, and the typical Female Role is Female Runner. Also, both men and women prioritize romance over sex. Here is where emotional connections dominate, but with a dynamic that leaves men struggling to balance their emotional needs. Women lead with love but keep relationships at an arm's length, making them the "Runners" in this quadrant. They are less likely to become overwhelmed by the emotional complexities of the relationship, often leaving men in a vulnerable and unsatisfied position. Women withhold sex and activate men emotionally, and men give love to get sex.

Key Characteristics:

- **Women Lead with Love but Give Nothing to Get Love**: Women engage in romantic connections and encourage men's emotional investment, but they withhold reciprocation in terms of vulnerability or attachment.

- **Female Runners, Male Chasers**: Men, in this quadrant, are the "Chasers," who often find themselves investing deeply in hopes of building an emotional connection and receiving sexual benefits. Women maintain their distance and give just enough to keep men interested without fully committing.

- **Omega Males**: Men in this quadrant tend to be emotionally sensitive and may have difficulty establishing boundaries. They are emotionally invested and look for a fulfilling connection but are met with an Unbalanced Dynamic.

- **Validated Relationships**: Women have Market Leverage and receive constant attention and validation from men, giving women the Relational Power in this dynamic.

- **Men Give Love to Get Sex, Leading to Emotional Overload**: Men hope that their emotional openness and affection will result in a deeper romantic and physical bond. However, due to women's lack of sexual interest, men become frustrated as emotional attachment grows, creating a sense of emotional overwhelm. A positive number multiplied by a negative number equals a negative number.

- **Sexual and Emotional Respect:** Women have no problem obtaining Sexual Respect, but men fail to obtain Emotional Respect.

- **Emotional Connections and Little to no Sexual Connection:** Because relationships are based on commitment, emotional connections are made. However, since both parties are not overly sexual, it's difficult to create and maintain sexual connections.

- **Good Intentions and Artificial Interest:** Women tend to have good intentions because they are relationship seekers. However, because their male counterparts tend to lack sexual depth, interest is maintained for financial purposes and emotional comfort.

- **Women are the Prize:** Women have High Sexual Market Value (Sexual Capital) and are Highly Emotional. However, because men in this quadrant are also Highly Emotional, and women in this quadrant are emotionally available, women are the prize because they provide the emotional fulfillment that the men are seeking. Also, the women are scarce, hence men compete for romantic achievement. Nonetheless, women date who they want and also tend to marry who they want.

Relationships in this quadrant are characterized by emotional intensity, with men developing strong attachments and women staying sexually detached. Although women are sexually unattached, they may have an emotional motive because of the comfort the men in this quadrant provide.

Summary of the Quadrants

These quadrants serve as a guide to understanding Dating Dynamics, with each offering a unique blend of psychological and emotional implications. The balance or imbalance in each section sheds light on who has Relational Power, who chases, and ultimately, how each individual may feel within a relationship. By recognizing these patterns, one can navigate the Dating Pool with greater awareness, avoiding unbalanced pursuits and one-sided attachments.

The Crisis of Connection: How Market Dynamics Are Fueling Modern Loneliness

The current Dating Market Crisis—characterized by rising loneliness, emotional disconnect, and relationship dissatisfaction—can be traced back to the complex interplay between **Sexual Market Value, Sexual Market Classification, Hypergamy,** and **Market Leveraging**. These concepts, rooted in both evolutionary psychology and modern social behavior, reveal a system that unintentionally leaves many individuals—especially men—**struggling to find a meaningful connection**, while others become disillusioned by mismatched expectations and one-sided dynamics.

Sexual Market Value (SMV) ranks individuals based on their perceived desirability in the Dating Pool. The reality is that a small percentage of high-SMV men attract the majority of female attention, creating a top-heavy system where **the few are oversaturated with options** while the rest go ignored. Meanwhile, women with high-SMV are often overwhelmed with male attention but find it difficult to secure long-term commitment from the men they desire most—many of whom have little incentive to settle down. This **uneven distribution of attention and opportunity** has created a class divide in dating, where the top-tier of men and women dominate the market and have Market Leverage, leaving average individuals isolated and overlooked.

Sexual Market Classification takes this further by categorizing people based not just on their SMV, but also on their sexual or emotional orientation—whether they prioritize sex or romance. This creates friction. For example, a highly sexual, high-SMV Alpha Male may attract many women, but struggle to offer emotional connection, while a low-SMV, emotionally available Omega Male is invisible to the women seeking excitement or dominance. These classifications reveal how many people are **either mismatched or misaligned**, with those prioritizing love often chasing partners who prioritize lust.

Hypergamy—women's tendency to date and marry "up"—only intensifies the crisis. Since most women desire men with equal or higher status, experience, and desirability, the Dating Market becomes a bottleneck, where all women compete for the top-tier men. Men, in turn, often practice **hypogamy**, seeking younger or less experienced partners, which further pushes average women out of contention. The result? Fewer committed relationships, more situationships, and a growing number of **emotionally unfulfilled individuals on both sides**.

All of this leads to the harsh reality of **Market Leveraging**: those with the most desirability, experience, or emotional detachment hold the most power. And because the power is concentrated in the hands of a few, **the majority feel powerless**—invisible, rejected, or constantly chasing something unattainable. As modern dating becomes more transactional, gamified, and filtered through digital platforms, the emotional toll is undeniable: **loneliness is at an all-time high**, not because people don't want love, but because the system is structured in a way that **keeps connection out of reach for the average person**.

Until individuals begin to understand and navigate these dynamics with greater awareness, and until society starts promoting relationship-building over superficial status markers, the dating crisis will continue—and so will the growing epidemic of emotional isolation.

The High-Value Double Standard: Why More Men Are Lonely

In the Dating Market, **a highly sought-after man** often finds himself with the power to distribute his attention, time, and intimacy among multiple women. Because of his high Sexual Market Value—whether due to status, looks, confidence, or resources—he becomes a scarce commodity that many women desire. As a result, the women who compete for him often end up **sharing him**, whether knowingly or unknowingly. He may not commit to just one woman but still maintains emotional or sexual access to several. This dynamic benefits the high-value man but leaves many women with only a **partial experience of him**—a fragment of his attention rather than exclusive devotion. However, even with partial experiences, a lot of women are able to avoid complete loneliness.

On the other hand, **a highly sought-after woman** typically operates under a different set of rules. When many men compete for her, she usually **selects just one winner**. She does not distribute herself across multiple men; instead, she chooses the one she deems most worthy and rejects the rest. This leads to a stark imbalance: **one man gets the prize, and many walk away with nothing**. The rejected men are left on the sidelines, often feeling invisible or undervalued in a dating landscape that increasingly favors the top tier of attractive, dominant men.

This disparity contributes to a growing phenomenon—**more men are lonely than women**. The majority of women are pursuing a small percentage of high-value men, while average men are left without connection, intimacy, or romantic fulfillment. Meanwhile, most women, even if they face their own emotional struggles, still have more romantic options and social attention than the average man. The result is a Dating Market where a few men are overindulged, and many men are **"underloved" and overlooked**. Therefore, contrary to popular belief, more women have Market Leverage than men.

Why Women Seem to Get Hurt More: The Limits of Hypergamy and Fitness Tests

Although men are generally lonelier than women, one of the key reasons women are often perceived to get hurt more than men in relationships is because they typically rely on **Fitness Tests** instead of **Loyalty Tests** when evaluating a man's worth. Fitness Tests are social and psychological challenges a woman subconsciously gives to gauge a man's **confidence, assertiveness, dominance, and emotional control**. These tests are part of the hypergamous instinct—designed to determine if a man is **strong enough, man enough, worthy enough, and "fit enough"** to be her partner. In essence, she's checking if he can lead, protect, and handle her emotionally. While these tests are effective at filtering out weak or indecisive men, they **don't reveal his character**, long-term intentions, or emotional depth. Therefore, Fitness Tests don't help women avoid One-sided, Unbalanced Relationships.

Hypergamy, by nature, focuses on a man's **status, strength, and ability to rise above competition**. But what it doesn't account for is **loyalty, commitment, or genuine emotional investment**. A man can pass every Fitness Test with flying colors, exhibit Alpha traits, and still have no intention of being faithful or emotionally available. This is where many women get blindsided—believing they've chosen the best option based on confidence and dominance, only to find out later that he was never in it for the long haul. Because the selection process focused on *how strong he is*, and not *how loyal or emotionally present he is*, the woman may end up emotionally invested in a man who is unwilling or incapable of reciprocating that investment.

This is why women often end up **hurt, confused, or betrayed**—not because they're overly emotional or naive, but because their instinctual and social filtering mechanisms are **testing the wrong traits**. By focusing on power and strength over sincerity and stability, women may attract men who can handle their energy but not honor their heart. To avoid this, women must learn to test for **emotional maturity, consistency, and long-term alignment**, not just dominance and confidence. Otherwise, the hypergamous filter becomes a trap—choosing men who can pass the fire but not stay through the storm.

The Flip Side: Why Men Tend to Do Loyalty Tests Instead of Fitness Tests

While women tend to use Fitness Tests to screen for strength, dominance, and confidence, **men typically use Loyalty Tests** to screen for commitment, emotional exclusivity, and long-term value. This difference stems from evolutionary pressures and relational priorities. Whereas women are wired to test a man's ability to **lead and provide**, men are more concerned with whether a woman will **stay loyal, remain emotionally faithful**, and not abandon him for a better option. Men instinctively want to know, *"Can I trust her when things get hard?"* and *"Will she still respect me when I'm not at my best?"* Therefore, Loyalty Tests do help men avoid One-sided, Unbalanced Relationships.

Loyalty Tests can take subtle or subconscious forms. A man might pull back emotionally or become less attentive to see if she will chase, remain patient, or stay committed. He might put her in situations where her values are challenged—observing how she reacts to attention from other men, how she handles conflict, or whether she's supportive in his low moments. These aren't tests of strength like the ones women use; they are tests of **emotional allegiance**. For men, a woman's ability to be trusted with his vulnerability—especially once he opens up—is the real test of her worth.

The problem arises when Loyalty Tests go unspoken or unacknowledged. A man may become cold or detached not to hurt her, but to **see if she will still be there** when he's no longer easy to love. This can lead to misunderstandings, especially if the woman interprets his behavior as disinterest rather than a subconscious test of her character. But beneath the surface, many men are silently watching, trying to answer one critical question: *Is she the kind of woman who stays?* This deep desire for loyalty, more than beauty or excitement, is often what determines whether a man chooses to commit or simply move on.

Fitness Tests, Loyalty Tests, and the True Source of Market Leverage

A **High-Value Man** with **High Sexual Capital** and strong **Market Leverage** can easily **pass Fitness Tests**—those subtle challenges women present to assess a man's confidence, dominance, and emotional strength. His charisma, status, and experience allow him to remain composed, unaffected, and often even more attractive under pressure. But as previously mentioned, **just because a man can pass a woman's Fitness Tests doesn't mean he will settle down with her**. In fact, many of these high-status men have the options and awareness to avoid commitment altogether, especially if the woman issuing the test offers only beauty without long-term value. The ability to pass Fitness Tests may qualify a man to *date*, but it doesn't obligate him to *commit*.

Ironically, **a man's ability to pass Fitness Tests is one of the most crucial indicators of his overall desirability**. Women are evolutionarily wired to be attracted to men who remain emotionally grounded, unaffected by pressure, and unshaken in their self-worth. This trait signals confidence, leadership, and security—the very things women subconsciously associate with protection and provision. This is why passing Fitness Tests increases a man's Market Leverage: it proves he's emotionally unshakable and has options, which makes him more desirable in the eyes of many women.

On the other hand, **a woman gains Market Leverage in a completely different way**. While her **attractiveness** gets her noticed and may open the door for romantic opportunities, it's her **loyalty, femininity, and emotional commitment** that determine whether she stays in the room. In a man's eyes, beauty may ignite interest, but **character earns commitment**. Men, from an evolutionary standpoint, have always prioritized **paternal certainty**. Because they cannot biologically confirm that a child is theirs without modern testing, men have historically valued signs of **faithfulness and modesty** as cues of long-term security.

This is why a woman's **ability to pass Loyalty Tests**—to remain devoted, emotionally exclusive, and non-promiscuous—**greatly increases her Sexual Market Value and Market Leverage**. In today's dating world, where surface-level beauty is everywhere, a woman who is both attractive and clearly loyal stands out. She becomes a rare combination: high in desirability *and* trustworthy. And that's what gives her lasting power in the Dating Market—not just to attract a man, but to **inspire him to invest**.

Striking a Balance

The Law of Market Leveraging isn't about assigning blame or reducing relationships to cold calculations. Instead, it's about awareness. Recognizing where leverage exists can help partners communicate openly and ensure that both feel valued and empowered. In the end, the healthiest relationships are not built on leveraging power but on mutual respect, shared goals, and an appreciation for what each partner uniquely contributes. However, understanding the dynamics of leverage gives you the tools to navigate the Dating Market with greater confidence and clarity.

Maximizing Leverage: Understanding the Struggles

For those seeking to improve their position in the Dating Market, the focus should be on **growth and self-awareness**:

- **For Alphas**: Use your leverage responsibly. While you may hold significant power, relationships built solely on sexual priority can lack depth and long-term fulfillment. Cultivating emotional intelligence can help balance your natural strengths.

- **For Omegas**: Focus on self-improvement to increase your sexual capital. This might involve building confidence, enhancing physical appearance, or developing social skills. Learning to set emotional boundaries and prioritize self-respect can also shift the Balance of Power in your favor.

- **For Betas**: Strive for balance by aligning your strengths with your priorities. Understanding where you naturally excel and where you need growth can help you maximize your leverage in the Dating Market.

By understanding **Sexual Market Classification**, individuals can navigate **The Law of Market Leveraging** with greater clarity and purpose, ensuring they cultivate relationships that are both balanced and fulfilling.

The Shift in Power: Overcoming the Struggles

The Balance of Power between dating and marriage can create a struggle, but both men and women can maximize their leverage by understanding and overcoming these dynamics. The power struggle for men usually comes in the front end and the power struggle for women usually comes in the back end. Since women date who they want, a woman who leverages her ability to date who she wants must use her leverage wisely and choose the right partner from her pool of viable options. That way she would overcome the back-end power struggle and maximize on her leverage and also marry who she wants. On the flip side, since men marry who they want, a man who leverages his ability to marry who he wants must use his leverage wisely and position himself as the best viable option the woman he wants has to choose from. That way he would overcome the front-end power struggle and maximize on his leverage and also date who he wants.

For Women: Leveraging the Ability to Date Who They Want

Women have the advantage in the Dating Market, but to ensure that they also marry who they want, they must approach the power shift strategically:

1. **Align Dating and Marriage Goals**: Women who seek marriage should prioritize relationships with men who share their long-term goals, minimizing the risk of time wasted on incompatible partners.

2. **Retain Leverage Through Growth**: Continuing to cultivate personal value—whether through career, self-improvement, or emotional resilience—ensures that women retain leverage even as the Dating Market Dynamics shifts toward marriage.

3. **Avoid Settling**: By maintaining standards and a strong sense of self-worth, women can maximize their ability to attract a partner who aligns with their vision for the future.

For Men: Leveraging the Ability to Marry Who They Want

Men often find that their leverage increases as they transition from dating to marriage. To maximize this advantage while ensuring healthy relationships:

1. **Expand Dating Options**: Instead of settling for "who they can," men can work on improving their social status, emotional intelligence, financial stability, or physical fitness to increase their appeal in the Dating Market.

2. **Date With Intention**: Men who use dating to understand what they want in a long-term partner are better equipped to transition smoothly to the Marriage Market.

3. **Respect the Power Dynamics**: Recognizing that leverage is not about domination, but mutual value can lead to healthier, more fulfilling relationships.

Balancing the Scales

Ultimately, the key to overcoming the power struggle and achieving a balanced relationship lies in **awareness and intentionality**. Both men and women can maximize their leverage by understanding their strengths and the dynamics at play, but the healthiest relationships come from mutual respect and shared goals—not a competition for attention or control. By navigating the shift in power thoughtfully, women can overcome the struggle by leveraging their dating options into long-term commitments with partners who align with their goals. Likewise, men can move beyond the limitations of "dating who they can" by using their eventual advantage in the Marriage Market to choose fulfilling, intentional partnerships. This delicate balance ensures that both partners feel valued, respected, and equally invested in the relationship's success.

Conclusion

The consequences of becoming and remaining absolutely powerless in a relationship cannot be overstated. Without Relational Power, you may find yourself tolerating things you would otherwise never accept—disrespect, neglect, manipulation, or even infidelity. Powerlessness creates an unhealthy dynamic where you feel bound to your partner, often in ways that are detrimental to your well-being. You may stay loyal, faithful, and submissive, even when those actions are not reciprocated. Such one-sided devotion is not love; it is self-sacrifice born from a lack of self-worth and a lack of Relational Balance, and an unhealthy dependency that traps you in a cycle of giving without receiving, of losing yourself in the process of trying to keep someone else.

The sad reality is that some people mistreat their partners, and often, it stems from traits associated with the *dark triad*: narcissism, psychopathy, and Machiavellianism. These traits lead people to view relationships as opportunities for power, manipulation, or personal gain rather than as partnerships built on mutual care and respect. Environmental factors, such as growing up in dysfunctional families, experiencing trauma, or adopting extreme ideologies, can also foster these destructive behaviors. People shaped by these factors often seek to exploit their partners rather than build meaningful, balanced connections, and foster mutual respect and love.

It's essential to understand that *it's not your job to fix someone who mistreats you*. No matter how much you love them, no matter how deeply you believe they can change, their growth is not your responsibility. Staying in a toxic relationship with the hope of "saving" someone will only drain you emotionally and prevent you from achieving the healthy and fulfilling relationship you deserve. Love is not about sacrifice to the point of self-destruction. And love alone cannot transform a toxic relationship into a healthy one. You deserve a relationship where respect, commitment, and balance are the foundations—not dysfunction or power struggles.

For some, the tendency to accept mistreatment is rooted in past experiences. If you grew up in an environment where love was conditional, neglect was common, or abuse was normalized, you may unconsciously seek similar dynamics in your adult relationships. You might settle for less than you deserve because it feels familiar or because you doubt your worth. Breaking this cycle begins with healing—addressing the wounds of your past, learning to set boundaries, and rediscovering your value. Loving yourself is not selfish; it is the foundation for every healthy relationship you will ever have. Only by loving and valuing yourself can you set the standards for how you deserve to be treated.

It is also critical to recognize that the issues discussed in this book are not exclusive to one gender. Men and women are equally capable of inflicting relational harm or experiencing heartbreak. In society, there are heartbreakers, and there are the heartbroken—and both men and women can occupy either role. Blaming the opposite sex as a whole only deepens division and distracts from the real issue: accountability. Rather than being combative, men and women should come together, offering support and understanding to those who have been hurt, and holding the heartbreakers accountable for their actions, regardless of gender.

At its core, this book is about balance—about creating relationships where power is shared equally, respect is mutual, and love is uplifting. A healthy relationship is not about power, control, attention, validation, or dominance; it is about partnership, where both individuals feel valued, empowered, and loved, walking side by side as equals. By valuing your worth, setting boundaries, and refusing to settle for less, you can break free from unhealthy patterns and attract the kind of love you truly deserve. As you apply the fundamentals, principles, and essentials in this book, remember that your happiness and well-being are nonnegotiable. You deserve a love that uplifts and empowers you—not one that diminishes or confines you. Always choose yourself first, and you'll attract the kind of relationship you truly deserve.

As you move forward, remember, it's never too late to reclaim your power and rewrite your story. You are worthy of a love that is kind, supportive, and balanced. Choose yourself, and the rest will follow.

Hopefully, by now, you understand the vital importance of grasping the dynamics of relationships. Relationships are not just about emotions or sex; they are also about the underlying Balance of Power, respect, and mutual understanding that sustains them. With the knowledge of the fundamentals, principles, and essentials outlined in this book, you are equipped to take a more informed and empowered approach to dating, relationships, your overall love life, and even your sexual experiences.

The **12 Laws of Dating Dynamics** are not just abstract ideas—they are actionable tools designed to guide you toward healthier, more fulfilling connections. These laws serve as a roadmap to help you Balance the Power in your relationships and avoid the pitfalls of one-sided dynamics. Whether you are currently in a relationship, navigating the dating world, or reflecting on past experiences, these laws are here to remind you of your worth and the kind of relationship you deserve.

This is about taking control of your love life, not through manipulation or games, but through understanding, self-awareness, and confidence. When you apply these laws, you set the foundation for relationships built on mutual respect, shared power, and genuine connection.

Remember, you have the power to create the love life you want, and it starts with you. Use what you've learned here to make better choices, to recognize red flags early, and to nurture relationships that uplift and inspire you. The goal is not just to find love but to find *balanced* love—love that empowers both you and your partner equally.

Here's to a future filled with healthy, fulfilling, and Balanced Relationships. May these laws help you navigate your journey with clarity and confidence as you build the love life you truly deserve.

Made in the USA
Middletown, DE
23 May 2025

75912268R00169